BETRAYAL

*How the
Clinton Administration
Undermined
American Security*

Bill Gertz

Since 1947
**REGNERY
PUBLISHING, INC.**
An Eagle Publishing Company • Washington, DC

Library of Congress Cataloging-in-Publication Data

Gertz, Bill.
    Betrayal : how the Clinton administration undermined American security / Bill Gertz.
       p.   cm.
    ISBN 0-89526-317-3 (alk. paper)
    1. United States—Foreign relations—1993–   2. Clinton, Bill, 1946– .
    3. National security—United States—History—20th century. I. Title.
E885.G47 1999
327.73—dc21   99-24248
                                                          CIP

Published in the United States by
Regnery Publishing, Inc.
An Eagle Publishing Company
One Massachusetts Avenue, NW
Washington, DC 20001

Distributed to the trade by
National Book Network
4720-A Boston Way
Lanham, MD 20706

Printed on acid-free paper.
Manufactured in the United States of America

10 9 8 7 6 5 4 3 2 1

Books are available in quantity for promotional or premium use. Write to Director of Special Sales, Regnery Publishing, Inc., One Massachusetts Avenue, NW, Washington, DC 20001, for information on discounts and terms or call (202) 216-0600.

TABLE OF CONTENTS

For Debra

"We, too, shall encounter follies; but if great, they will be short, if long, they will be light; and the vigor of our country will get the better of them."

—Thomas Jefferson, 1806

PART I

Betrayal

CHAPTER ONE

The Clinton Method: Foreign Policy Cover-up

I n August 1998 President Bill Clinton went on national television and told the American people he had "misled" them by covering up his sordid sexual affair with a young White House intern. It was a shocking admission of guilt from a man holding the most powerful office in the world.

But the president has yet to admit, possibly even to himself, that he is guilty of a far more devastating cover-up: his administration's willful failure to "provide for the common defence," as the Constitution demands. His wrongheaded policies affecting our nation's security, and his cavalier cover-up of this misconduct, amount to betrayal—a betrayal that has left the United States weaker militarily as its enemies grow stronger and the world becomes more dangerous. He has squandered the Cold War victory that he inherited from his predecessors, presidents who understood the realities of global power politics that are apparently beyond Clinton's grasp, or that he has no interest in learning.

By making the economy his top priority, Clinton has shortchanged vital military and intelligence programs, diverting some $80 billion a year from defense and spending it on domestic programs that reward corporations and political supporters. His use of military force has been haphazard and ineffective, calculated more to divert public attention from his personal problems than to advance any strategic national security goals.

A deep suspicion of the military and its crucial role in the nation's survival has permeated the Clinton administration, leading to repeated misuse of the armed forces for peacekeeping and humanitarian functions for which they are ill suited. This in turn has led to confusion and low morale among the men and women in uniform on whom the nation's safety depends. The best and the brightest are finding it difficult to justify their choice of a military career in the face of such hostility and maladministration, and many are leaving the ranks. Recruitment is down, and as a result standards have been lowered to fill enlistment quotas.

President Clinton has turned upside down President Dwight D. Eisenhower's warning about a too-powerful military-industrial complex. Using the end of the Cold War as cover, and to please corporate bigshots targeted for campaign contributions, Clinton has loosened export controls on several high-technology sectors, including U.S. high-speed computer manufacturers, software makers, and communications satellite makers who want to sell to China.

Two such companies are Loral Space & Communications, Ltd., and Hughes Electronics, both the subject of a federal investigation to determine how they passed embargoed militarily-useful rocket technology to Beijing without licenses. At the time of the weapons technology transfers, Loral was headed by Bernard Schwartz, who has given hundreds of thousands of dollars to Clinton and the Democratic Party. Hughes was headed by C. Michael Armstrong, who was named head of the influential President's Export Council after lobbying vigorously—and successfully—for the easing of U.S. national security export controls. Shortly after the "decontrols" took place, American supercomputers began showing up in both Chinese and Russian nuclear weapons development centers—helping to build nuclear arms that might one day be turned against the United States.

The president, at the urging of Armstrong and other export-hungry businessmen, has consistently opposed the imposition of sanctions on nations that engage in the sale of dangerous weapons of mass destruction technology and equipment. In a rare moment of candor, during a White House meeting in April 1998, Clinton explained, "What happens if you have automatic sanctions legislation is it puts enormous pressure on whoever is in the executive branch to fudge an evaluation of the facts of what is going on." This frank admission of deceit captured the essence of the administration's foreign and defense policies. Bill Clinton and his administration have relied heavily on this "fudge factor"—deliberately ignoring, playing down, or covering up dangerous developments abroad that affect vital U.S. interests.

While Clinton has shown flexibility on virtually every political issue he has faced, he has stood firm on one: long-range missile defense. There will be none on his watch.

Appeasement diplomacy and White House spin-control are the Clinton substitutes for missile defenses. A case study is the radical communist regime in North Korea. When North Korea began developing nuclear weapons in the early 1990s, the Clinton administration "solved" the threat with a deceptive agreement. The hardline communists in Pyongyang promised to halt the nuclear arms program in exchange for two replacement nuclear reactors that would, so Clinton asserted, be less useful in developing weapons. But within four years of the agreement, U.S. intelligence agencies revealed that North Korea was engaged in a second, covert nuclear weapons program that circumvented the agreement. Pyongyang then shocked the world by test-firing its first intercontinental-range missile, capable of hitting U.S. territory with nuclear, chemical, or biological warheads.

> The Clinton administration has covered up its mistakes, and, when facts leaked out, simply brushed them off as trivial, or lied outright.

The list of administration failures is a long one; this book will deal with the most egregious. Central to all of them, however, is the inescapable conclusion that President Clinton and his top advisers have covered up the seriousness of their mistakes, and, when facts leaked out, simply brushed them off as trivial, or lied outright.

This betrayal of American national security so angered some intelligence, defense, and foreign policy officials that they responded in the only way they knew how: by disclosing to the press some of the nation's most secret intelligence. The disclosures ranged from secret Chinese arms sales and intelligence operations against the United States to highly detailed reports linking Russian officials with secret arms sales to Iran, from sensitive internal negotiations with Moscow to dangerous foreign weapons developments that have sharply contrasted with Clinton's misguided belief that the world is growing more peaceful. Many of these officials, whose anonymity is their only protection from political retaliation, have been criticized by administration political appointees for risking national security by disclosing this information.

But the fact that these unsung heroes have jeopardized their careers to expose wrongdoing only underlines the great danger to our country brought about by the Clinton administration. I have worked with many of these people in my fourteen years covering defense and national security affairs, and I regard them as both dissidents and patriots. To a great extent, this book is their story as well as my own.

CHAPTER TWO

The Kapitan Man

> *"A year from now everybody is going to deny this*
> *ever happened, and you and I are going to be two*
> *poor shmucks with bad eyes for the rest of our lives."*

—Canadian Air Force Captain Pat Barnes to U.S. Navy Lieutenant Jack Daly

O n April 4, 1997, a Russian merchant ship suspected of spying on U.S. nuclear missile submarines was photographed by a Canadian military surveillance helicopter that had been tracking the ship in U.S. territorial waters north of Puget Sound. During the encounter, someone on the Russian vessel fired a laser at the helicopter, permanently damaging the eyes of the Canadian helicopter pilot and a U.S. Navy intelligence officer working with the Canadians. The incident was kept secret by the Clinton administration for weeks. The president and his advisers did not want to publicize a hostile action that would upset its conciliatory policy toward Russia. This is the inside story of the incident.

The phone rang in the middle of the night at the Canadian home of U.S. Navy Lieutenant Jack Daly. It was the intelligence center at Canada's military base near Esquimault on Vancouver Island. A suspected Russian spy ship that for years had been masquerading as a merchant vessel was at the mouth of the Strait of Juan de Fuca and heading into Washington State's Puget Sound. Daly was ordered to secretly photograph the ship. It was a mission that would change Lieutenant Daly's life—and his opinion of the U.S. government and the U.S. Navy he loved so much.

Daly was a foreign intelligence liaison officer with the Maritime Forces Pacific, a joint command staffed by about 1,500 Canadian

Navy, Air Force, and Army personnel whose job is to defend Canada's West Coast. These Canadian forces work closely with the U.S. Navy.

Once airborne, the aerial surveillance seemed routine. Daly was tethered securely to a harness that allowed him to move around inside the Canadian Forces CH-123 helicopter. He was holding one of the newest pieces of equipment used by the Office of Naval Intelligence (ONI) to spy on foreign ships: a Kodak DCS-460 single-lens reflex digital camera. The converted Nikon takes crisp photographs that can be downloaded directly into a computer.

The target was the *Kapitan Man*, one of two Russian merchant ships that had been spying on the nine U.S. nuclear missile submarines based nearby with Submarine Group Nine in Bangor, Washington.

"When I first got up to Esquimault I knew I would be working in the Canadian Joint Intelligence Center as a liaison officer," Daly recalled. "But when I arrived, the J-2, Canadian Lieutenant Commander Ted Parkinson, informed me that their plans were to utilize me as operations officer within their intelligence organization." The job involved him in the production, collection, and dissemination of intelligence to the command. The Canadians had specifically asked the Navy to provide someone with a background in merchant shipping.

Traditionally, Soviet Navy spy ships had been disguised as fishing vessels and were known as AGIs, for Auxiliary, General Intelligence. Since the collapse of the Soviet Union in 1991, however, merchant ships owned ostensibly by Russia's Far East Shipping Company (FESCO) became Russia's primary spy vehicles. For decades during the Cold War, Russian ships were barred from visiting key ports in the United States. Then in 1992 the ports were opened to merchant vessels as part of a policy of wooing Moscow. Seattle was a particularly sensitive port because it was home to one of the United States' most important strategic weapons: the ballistic missile submarine. The other elements of America's nuclear deterrent—land-based intercontinental ballistic missiles (ICBMs), the U.S. Minuteman I and II, and giant ten-warhead MX systems—were based in fixed silos and thus were easy targets for foreign missiles. U.S. strategic bombers were also vulnerable to foreign air defense systems and fighter aircraft. Only the submarine force provided true stealth and near invulnerability in strategic warfare.

Tracking these submarines was a job assigned to Russia's "merchant ships." However, intelligence reports indicated that these ships were also involved in transporting illegal contraband for the growing Russian Mafia.

TRACKING THE "MERCHANT SHIPS"

By April 4, 1997, when Daly was ordered to photograph the Russian ship, the *Kapitan Man* had been under international surveillance for days, as it made its way across the North Pacific and down the coast from Alaska, where it spent a few days suspiciously loitering around the U.S. Air Force listening posts in the region. Like Russia's "fishing vessel" spy ships, the *Kapitan Man* sported an unusual array of antennae, far more than were needed for communications and navigation.

Back in 1993 a search of the *Kapitan Man* had produced this tantalizing piece of intelligence: Deep inside the ship in a remote forward compartment lay a dozen electronic buoys. The T7 buoys could be used for collecting underwater sounds. A data sheet on the device states that it can be used "at increased depth for improved sonar prediction in ASW [Anti-Submarine Warfare] and other military applications." The compartment also contained about fifteen black canister devices that were XBTs—probes used for ASW monitoring. The ship also had a photo-processing lab, unusual for a "merchant vessel." The secret forward compartment also appeared to one investigator to have been booby-trapped and sprayed with dog repellent in an apparent attempt to prevent the use of police dogs to discover smuggled drugs or aliens.

> **Russia's "merchant ships" were tracking U.S. submarines and transporting illegal contraband for the growing Russian Mafia.**

The search of the *Kapitan Man* not only created deep suspicions that the ship was spying, but worse, the devices appeared to be part of a plan for deploying "permanent sensing devices" on the floor of Puget Sound to track U.S. nuclear missile submarines. A report on the search said that Customs Service investigators considered boarding the vessel a second time, but "it was decided that such a boarding would not be a good idea as it could reflect negatively and be a distraction to the meetings between President Clinton and President Yeltsin, which were occurring nearby on the following two days, at Vancouver, B.C."

About the same time, a fisherman had called the Coast Guard to report seeing the Russian ship throw a metal cylinder overboard in Puget Sound just before one of the U.S. nuclear submarines headed outbound. The cylinder was never recovered, but it was part of the Russian effort to set up a system of listening devices to record the unique sound "signature" a submarine makes when it passes through the water. With this knowledge, Russian hunter submarines could track the target submarines and kill them with high-tech wake-homing torpedoes in time of war.

Daly first warned ONI headquarters in December 1996 that the Russians were spying on U.S. submarines. His classified cable laid out the facts that made the *Kapitan Man* and its sister ship, *Anatole Koleshnichenko*, more than just merchant vessels: They were not following the navigational routes of merchants. They had spent an unusual amount of time around key installations in the Aleutians, up to forty hours at a time and far more than could be claimed for legitimate efforts to avoid bad weather. They seemed particularly interested in naval facilities on Adak Island, Alaska, near Attu Island, where the Air Force operates Cobra Ball reconnaissance aircraft and Cobra Dane intelligence radar posts, as well as the U.S.-Canadian eavesdropping center located on Canada's Queen Charlotte Islands. And finally, the two ships made regular trips every four to six weeks to the West Coast of the United States. The visits were often made without bringing or picking up any cargo.

Daly's report received no comment from ONI headquarters. "Maybe it was the holidays and it just fell through the cracks," Daly said. "I made a number of phone calls [asking] have you read this? Does this mean anything to anybody?"

The Central Intelligence Agency (CIA) and National Security Agency, however, received copies of the cable and were interested in the two ships. In the past, both agencies had received intelligence reports linking the *Kapitan Man* and *Anatole Koleshnichenko* to illegal drug smuggling. A Russian seaman who worked for FESCO, owners of the ships, told the Navy in 1994 that Russian organized crime groups were using FESCO ships to smuggle contraband, including narcotics, weapons, furs, gems, and illegal aliens. At the end of the Cold War, the National Security Agency had disbanded its analysis center for tracking the communications of international merchant vessels. The job now fell to the ONI, which set up a special cell to monitor those ships' movements. And so Daly and the intelligence unit in Esquimault continued to note incidents of suspected spying. The ships had a couple of encounters with the U.S. Ohio-class missile submarines, called "boomers" in Navy parlance. "These FESCO vessels," Daly reported, "were either delaying their arrivals or departures and one of them stopped in the Strait of Juan de Fuca claiming to have an engineering problem or weather avoidance."

The ships had been built in the 1970s by the Soviet Navy as troop and equipment ships. They were similar to U.S. "Ro-Ro" freighters— roll-on, roll-off—used by the Navy to bring equipment near potential hot spots overseas, such as the Persian Gulf and Northeast Asia. After the dissolution of the Soviet Union, the ships were overhauled by the Russian government, which controls some 20 percent of FESCO.

In January 1997 Daly and U.S. Navy Chief Petty Officer Scott Tabor were invited to a meeting of a secret intelligence group in Seattle. The group was called Project 139, a number derived from the U.S. Coast Guard's Thirteenth District and the Navy's Submarine Group Nine. It also included agents of the civilian-run Naval Criminal Investigative Service, which had counterintelligence duties within the Navy. Daly and Tabor went to their first and only meeting of Project 139 in Seattle that month and were told they would be allowed to take part in future meetings if they were "deemed worthy." The meeting ended abruptly when members of the group objected to Daly saying he would have to contact his commanding officer, Admiral Michael W. Cramer, the director of naval intelligence, about participating in the project. Project 139 had been monitoring Russian ship movements into Seattle since the early 1990s, but did not have the resources to do a good job, according to Daly. "Their activities were uncoordinated, and they did not have a full grasp of what was going on, nor the capability to monitor," he said. The group depended mostly on the Coast Guard's ship traffic monitoring system for its information. The system was limited because it worked only after the target had come into local waters.

Russian military spying had also come up during a joint U.S.-Canadian military exercise a year earlier, in November 1996. As part of officer training, a group of ships conducted a simulated war at sea. The *Anatole Koleshnichenko* sailed right through the middle of the exercise. Rear Admiral Russell Moore, the Canadian Forces commander of the Maritime Forces Pacific, dispatched a ship to shadow the *Koleshnichenko*. Other maritime patrol aircraft also followed the ship. The incident made it clear to the Canadians that the Russians were spying on their exercises and that the ships needed watching.

The Russians, incidentally, were not the only ones to practice nuclear submarine spying; in May 1996 the Canadians had detected a Chinese merchant ship spying in the northwest waters. But the Russians continued to be the main offenders.

On March 17, 1997, a group of senior Navy intelligence officers went to Esquimault, and Daly briefed them on what was being called the "anomalous activity" of the Russian merchant ships. The group included Admiral Cramer, Admiral Moore, and several other senior officers. "I briefed them on everything I saw," Daly said. He also told his superiors what was required. The most immediate need was for high-resolution imagery—of the *Kapitan Man* and other FESCO vessels involved in spying. The photographic reconnaissance mission was ordered.

Within a couple of weeks, U.S. and Canadian intelligence learned that the *Kapitan Man* had left its home port of Vladivostok en route to

Seattle. The Canadian government circulated a report labeled "Secret Spoke" on April 2, 1997. It said, "The vessel is expected to arrive in Tacoma, Washington, on 4 April. *Kapitan Man* was last located in the vicinity of 5310N 14950 on 2 April." That put the ship several hundred miles south of Vladivostok in the middle of the Sea of Japan.

Before it reached Tacoma, however, the *Kapitan Man* hovered off the coast of Queen Charlotte Island, north of Vancouver. The move was suspicious because the ship was on the leading edge of a storm that it could have avoided by sailing south. "That got the attention of the admiral and myself," Daly said. Furthermore, the *Kapitan Man* was not alone. The *Anatole Koleshnichenko* was also en route to the United States. As they passed through the Aleutians, the ships took separate courses. The *Koleshnichenko* held the Alaska coastline, and the *Kapitan Man* followed a direct route toward the Strait of Juan de Fuca. In addition, Daly said, "I did receive a report on April 7, 1997, that there was an intelligence officer on board the *Kapitan Man.*"

Daly said Admiral Moore told the intelligence center to come up with a "collection plan" for close-up photographs of the ships. "For some reason the Canadians passed this off to me and Chief Tabor," Daly said.

The plan called for catching both ships as they sailed through the strait, where the ships would have to stop or slow down near Port Angeles to pick up a harbor pilot. The idea was to use Canadian CH-124 Sea King helicopters based at Victoria International Airport to photograph the vessels. CP-140 aircraft (the Canadian equivalent of the U.S. Navy's P-3 Orion maritime surveillance planes), based in Comox, north of Victoria, were also used. The aircraft were told to remain on standby for immediate launch as soon as the Russian ships were spotted entering the Strait of Juan de Fuca.

"I made the decision that I would go up in the helo, as opposed to Chief Tabor or a Canadian enlisted man," Daly said, "if for no other reason than I was the one most familiar with the camera." Daly had used the Kodak DCS-460 to covertly photograph the *Koleshnichenko* in November during a visit to Seattle.

THE LASER

Early on the day of the mission, the watch officer at the Joint Intelligence Center in Esquimault was on the phone. It was 3:30 AM. "The *Kapitan Man* is inbound about to enter the strait," the officer said. "It's just outside Buoy Juliet," the last designated marker at the mouth of the Strait of Juan de Fuca.

Daly showered, grabbed his flight suit, and headed for the base. Reports continued to flow from the U.S. Coast Guard's vessel traffic management system to the intelligence center showing the ship's movement through the one hundred–mile strait. The squadron was notified to launch and to expect two men to join the crew. Along with Daly on the helicopter was Canadian Navy Lieutenant Ivan Allaine, who worked as an intelligence officer with Daly at the center in Esquimault. The air crew was briefed on the mission: The target was the *Kapitan Man*. The helicopter would make several passes around the ship. Daly sat on the port side of the helo in a jump seat. He was hooked up to a safety line.

The aircraft took off about noon and flew southeast from the military side of Victoria airport. As they reached the water, Captain Pat Barnes, the pilot, notified Daly of an unexpected development. "We've got an outbound boomer on the surface," Barnes said. The huge black submarine was the USS *Ohio*. It had just finished an unscheduled visit to its home port of Bangor to drop off a crew member who had fallen ill. Because its missions are secret, the submarine was not supposed to be on the surface. As a result, it had just had a direct encounter with the Russian spy ship *Kapitan Man*. Daly asked Barnes if they could make a pass over the submarine, but Barnes told him the pass would upset the boomer's captain. The *Ohio* was moving at about ten to thirteen knots. Daly asked the navigator on the helicopter to gauge how close the *Kapitan Man* had come during its pass of the nuclear missile submarine. His calculation: within a thousand yards. "If we had launched five minutes sooner, I would have been able to photograph both vessels in the same frame," Daly said.

A few minutes later, three merchant ships came into view. The *Kapitan Man* was the middle vessel. To avoid looking too obvious,

Daly directed the pilot to fly over the last vessel in the line. It was the U.S.-flagged container ship *President Jackson*. The helicopter made a single circle over the *Jackson* and then headed east for its several passes over the *Kapitan Man*. It was about 12:30 PM. Daly was wondering whether they would see anyone on the deck of the Russian ship and whether he would be spotted in his olive drab flight suit—distinct from the helicopter crew's blue flight suits.

Daly never suspected the Russians had a laser on board. "They were a commercial vessel," he said. "If anything I would have expected a gun of some kind, but never in my wildest dreams did I expect a laser. I did expect someone taking pictures of me taking pictures of them."

The State Department had taken the extraordinary step of interfering with a military investigation.

The three passes of the helicopters seemed uneventful. The pilot and crew chief said they had seen Russian personnel on deck. Captain Barnes notified the command center in Esquimault of the exact location of the helicopter and the *Kapitan Man*. After three circles, the chopper flew directly over the top of the ship. That was it. The mission was over, and they all headed back to Victoria. "As far as I knew," Daly said, "the camera was working and the mission was successful."

After reaching the airfield, the crew held an informal debriefing session. The crew reported seeing someone on the bridge holding what appeared to be a pair of binoculars. Lieutenant Allaine, the Canadian intelligence officer, recalled seeing a man on deck with his arms crossed over his head. But he could not discern whether it was a signal to the helicopter. Daly then drove back to his office at Esquimault to download the digital photos from the camera. Around 4:00 PM on that Friday afternoon, he handed the camera to Chief Tabor, who put the images in the office computer. Tabor was trained by the Navy in imagery technology and analysis. Daly then went into his office to make some notes on the mission. Around 5:30 Chief Tabor walked into the office and asked a strange question:

"Are you having any problems with your eyes?"

"Yeah, my right eye is bugging me," Daly replied. "I guess I must have gotten something in it when I stuck my head out the door because of the wind."

"Are you experiencing any kind of headache?"

"Yeah, I have a real bad headache."

"Well, I think you better take a look at this."

He handed Daly one of the photographs just taken of the *Kapitan Man*. It showed a red dot of light coming from the bridge of the ship. "I think you may have caught a laser beam in this picture," Tabor said. "I know this is supposed to be the running light area, but the signature of the light in this picture just doesn't look right to me."

Tabor, who had been trained in Russian laser systems at ONI headquarters, pointed out that the light in the photo had a white center and had an unusual "halo." Daly immediately telephoned the 433rd Squadron at Victoria International Airport, where the helicopter unit was based. It was about 6:00 PM when he reached the colonel in charge of operations for the unit. He told the colonel to contact everyone on the surveillance flight. "I have reason to suspect that we may have been lazed during that flight over the *Kapitan Man*," Daly said. "Please notify the crew and if anyone is experiencing any type of eye irritation or any discomfort whatsoever, to call us."

Daly's right eye, the one he had used to look through the viewfinder of the camera, was irritated. "It felt as though someone had jabbed me right in the eye with a finger," he said. There was also a burning sensation, the feeling experienced by looking underwater in a swimming pool with too much chlorine. "The headache was a headache I had never experienced ever before," he said. "It was isolated to the right side. A real strong ache." Daly's initial reaction was disbelief. "Why would they do something like this?" he asked. Tabor reminded him of the Russians' use of lasers to blind U.S. pilots and military observers in the past.

The former Soviet Union had often used lasers for military purposes. Tabor recalled that during the Cold War the Russians would fire lasers at pilots. Aircraft crews had been warned to don protective eye gear, but pilots spotting intelligence ships had nevertheless been injured. Intelligence officers working on the border in East Germany had actually been fired on by lasers. As recently as October 1998, two U.S. Army helicopter crew members had had their eyes injured by a laser while flying a mission as part of the U.S. peacekeeping force in Bosnia. And in 1998 the Human Rights Watch group obtained a declassified U.S. intelligence report that stated, "Russia leads the world in the development of laser blinding weapons." But the use of a laser against a Canadian helicopter was not something most officials in Washington expected from America's former enemy.

"I began to think it was plausible," Daly said. "But was it probable? It was going to take a lot more to convince me that it wasn't something in my eye after I stuck my head out the [helicopter] door. I wasn't close to being convinced."

Tabor told Daly to see a doctor right away, but Daly was too busy getting ready for a trip to a conference in Australia. Still, "While I was driving home, the pain seemed to get more severe," Daly said. "Any time a car came at me I seemed to get sudden surges of pain, and the oncoming headlights were absolutely blinding." All but convinced, he drove to the emergency room at Victoria General Hospital and told a nurse, "I would like someone to look at my eyes. I may have looked at a laser."

The examination was limited to the outside of the eyes, which according to the doctor showed signs of "abnormalities." A later examination by doctors who specialized in the effects of lasers would uncover lesions—small spots—in the lower half of the eye. The doctor at Victoria General, however, who had treated workers from a nearby shipyard for arch welding burns and debris in the eyes, said, "I don't know what to do for you. I have never treated anyone for this before."

The next morning cast aside all of Daly's doubts about his injuries. Daly awoke with a sharp pain in his eye. He went into the bathroom and looked in the mirror. There was a large blob of blood inside the white part of his right eye. He immediately called the desk officer on duty at ONI headquarters and told him what had happened. He then called Bremerton Naval Hospital and was told no one there had expertise in optical laser burns. So Daly found an eye doctor in Victoria, who discovered the eyeball was swollen.

Later that day, around 10:00 PM, the phone rang. It was Captain Pat Barnes. "Jack, it's Pat. I just wanted to see how you're doing," the helicopter pilot said.

"It still hurts like hell," Daly said. "It feels really gritty."

"Well, Jack, I got news for you: my eye's all fucked up too," Barnes said. The symptoms were eerily similar. The pilot explained that when he awoke in the morning he saw a blob of blood in his right eye and it felt as though someone had thrown a bucket of sand in it. He had also had a severe headache the night before. Daly told him to get to a doctor.

THE INVESTIGATION BEGINS

A meeting was called the next morning at the intelligence center, and the Canadians drew up a "significant incident report," outlining an encounter with a laser while photographing the *Kapitan Man*. Admiral Moore was briefed, and Daly called ONI headquarters to explain that the Canadians would soon be distributing facts about the incident to the U.S. Navy, to the office of the chairman of the U.S. Joint Chiefs of Staff, to the National Military Command Center, to the chief of naval operations, to the White House situation room, and to the State Department watch center.

Daly phoned the home of his ONI supervisor, Captain Eric Meyers, and told his story. Meyers responded, "Why the heck would they do something like that?" Meyers ordered Daly to write a report outlining the incident to the ONI and the commander in chief of the Pacific Fleet, based in Hawaii.

Daly also talked to Brad Millard, a civilian analyst at ONI headquarters. Millard asked Daly why he had waited two days to report the incident. "Because of the ramifications," Daly said. "This could be construed as a hostile act in U.S. waters involving a Canadian helicopter and a Russian-flagged merchant vessel. We wanted to make sure we had some evidence before we said anything."

"Get the report out as soon as you can!"

White House and State Department policymakers were alarmed because the incident could upset U.S.-Russia relations. And so the public knew nothing about it until May 1997, when a top-secret Joint Staff report was leaked to the author. (The Pentagon would not disclose the identity of the military officer who wrote the report, and efforts to track him down were unsuccessful.)

According to the report, the *Kapitan Man* "was transiting the inbound lane of the Strait of Juan de Fuca (U.S. territorial waters). This ship is known to the intel community and is suspected of having submarine detection equipment on board."

The surveillance by the Canadian helicopter was described in the report as "a fairly routine operation." Around 9:00 PM on April 6, the entire military chain of command was notified of the incident. According to the top-secret report, shortly after the first news reached Washington, the Department of State "contacted us to ask what DoD [the Department of Defense] intended to do about the situation."

"At the time, the details did not support taking action against the merchant vessel," the document states. General John Shalikashvili, the chairman of the Joint Chiefs of Staff, ordered the operations directorate to get more information.

"The focus of the operation was to collect pictures of the antenna array aboard the merchant vessel," the Joint Staff report said. "A total of thirty frames were taken with frame number sixteen showing definitive evidence of an emanation coming from the bridge area of the merchant vessel. Initial medical exams indicated some eye damage to both the pilot and the U.S. lieutenant, but none that is considered permanent."

Daly would wonder later where that information came from, since more than two years after the incident he is still suffering from severe eye pain and headaches. And Pat Barnes, still in pain from the effects of the incident, had his flying career cut short.

The report from Canada to the Joint Staff also stated that "the subject merchant vessel's sister ship (*Anatole Koleshnichenko*) was currently transiting the inbound lane with an unknown destination. MARPAC HQ [Maritime Forces Pacific, the Canadian military designation] had this vessel under observation earlier in the day." The

Pentagon would later mislead news reporters by claiming in public it had no evidence the ship was engaged in spying.

At 1:30 AM on Monday, April 7, the Joint Staff's deputy director of operations, known as the DDO, talked to Thomas Lynch, the State Department's director of Russian affairs, who said the department would "concur with DoD if we had reason to detain the vessel," and the decision was made to hold up the ship after consultations among General Shalikashvili and the deputy secretary of defense, John White. "This was based on a discussion DDO had with Lt. Daly, the American on the Canadian helo—there is enough evidence foul play occurred." The Coast Guard was ordered to detain the ship, which was set to depart that day at 6:00 AM.

What Lynch did not say was that the State Department had notified the Russian embassy in Washington that a search party would be boarding the ship. The tip-off gave the Russians time to notify their vessel of the planned inspection so that any lasers on board could be disposed of or hidden. The National Security Agency later confirmed exactly that through an intercept—officials at the Russian embassy in Washington had directed an official at the Russian consulate in Seattle to have the *Kapitan Man*'s captain get rid of the laser range-finder on board. But a later translation of this electronic intercept, interestingly, caused the National Security Agency to revise its earlier conclusion. Instead, all that was discussed, the agency concluded, was *whether* the ship carried a laser range-finder on board. Either way, the State Department had taken the extraordinary step of interfering with a military investigation.

THE COVER-UP

When the author broke the story in the *Washington Times* on May 14, 1997, State Department spokesman Nicholas Burns confirmed there had been discussion of the incident between senior officials at the department and the Russian embassy before the search of the vessel. But, Burns added, "We protested this incident forcefully to the Russian government. The Russian government in turn promised to cooperate with an investigation." The spokesman also denied that any restrictions had been placed on the Coast Guard and Navy search team. "There were no conditions placed upon the Coast Guard during that search—no conditions certainly on the part of the State Department. We wanted there to be a full search, as did the Pentagon, as did the Coast Guard."

Burns lied—and a secret State Department document proved it. An interagency group led by Robert Bell, Clinton's top arms control advocate at the National Security Council, had taken part in a "Secure Video Teleconference System" (SVTS) meeting on April 7. "The nine-member boarding party has instructions to search *public* areas of the ship for a laser [emphasis added]," State Department official Jonathan Kessler wrote in a secret memorandum on the SVTS meeting. "SVTS participants decided that if the crew of the vessel cooperates with the boarding party by admitting to illuminating the helicopter with a laser, and shows the party the laser, the case will be handled through Naval channels, although the search party will continue to search the vessel. If the *Kapitan Man* crew is uncooperative, a second SVTS will be convened April 7 to decide on a further course of action."

The crew did not cooperate. "The CG/Navy team aboard the *Kapitan Man* found no laser or any trace of a laser," Kessler wrote on April 8. "The American helo crew member Lt. Daly along with the Canadians left Canada at [midnight] 4/8 for San Antonio for further medical tests to confirm laser burns. The tests are scheduled to be completed around [noon] 4/8."

During the second videoteleconference on April 7, "the conferees could not agree on a course of action," Kessler stated. "State and NSC [National Security Council] opted to let the *Kapitan Man* leave Tacoma. DoD (except for the Coast Guard) wanted to detain the vessel until tests are completed on the helo crew."

At 12:15 AM on April 8, the National Security Council set up a conference call on the secure telephone system with Jan Lodal, a deputy undersecretary of defense for policy; James Steinberg, the National Security Council's executive director; Strobe Talbott, the deputy secretary of state; and James Collins, who was designated as the next ambassador to Russia. No military officials took part in the discussion, and the decision was made to let the *Kapitan Man* leave Tacoma. The ship sailed Tuesday morning, April 8.

Daly was helpless to intervene because he and the helicopter crew had been booked on a commercial airline flight to San Antonio. The U.S. Army Medical Detachment there was the premier facility for studying the effects of laser burns. But before Daly left, a call came in from the ONI. Did he know anyone who could go on the Coast Guard boarding party? Sure. Daly recommended a Navy friend based at the Whidbey Island Naval Air Station. Within an hour, however, Daly was informed that the boarding party had conducted a mere two-hour search. Captain Meyers, the ONI supervisor, said "all indications are they didn't find anything" on the ship, confirming what Jonathan Kessler of the State Department wrote. That would be contradicted by a member of the boarding party who reported that the searchers had been confronted by a group of Russian sailors in front of a locked compartment and were denied entry. The inspectors did not press to enter because they had a two-hour time limit.

"That was my first indication something was not right about this," Daly said. "It didn't make sense that it would go down like this." During the flight to San Antonio, Pat Barnes told Daly, "You know something, Jack, a year from now everybody is going to deny this ever happened, and you and I are going to be two poor shmucks with bad eyes for the rest of our lives."

In San Antonio, Daly and Barnes were examined and tested for several days. Bruce Stuck, the head of the medical group, told Daly there was interest in his case "at the highest levels" and that President Clinton was being briefed on a daily basis about his health.

Daly was discovered to have four to five faint lesions on the retina of the right eye, and the doctors believed the cause of the injuries was a "repetitive pulsed laser." The Army experts believed the laser type was a Neodymium-Yttrium Aluminum Garnet laser, or Ng-YAG, perhaps emanating from a laser range-finder. But laboratory tests in San Antonio were unable to duplicate the light seen in the pictures of the

Kapitan Man. One possible explanation is that the Russians used a handheld laser that combined a visible-light, red laser pointer—such as is common in lecturing aids—with a dangerous invisible-light laser.

Daly felt a certain relief at the conclusion. "We were essentially correct something had happened to us that involved a laser," he said. "But also at the same time there was a degree of disappointment because there was no physical evidence on Pat's eyes, because now this made the problem 'an anomaly.'" Though Barnes was suffering the same painful symptoms as Daly, no lesions were detected. Nevertheless, Daly said, "I knew for the most part that his flying days were numbered."

The doctors believe that Daly might have suffered greater damage because the laser's effect was magnified by the lens of the camera.

On April 27, more than two weeks after the incident, Daly and Tabor flew to Washington for a debriefing at ONI headquarters. Daly reviewed the files on the affair at the ONI collection analysis center, where a crisis action team had worked on the issue. Daly found that information he had relayed to headquarters had been reported inaccurately. He also discovered that the Russian embassy had been informed of the plan to search the *Kapitan Man.* "It didn't take a rocket scientist to figure out they were going to notify the consulate in Seattle," he said.

Despite all the evidence and despite Russia's track record with laser weapons, the Clinton administration let the Russians off the hook.

At a meeting with ONI officials, including Captain Meyers, the questioning got heated. According to Daly, Chief Tabor's credentials for analyzing photography came into question. "What qualifies you to make this call?" Meyers demanded to know. Daly interjected: "If he hadn't brought it to my attention I'd be sitting here saying, 'What the hell's wrong with my eyes?'" Daly remembered that, after Meyers left the room, Fred Frederickson, a civilian analyst for the Navy, commented, "You know, Jack, I think you're getting screwed for this."

"What do you mean?"

"There's no doubt in my mind this thing happened, but because of the implications and ramifications for this, I think you're getting screwed over this."

As the meeting continued, Daly suggested to the officials at the ONI that an independent investigative team be formed, employing laser experts. Daly recalled that, after lunch, another analyst, Commander Joseph Hoeing, confided to the lieutenant, "You do not know the pressure I am under to sweep this under the rug." Daly remembered, "As soon as I heard those words, I knew I was in trouble. The first thought that came to my mind was that this was a cover-up. Hoeing was under pressure to sweep it under the rug." Hoeing declined an interview with the author regarding the *Kapitan Man* incident. "That's a matter I'm not going to discuss," he said.

When the story became public in May 1997, the ONI investigation had been under way for about two weeks. Defense Secretary William Cohen, however, made no mention of the ONI's ongoing probe when he announced that the military's Joint Staff would conduct an investigation. Meanwhile, the State Department denied that the search of the *Kapitan Man* had been limited, and spokesman Nicholas Burns rejected the characterization of the department as having "acted like wimps" in dealing with the issue. But he offered curious explanations for how the matter had been handled. "Well, you see, we haven't been able to establish exactly the source of the laser," he said. A reporter then asked for a description of the protest the U.S. government lodged with the Russian embassy on the Sunday before the ship was searched.

"We were protesting the fact that an unusual activity occurred, a laser was shot at a helicopter, which didn't harm the helicopter, but unfortunately harmed one of the people in the helicopter," Burns said, ignoring the injured Canadian pilot, Pat Barnes. "We just felt that it was important enough to search the vessel and ask the Russians to fully cooperate with the search of the vessel and any other further investigative work that needs to be done subsequent to this whole incident. The Russians said they would cooperate with us," Burns said.

The truth is, the Russians did not cooperate. In fact, the National Security Agency intercept suggested they took steps to cover the incident up. It confirmed other suspicious information—that the crew of the *Kapitan Man* refused to allow the Coast Guard inspectors to look at all areas of the ship, and that there was no way the entire vessel could have been searched thoroughly within the two hours allowed the party to search for the laser.

Under later questioning from reporters, Pentagon spokesman Ken Bacon admitted that not all areas of the ship had been searched. The boarding party was "granted access to every part of the ship to which they requested access with one exception: There was a library to which the crew could not find the keys, and they did not go into that library." Bacon acknowledged it was possible the laser had been hidden in the library. But, the official spokesman insisted, Lieutenant Daly's injuries were "not compatible with a laser having been used on the ship." Pressed to explain his unusual statement—that a laser had been fired but that it had not come from the *Kapitan Man*—Bacon said, "I think you have to describe this as a mystery."

> **"I was betrayed and sacrificed by our government for a political agenda, one that believes our once most-feared foe has, overnight, become a friend we can trust."**
>
> —LIEUTENANT JACK DALY

The formal report issued to the public concluded:

> The Department believes that the eye injury suffered by the American naval officer is consistent with injuries that would result from exposure to a repetitive pulsed laser. Available evidence does not indicate, however, what the source of such an exposure might have been. Specifically, there is no physical evidence tying the eye injury of the American officer to a laser located on the Russian merchant vessel. The Department is not closing this investigation. There will be additional medical examinations. The Department will analyze any new information that might become available to identify the source of the injury.

The cover-up had been complete. The official Pentagon version was that someone or something fired a laser at the Canadian helicopter, injuring a U.S. military officer. But it was not from the *Kapitan Man*. The Russians had been let off the hook, and the Clinton administration's pro-Russia policy remained intact, despite all the evidence and despite Russia's track record with laser weapons.

A Navy admiral told me privately that the State Department's tip-off to the Russians was an obvious attempt to block the investigation. It made sure that U.S. inspectors would not find any signs of a laser during the search. "You can't search a ship if you tell them you are coming," he said. The admiral also questioned the official Pentagon explanation that the red light photographed by Daly on the bridge of the Kapitan Man was one of the ship's running lights and not a laser. "It was broad daylight," the admiral said. The only explanation for the red light was that it was some type of laser pointing device.

All in all, Daly felt that the ONI had bungled the investigation in ways that could not have been accidental. The final, public report was rife with errors and inaccuracies, and Daly's efforts to get ONI headquarters officials to fix them were fruitless. He was particularly upset because the defense secretary had said publicly that the eye damage was temporary.

Daly was ordered not to talk to any media, print or electronic, about the experience. The report did not mention Barnes and his injuries at all. The reason was clear: Place all the onus on a single person, discredit his account, and the matter could be disposed of with little or no consequence—a classic bureaucratic tactic.

Though Daly admits that he should have protested louder and sooner, he worried about the damage to his career. The damage happened anyway. After he agreed to be questioned by two staff members of the House Intelligence Committee who were looking into the matter, Daly was told by a Pentagon friend, "Big Navy questions your loyalty." It seems he was not supposed to have spoken to Congress. By the summer of 1998 Daly had been passed over for promotion to lieutenant commander. Then in January 1999 Daly was given a less than stellar military evaluation, and, worse, it was suggested that he undergo a psychiatric evaluation, a tactic used against whistleblowers who make waves. His career was obviously over.

Daly finally went public with his story in testimony before the U.S. House of Representatives on February 11, 1999. "In essence, this incident left Captain Barnes and I as victims of what could be argued was a hostile act in an undeclared war, an act of terrorism, and at a minimum, a federal crime," Daly said.

"I felt I had been betrayed by my country," Daly said in an interview with the author. "Pat Barnes felt the same way. Betrayed and sacrificed for a political objective. The only thing that was laid out to me [by Navy superiors] was to forget about it and move on."

Daly felt that the ONI had done everything it could to disprove the incident had ever happened. "I knew I might have to take one for the team, but I never expected the home team to run and hide and leave me alone on the field. I was treated as a traitor and a lunatic." During a meeting with the new director of naval intelligence, Rear Admiral Lowell Jacoby, Daly's appeals for help in resolving the incident were dismissed on the grounds that it had taken place before Jacoby had assumed command. Jacoby appeared before the House Armed Services subcommittee the same day Daly testified, and he did not dispute the lieutenant's alarming charges about a cover-up. "He's described the problem," Jacoby said. That was it. End of story. No other action was taken. So much for the Pentagon's claim that the investigation is still open.

TRUST BETRAYED

Daly left Canada in early 1998 and on February 28, 1998, became an intelligence officer with the Marine Corps Amphibious Group-3, based in San Diego. The Foreign Intelligence Liaison Officer (FILO) program that launched the U.S.-Canada intelligence program, and of which Daly was a part, is being disbanded as a result of the incident.

The pain, however, continues, and has affected both his eyes. "There are days when it seems worse than others," Daly said. "Most of the time it's like a really bad toothache—a constant ache in the eyes themselves. Other times it feels like I just got an elbow or a fist in the eye. At times the sensation is like eating ice cream too fast." On occasion, the pain resembles someone "sticking a needle in the corner of my eye." Daly is bitter about the handling of the affair. "I just want justice. I want to see somebody held accountable for the way it was handled." He also wants medical attention and, most of all, a full hearing on the incident and its handling.

Why the cover-up? "I firmly believe it was seen as jeopardizing our relations with Russia," he said. "Bill Clinton has said he doesn't want to be the guy who blew the opportunity for everlasting peace with Russia." Daly believed he was viewed by the powers in Washington as a "fly in the ointment," and he noted that his case was never discussed in the nine meetings between Vice President Al Gore and Russian Prime Minister Victor Chernomyrdin, who was ousted in August 1998.

Daly is especially bitter about the cover-up because the real threat to national security—Russian spying—is being ignored and is ongoing. "Why should the government lie to its own people when our national security has been compromised?" he asked. "And it continues to be compromised with impunity. I want to see those damn vessels restricted from ever entering that port. Send them to Los Angeles or Long Beach where they can't do any damage.

"If some guy said to me there may be some benefit in what happened, I could have accepted that," Daly told me. "Instead exactly the opposite has happened.

"The Clinton administration chose to hide the truth, this time because the perpetrators are Russian and the 'Cold War' is over," Daly went on. "I know for a fact that this is not entirely true, and I literally have the scars from this hostile act committed in U.S. waters to prove it. I firmly believe that our national security is in jeopardy. I believe someone on board the *Kapitan Man* was using a laser that was capable of recording the acoustic signature of the propeller on the USS *Ohio*. When we flew over the ship, [the laser] was turned on us knowing it would cause harm.

"Pat Barnes and I suffered irreparable eye damage resulting in permanent retinal damage. Pat was permanently grounded as a result of this incident and has lost all flight qualifications. He will never fly again. Both of us are in constant pain from this incident with little expected relief, as there is no effective medical treatment. Captain Barnes and I suffer constant agonizing pain in our eyes and our vision continues to worsen.

"Even if it had been a bullet and not a laser I am sure that there would still have been a cover-up. Pat and I were victims of an act of war or, at least, an act of terrorism. The use of lasers to ward off surveillance is a violation of the Certain Conventional Weapons Convention, Protocol IV. The intelligence community has evidence that this vessel and others like her are associated with the Russian military."

Many Americans fail to understand that the apparent improvement in relations between Washington and Moscow has not ended the deadly game of spy versus spy. Daly knows otherwise. He also believes Vice President Al Gore is to blame. "This incident was viewed as a possible stumbling block in U.S. relations with the Russians, including but not limited to big business investment under the Gore-Chernomyrdin Commission and the then-pending Russia-NATO agreement," he said.

"Despite being injured in the line of duty," Daly continued, "I was betrayed and sacrificed by our government for a political agenda, one that believes our once most-feared foe has, overnight, become a friend we can trust," he said. Daly believes a dangerous precedent has been set. The message to the Russians is: "You can get away with an intentional hostile act within U.S. borders and not only will your crime go unpunished, your illegal acts will be denied and your getaway assisted by the U.S. government."

Daly recalled, "When I enlisted in the Navy in 1982 I took an oath that I have repeated several times since, '...to protect and defend the Constitution of the United States... against all enemies foreign and domestic....' I believe very deeply in those words. Little did I ever expect that my own government would one day become an enemy.

"There will be those who will claim that this cover-up was conducted 'for national security reasons.' The culprits will use this as a veil to hide behind when it is our national security that they have jeopardized and our nation they have weakened. In fulfilling my duty as a naval intelligence officer I was betrayed and sacrificed so that our continuing relations with Russia would not be jeopardized, despite their continued illegal activities in our waters and on our soil.

"Secretary of Defense William Cohen not long ago stated to the press, during the Monica Lewinsky debacle, that he didn't believe that President Clinton 'would ever take risks with our national security.' However, I am living proof that he has."

Further proof of Daly's political suspicions came in a classified 1996 memorandum leaked to the author, revealing President Clinton's promise not to allow any events to embarrass Russian president Boris Yeltsin. (Part of the memorandum is quoted in Chapter 8.) In that regard, the *Kapitan Man* was only the thin end of the wedge of American surrender to foreign threats.

PART II

Threats

CHAPTER THREE

Nuclear Nightmare (Part One)

"Continuing turmoil and political uncertainty in Russia, as well as disarray in the armed forces, have raised concerns about the prospects for unsanctioned use of Russian nuclear weapons."

—Top-secret CIA report, 1996

On January 25, 1995, a scientific rocket blasted off from a launch pad in Norway, and the world came closer to nuclear war than it did during the Cuban missile crisis. The Norwegian rocket was launched early in the morning to study the aurora borealis, the beautiful natural phenomenon also known as the Northern Lights. But nearby Russian military forces detected the rocket launch and mistook it for a submarine-launched ballistic missile heading for Russia. The Norwegian government had notified Russia's foreign ministry about the scientific rocket launch well in advance, but for some reason the Defense Ministry never got the message. Instead, Russia's Missile Alert Warning System picked up the signature of the rocket as it headed skyward. Russian officers had only minutes to decide if their country was under attack.

The officer in charge of the strategic warning center remembered how officers had been fired after Mattias Rust, a young German, landed a small airplane on Moscow's Red Square in 1987, without ever being spotted by Moscow's vaunted air defenses. With that in mind, the air defense officer acted. Alarms signaled senior military leaders of a possible nuclear attack. Duty officers ran down the corridors of Russian ministries to notify President Boris Yeltsin, Defense Minister Pavel Grachev, and Chief of the General Staff Mikhail Kolesnikov.

This was not the first time the Russians had been alerted to a potential attack. Since 1990 Russian nuclear forces had gone to heightened alert status at least four times. Former CIA analyst Peter Pry, in his book *War Scare*, notes the still-present danger of a nuclear-capable Russia: "The Russian military's continued fixation on surprise attack scenarios into the 1990s, combined with Russia's deepening internal problems, has created a situation in which the United States might find itself the victim of a Russian preemptive strike for no good reason, but just because of a war scare born of Russian domestic troubles."

Russian tracking data indicated the Norwegian missile was possibly headed directly for the Kola Peninsula, where most of Russia's nuclear missile submarines are based. A deadly air-burst nuclear detonation in the area could disrupt Russian military communications. And the resulting "electromagnetic pulse" could cripple the Russian Army's ability to communicate—and counterattack.

Boris Yeltsin activated his *Cheget*, which contains the nuclear button. The *Cheget* has a display screen showing attack assessment data. On the left side is a status indicator screen, with several switches and six buttons, two-inches square. Two red buttons and a single yellow button offer three nuclear strike options; a white button, if pressed, orders no nuclear retaliation; another button can cancel a nuclear attack; a final button authorizes the Russian military to use nuclear weapons. No Russian leader had ever activated the *Cheget*.

Congressman Curt Weldon, Pennsylvania Republican and chairman of the House National Security subcommittee on military research and development, notes, "President Yeltsin was one decision point away—less than several minutes away—from launching an all-out nuclear attack on the United States. This was the closest the U.S. and Russia have ever come to nuclear Armageddon, far closer than during past incidences of international tension like the Cuban Missile Crisis. The idea that we came so perilously close to nuclear war as a result of a miscalculation, rather than any sort of provocative action, should be a cause for considerable concern both in Russia and the United States."

Yeltsin didn't act. The Norwegian missile eventually landed near Spitsbergen, some 650 miles away from Russian soil.

Despite the real danger, outside Russia almost nothing appeared in the press about the incident. The *Washington Times* published a short editorial with the headline "Nuclear Nightmare in Norway" based on a brief Russian Interfax news report.

NUCLEAR INSECURITY

The Clinton administration has tried to keep such incidents secret, lest the American public become alarmed at how dangerous America's Russian "ally" is. One of the early but largely unnoticed acts of the Clinton administration was the dismantling of the Energy Department's special intelligence program that monitored Russia's

> **The Russians asked for help with "methods to ensure that 'drunks' and 'psychotics' do not gain control of nuclear weapons."**

nuclear arsenal. According to those involved and department documents, not only was the so-called "Russian Fission" monitoring program halted in 1993, but its records were destroyed. Congressman Weldon called the act "a prime example of how any information that contradicts the Clinton administration's save-Yeltsin foreign policy is at best unwelcome or, worse, completely suppressed."

The Energy Department, however, was only one of several agencies responsible for monitoring nuclear affairs in Russia. Among the others were the CIA, the Defense Intelligence Agency, and the National Security Agency, and the unsettling reports from these agencies proved harder to ignore or keep secret. One "Top Secret" report produced in September 1996 by the CIA's Office of Russian and Eurasian Analysis and the Office of Weapons, Technology, and Proliferation was leaked to the author by officials in government who felt its findings should be shared with the American public. The report stated: "The Russian nuclear command and control system is being subjected to stresses it was not designed to withstand as a result of wrenching social change, economic hardship, and malaise within the armed forces. Moreover, some evidence suggests that, despite their official assurances, high-level Moscow officials are concerned about the security of their nuclear inventory. Adding to our concerns are significant gaps and inconsistencies in our information about the command and control of Russian nuclear weapons."

In essence, the report said the Russians are sitting on a powder keg that includes 7,500 deployed strategic nuclear warheads and 4,400 battlefield nuclear weapons. Additionally, the Russians are believed to have 10,000 more nuclear warheads in storage and a total of 21,900 nuclear warheads. Moreover, the CIA reported that Strategic Rocket Forces "have the technical ability to launch without authorization by political leaders or the general staff." Agents in the field "have repeatedly warned that the controls over some tactical nuclear weapons are poor," and Russian nuclear missile submarines, according to some intelligence reports, are believed to have on board all that is needed to launch their missiles in an "emergency." The CIA report went on:

> We continue to assess the possibility of unauthorized launch or nuclear blackmail as low, because many of the safeguards built into the old Soviet system are still in place. A severe political crisis, however, could exacerbate existing problems in military-political relations and widen internal fissures in the armed forces, especially if control of the military—already demoralized and corrupted—were to break down. Such a crisis could raise concerns about nuclear control.
>
> An array of evidence indicates that political authorities could not prevent the general staff from launching nuclear weapons on its own initiative.
>
> Nuclear armed units conceivably could become involved in conspiracies to threaten or blackmail perceived enemies or political authorities; a rogue submarine crew might have the autonomous ability to launch at least tactical nuclear weapons.

The report concluded that, although the Russian government has maintained that nuclear weapons remain under control, "some evidence suggests that Moscow authorities are concerned about the security of their nuclear stockpile." A case in point: A senior official of the Yeltsin government "privately agreed that concerns raised by the West with regard to Russian nuclear security were justified."

According to the CIA, the Russians had also asked for help with "methods to ensure that 'drunks' and 'psychotics' do not gain control of nuclear weapons. Russian officials privately have expressed fear of nuclear blackmail and have singled out the Russian Far East, where troop living conditions are particularly deplorable, as an area of concern where nuclear weapons might fall into the 'wrong hands.'"

The leak of this report was an extraordinary event, but the CIA played it down, telling reporters that the real highlight of the report was its conclusion that the prospect for an accidental missile launch was low. Asked about the report during the Pentagon's regular press briefing, Kenneth Bacon, the assistant secretary of defense for public affairs, said: "I don't want to comment on a report that should not have been leaked to the press, a classified report. Just let me tell you that it's been said from this podium... that the Russian Strategic Rocket Forces are probably their most elite or among their most elite forces. We believe that they're well disciplined, and well commanded.... We think they've taken prudent steps to keep the forces safe and secure.... We think that they generally have good security for their forces."

Translated, that meant that the president was intent on maintaining the fiction that Russian nuclear arms were secure because, were they not, the United States would need better defenses, especially missile defenses that Clinton vehemently opposed as upsetting to his arms control agenda.

But the September 1996 CIA report would not go away. It was followed by more bad news about Russian nuclear weapons control. Russian Defense Minister Igor Rodionov offered a blunt warning to Yeltsin in a letter he sent in early February 1997. "The worst thing of all is that I, the defense minister, am presiding over destructive processes in the Army and can do nothing about it," Rodionov wrote, referring to money owed to Russian troops. Then at a press conference, Rodionov dropped this bombshell. He told reporters in Moscow he was "concerned, first and foremost, about the declining reliability...

of the command and control system for strategic nuclear forces," including problems with nuclear control. "Uncontrollable processes, both in terms of hardware and servicemen, could develop," he warned. "The components of Russian command centers have already been pushed to operate twice or thrice as long as their useful life. Today, no one is able to guarantee the reliability of our command and control systems.... Russia may soon approach a threshold beyond which rockets and nuclear systems become unmanageable."

For his candor, Rodionov became the immediate target of a Soviet-style press campaign of denunciation. Yeltsin then ordered Prime Minister Victor Chernomyrdin to conduct an assessment of the nuclear missile command structure, which he soon declared safe. "Nuclear missiles will not take off by themselves," Chernomyrdin said. But he acknowledged that Russian nuclear missile forces were facing problems and needed new equipment to fix them.

Interestingly, during the dissolution of the Soviet Union, Chernomyrdin took over an entire defense industry plant and later sold it, stashing millions of dollars in foreign bank accounts. Chernomyrdin was also a favorite of Vice President Al Gore, and the two held regular meetings as part of a U.S.-Russian binational commission that was couched in secrecy and appeared to be a U.S. government attempt to pressure American businesses to invest in the crumbling and thoroughly corrupt Russian economy.

Russian Colonel Robert Bykov, a career strategic missile officer and a consultant to the Duma (the lower chamber of the Russian parliament) on military affairs, affirmed that "Rodionov is absolutely correct" about the dangers of nuclear forces. In an article in the newspaper *Komsomolskaya Pravda*, Colonel Bykov wrote: "We could launch an accidental nuclear strike on the United States in the matter of seconds it takes you to read these lines." Bykov revealed that nuclear command and control systems were put in place in the 1970s and that he took part in testing the system. As early as the 1980s, the equipment was falling apart and components were malfunctioning. "Even during my period of service, the equipment ceased functioning properly on more than one occasion, or certain parts of it spontaneously went into 'combat mode.' You can imagine what is happening now." The equipment designers who developed the system and are needed to maintain it have left the armed forces and defense industry and cannot be located, he noted. "The missile attack early warning system is disintegrating not on a daily but an hourly basis. But the person who states this openly is condemned." The Strategic Rocket Forces officer corps is also struggling with "psychological weariness," he added.

"Very few people," Bykov wrote, "can imagine the danger presented by the unstable psychological state of the duty-shift personnel of a strategic nuclear forces command and control center. Officers manning control desks are also people, and their patience is not infinite. Which is why we have no guarantee today that some Herostratos will not turn up in Russia's missile forces." Herostratos was the man who in 356 B.C. set fire to the ancient Greek temple at Ephesus, one of the Seven Wonders of the World, merely to perpetuate his own name.

> **Russia is embarked on a major nuclear buildup while, at the same time, the U.S. is sending over $1 billion to help the Russians "dismantle" nuclear weapons.**

What is not one of the Seven Wonders of the World is Russia's command and control system. Russian Strategic Rocket Forces chief Igor Sergeyev, now Russian defense minister, has complained that the nuclear communications use lines that are only slightly better than Russia's public telephone system. "They are, in other words, archaic and unreliable," according to the CIA.

Key Russian command and control equipment manufacturers have not been paid. Power cutoffs at sensitive facilities, including strategic command posts, are increasing. And in one case, communications with an operational nuclear missile base were disrupted after thieves stole communications cables.

President Clinton has tried to paint a brighter picture of Russia by trumpeting the "detargeting" of American sites by the Russian military, the result of the Clinton-Yeltsin summit in January 1994. Anthony Lake, the president's national security adviser, in a speech in

April 1996 said, "Today, because of our steady engagement with Russia and the new independent states, America's cities and families are no longer targeted by Russia's missiles." The president adopted the quotation as a campaign slogan whenever he would boast about his administration's arms control successes.

Yet, as the CIA noted in a secret report to Congress, "detargeting" is a purely symbolic step that does nothing to affect the targeting of strategic nuclear missiles. The measure was like pointing a gun at someone and telling them not to worry because it isn't loaded. "Placing ICBMs [intercontinental ballistic missiles] in a non-targeted status does not remove them from combat duty and only slightly reduces their readiness. For Russian ICBMs, detargeting means that targeting and flight data have been downloaded from the missile's onboard computer and replaced with a zero or null target set. Such data, however, remains stored in the fire control computer and can be reloaded into the missile's onboard computer within a few minutes. The impact of detargeting on combat readiness is thus easily reversible and cannot be monitored by national technical means," the euphemism for electronic intelligence-gathering systems. The CIA concluded that "unless a missile is actually demated from its warheads, defueled and removed from its launcher, the intelligence community is unable to monitor a change in its combat status."

Russian nuclear missile submarines on pierside duty or on patrol in peacetime operations have all the targeting data they need to launch their missiles stored on computer tapes within safes on the submarines. A signal from on shore authorizes the commanding officer to remove the tapes and load the targeting data into the missiles. "The detargeting agreement thus required no change to Russian procedures and did not change Russian SLBM [Submarine Launched Ballistic Missile] readiness (nor that of U.S. SLBMs)," the CIA said.

Worse, the "political commitment" to detargeting is not a treaty obligation and cannot be verified. "Effective verification would not appear feasible, nor would attempts at verification make sense, given the fact the process can be reversed within a short period of time," the CIA added.

Not only is "detargeting" unverifiable, but so is the use of American aid money designated to help the Russians disarm their nuclear forces. In 1995 the General Accounting Office (GAO) noted that, despite apparent irregularities, Moscow refused to permit American audits of the $1.25 billion in U.S. disarmament aid sent to Russia. In one case, the International Science and Technology Center in Moscow received $21 million in Pentagon funds, yet no restrictions were placed on the money, and it went to more than just "former" weapons scientists. "We found that scientists receiving center funds may continue to be employed by institutes engaged in weapons work," the GAO said. "Recipients of two center grants at three different institutes told us that they had been involved in nuclear weapons testing and nerve agent research." Other Russians employed part time by the U.S.-funded center also helped develop Russian weapons of mass destruction, the GAO reported.

In February 1999 the GAO issued another report stating that Russian weapons scientists were using U.S. funds earmarked for weapons dismantling to develop weapons of mass destruction. According to the report, some $24 million in Department of Energy money had gone to Russia. Though the GAO was unable to determine how much of that money went to help scientists focus their efforts on nonweapons programs, what was clear was that some of the money was being misused. "Some scientists currently working on Russia's weapons of mass destruction are receiving program funds," the report noted. In response, Senator Jesse Helms, North Carolina Republican and chairman of the Senate Foreign Relations Committee, stated, "It is absolutely unacceptable for the Clinton administration to donate the U.S. taxpayers' money to Russian scientists who spend their time working on poison gas, biological agents, and new nuclear weapons designs for the Russian government. That must stop."

In an attempt to explain, the Clinton administration called on Rose Gottemoeller, director of the Department of Energy's Office of Non-proliferation and National Security. Before taking the Energy post, Gottemoeller had endorsed a radical National Science Foundation study that had called for the complete elimination of U.S. nuclear weapons, an arsenal that was still needed to counter the remaining Russian nuclear force and China's nuclear arsenal. In 1998 Republicans in Congress blocked her appointment to a senior Pentagon post because of her left-wing views on nuclear deterrence, and she ended up getting her senior position at Energy, which is in charge of handling and developing nuclear weapons for the Pentagon. Gottemoeller praised the program of American aid to Russia, and, contrary to the GAO's evidence, she claimed that no U.S. funds were helping build new Russian weapons. Again, the Clinton method was to deny and mislead when it came to dangerous and unpleasant facts about Russia's weapons.

Dr. J. Michael Waller, a specialist on Russian reform with the American Foreign Policy Council, is one of many who cites the GAO report and says continued financial aid to Russia is contrary to America's national security interests. "The Clinton administration has never sought to ensure that U.S. aid is not used to benefit Moscow's nuclear weapons modernization programs."

THE BUILDUP GOES ON

Unlike the United States, which has no new nuclear weapons in development, Russia is engaged in a major strategic arms buildup that includes new long-range land-based missiles and a new class of long-range ballistic missile submarines, as well as continued development of a massive underground strategic defense program of secret bunkers and command centers for waging nuclear war.

Russia's First Deputy Prime Minister Yuri Maslyukov, a member of the Russian Communist Party, said in 1998 that strategic nuclear "rearmament" remained a top priority despite Russia's severe economic crisis. Moreover, "Along with rearmament of Russia's strategic nuclear forces, it is necessary to seek in a diplomatic way a limitation and reduction of the nuclear potential of the United States," Maslyukov said.

Each year Russia plans to produce between thirty-five and forty new Topol-M ICBMs, a modernized version of the world's only operational road-mobile ICBM, the SS-25. The Topol was first deployed in late 1997. Maslyukov said that in addition to mass production of the missile system the Pentagon calls the SS-27, Russia will continue "pressing home the fact that the Americans have a multiple superiority over Russia in the number of warheads and so must reduce their nuclear force."

The strategic forces modernization in Russia was the subject of a closed-door meeting led by Yeltsin in August 1998, when the Russian Security Council—Moscow's counterpart to the White House National Security Council—decided what to do about the arsenal in the face of a major economic collapse in Russia. Andrei Kokoshin, the council secretary, disclosed later that Moscow had decided to continue maintaining a robust nuclear force composed of land-,

Russia has been building a nuclear bunker the size of the Washington, D.C., metropolitan area.

sea-, and aircraft-based nuclear systems. "The resolutions passed by the Security Council envision preservation of the three-component structure of the nuclear forces... until the year 2010 and beyond that date," Kokoshin said. "The Russian [strategic nuclear forces] will make a transition from six types of ICBMs to one type for both stationary and mobile systems—the recently developed Topol-M missile. The first missile systems of this type were put in the state of operational readiness last year [1997]. According to tentative estimates the system will be used until the year 2020."

In other words, Russia is embarked on a major strategic nuclear modernization program while, at the same time, the United States is sending over $1 billion to help the Russians "dismantle" nuclear weapons. This buildup has gone on without any effort by President Clinton to discourage the Russians from spending millions on weapons that directly threaten the United States.

The Russian military buildup is across the board. It includes improvements to Tu-95 and Tu-160 strategic nuclear bombers as well as the long-range cruise missiles they carry. The bombers will be used until 2015 and longer, according to Kokoshin. For sea-based nuclear forces, Russia will continue to maintain a high combat readiness for its nuclear missile submarines. The new submarine is called the "Borei-class strategic missile boat"; construction began on the first submarine in November 1996.

Colonel General Vladimir Yakovlev, commander of the Strategic Rocket Forces, revealed that Russian nuclear forces have only slightly decreased their combat readiness since the collapse of the Soviet Union. He said the forces are at 90 percent of the combat effectiveness they had during the Cold War and described the SS-27 missile as the weapon of the twenty-first century. "They are second to none and by some parameters exceed all existing weapons of this kind," he said. However, General Yakovlev also said 62 percent of Russian missiles are operating beyond their life expectancy, and strategic command and control for all systems are now 71 percent beyond their operational life. In other words, the missiles, and the systems that control them, are deteriorating. Nuclear forces will continue to be the most important element of Russian armed forces because "we are lagging in conventional forces," the general added. "Depending on financing, we will try to keep 450 to 650 launchers fully deployed." Deploying 450 new strategic missiles by 2005 will require about 700 billion rubles, or $42 billion. According to Yakovlev, ten silo-based and mobile Topol-M systems will be commissioned annually until 2001; starting in 2002, thirty-one systems will be commissioned annually.

The buildup is not limited to offensive missile systems. "We are planning other measures also," Kokoshin revealed. The statement prompted renewed focus within the U.S. intelligence community on the huge strategic underground complex being built in the Ural Mountains several hundred miles east of Moscow. The facility, known as Yamantau Mountain, is part of continued underground construction costing Moscow billions of dollars. Yamantau Mountain, which appropriately translates into "Evil Mountain" in the local Bashkir language, is a secret installation, said by U.S. intelligence officials to be as large as the area inside the Washington Beltway, the highway that rings America's capital city.

The Russian government publicly acknowledged the secret bunker for the first time in a budget report published in Moscow on March 4, 1997. It was listed among "Defense Ministry facilities." Two secret "numbered" cities were built to house the 30,000 people involved in its construction. The cities are known as Beloretsk-15 and Beloretsk-16 and are located about 850 miles east of Moscow. The construction activity in the remote mountainous region includes the Beloretsk-Karlaman railroad and the Beloretsk-Ufa highway. A Russian newspaper described the facility as a "bunker for leadership" in the event of war and noted that "several billion" rubles had already been invested in the work as far back as 1992.

After the *New York Times* wrote an article about Yamantau, the Strategic Rocket Forces issued a statement suggesting that nuclear missiles may be secretly deployed at the site as part of what has been called the "dead-hand doomsday system," a nuclear command program designed to fire nuclear missiles automatically in the aftermath of a first strike on Russia. Pavel Felgengauer, considered one of the most informed and well-connected news reporters of Russian defense affairs, quoted "competent Russian sources" in April 1996 as saying such an automatic nuclear attack system was being developed and was nearly ready to operate. "But it is said that the bunker under construction in the Urals is 'not quite' part of this system," Felgengauer wrote. So what is it?

In 1998 U.S. Air Force General Eugene Habiger, then commander of U.S. nuclear forces, was given a tour of Russian strategic nuclear bases. When he returned to America, a reporter asked about the secret of Yamantau Mountain. General Habiger replied, "Another senior [Russian] official, very senior official, and I had a discussion and that's one of the issues I brought up. I said, We've got folks in the United States who think you're committing a technical foul by, you know, you've... got 20,000 people working there. You've got a lot of resources going to this place. Why don't you just take an American down there and show them what you're doing? And he said, 'Got it.' I don't know what's going to happen."

"Did they tell you what it was all about?"

"Yes. It's the same story that I got from General Sergeyev over a year ago and it is not military-related. It is a national crisis center. That's the way it was described to me. I said you need to put it to bed."

The Russians never did "get it," and the issue was never put to bed.

It seems that the commander of the U.S. nuclear arsenal did not really want to know what the true nature of the activity at Yamantau was and how it would fit into calculations for a nuclear war with the United States. His only interest was in having the Russians dispose of the problem.

Habiger was typical of the weak military leaders President Clinton selected for top positions. As America's most senior nuclear war-fighting commander, Habiger should be the most skeptical and most worried about the obvious dangers posed by the Russian nuclear force. But instead of making an honest assessment of the dangers of the Russian nuclear arsenal, Habiger appeared to be most gullible and tried to do everything possible to explain the threat away. An officer who traveled with the four-star general said privately that the Russians had duped him during the visit by showing him only the facilities that were in good shape.

The reason became clear as early as 1996. U.S. aid money to Russian weapons dismantling did not come without strings. U.S. legislation mandates that no funds can be spent in Russia until the Clinton administration certifies that Moscow is "forgoing any military modernization program that exceeds legitimate defense requirements." A multibillion-dollar nuclear command bunker the size of a city would obviously justify curbs on the hundreds of millions of dollars the administration was giving the Russian military.

On March 17, 1997, the CIA's premier daily intelligence publication, the top-secret "National Intelligence Daily," which is a compilation of the most important of various intelligence articles on world events, contained an article on the extension of a secret railway line leading to Yeltsin's dacha outside Moscow. "The underground construction appears larger than previously assessed," the CIA said. U.S. defense attachés in Moscow and satellite spy photographs, the CIA said, had revealed that work was moving ahead on a deep underground sub-way—hundreds of feet below the surface and thus able to survive a nuclear attack—designed for "rapid evacuation of leaders during wartime from Moscow." The Russians had nearly completed building a "relocation bunker" outside Moscow separate from the Yamantau Mountain complex, and another large underground facility north of that called "Kosvinsky Mountain." "Satellite imagery shows continued excavation at the deep underground complex at Yamantau Mountain and new construction at each of its aboveground support areas," the CIA went on. "Work continues on a nuclear-survivable, strategic command post at Kosvinsky Mountain." The report said Yeltsin and his prime minister, Victor Chernomyrdin, endorsed the projects. The CIA reported that in January 1996 authorities at Yamantau had barred defense attachés from going into the facility, citing a decree issued by Yeltsin in November 1995 that ordered the project kept in the dark. The report also revealed the Russian government's funding for Yamantau and noted that Cherno-myrdin sent a congratulatory telegram to the tunneling company that was building both the Moscow VIP subway evacuation system and the Yamantau complex.

While the Clinton administration trumpets its arms control "achievements," it never mentions that Russia is developing nuclear missiles aimed directly at the United States.

"Two decrees last year on an emergency planning authority under Yeltsin with oversight of the underground facility construction suggest that the purpose of the Moscow-area projects is to maintain continuity of leadership during nuclear war," the CIA concluded. "The command post at Kosvinsky appears to provide the Russians with a means to retaliate against a nuclear attack; the rationale for the Yamantau complex is unclear." When, at the height of the Cold War, U.S. national security officials spoke of prevailing in a nuclear conflict, liberal arms control advocates were aghast. Yet many of those same officials were now in positions of power, and they kept the American public in the dark about information revealing Moscow's multibillion-dollar efforts to do just that, and dismissed such reports as insignificant when they were highlighted in the press.

"It shows they take the threat of nuclear war so seriously that they're willing to spend scarce resources on it," said former CIA analyst Peter Pry. "These things are tying down billions of dollars... that could go into other enterprises the Russians need—for example, providing housing for Russian military officers."

Added Pry, "This is a manifestation of the Russians' continued war-fighting attitudes. They believe in the idea that you can survive and prevail in a nuclear conflict. These kinds of facilities are designed to survive for weeks and months."

By contrast, U.S. nuclear protective facilities have largely been shut down. The leadership protection facility underneath the luxurious Greenbriar resort in West Virginia has long since been abandoned, along with a facility in Virginia known as Mount Weather.

The mystery of the Russian strategic defenses prompted almost no public concern from the Pentagon after the CIA report was made public by the author. "We do not regard the program as a threat," said Pentagon spokesman Ken Bacon. "It is not an offensive program. It's a program to protect their officials. We don't understand why they're continuing to do this, but they are."

A reporter asked the spokesman, "Does the United States discuss this issue with Russia? About maybe how these funds would be better spent elsewhere?"

"First of all, money that's being spent on digging tunnels is not being spent on developing new missiles; it's not being spent on developing new offensive capabilities. I think that's a very important distinction. These are [spent] on defensive measures. We are worried primarily about offensive measures."

Then again, the civilian political leaders at the Pentagon do *not* seem concerned about Russia's new offensive weapons, and the United States does *not* know whether the Yamantau complex is involved in offensive strategic weapons development. It may well be. In any event, the Pentagon viewed the exposure of the deep underground construction as merely another inconvenient distraction in its pro–arms control policy. "I think this development, which has been going on for a long while and is not new, deflects attention from two more important developments," Bacon said.

What were those developments? The Strategic Arms Reduction Treaty (START) and the meaningless and unverifiable detargeting accord. While the Clinton administration loudly trumpets these "achievements," it never mentions that Russia is continuing to develop nuclear missiles aimed directly at the United States. The START I arms treaty was concluded during the Bush administration. The Russians, however, began violating it by disposing of their missiles as space launchers, which was banned. In response, John Holum, President Clinton's top arms adviser, led the effort to change the treaty to make that action legal, and then claimed it as an arms control success. The START II treaty, which has been ratified by the United States Senate, was stalled in the Russian parliament for years. And the Russian government was able to blackmail the Clinton administration by threatening to reject the treaty each time Moscow objected to U.S. actions, such as plans to build missile defenses or the U.S. military action against Iraq. Fortunately, Congress had made U.S. compliance with START II nuclear arms reductions conditional on Russian Duma ratification. However, with the treaty's prospects dim, the administration secretly drew up plans for a START III pact that the White House has said will be presented to Moscow as soon as START II is either approved or rejected. Some arms control critics view the treaty as much less valuable than the president claims and argue that Russian missiles might actually be safer rusting away in their silos and launch tubes than if they were dismantled, allowing individual pieces to be sold or transferred illegally. For the Clinton administration, however, the prospect of arms control with Russia was viewed as the most important national security imperative, even if the United States was the only treaty partner that could be counted on to fully abide by its obligations.

Several weeks after the Russians announced their strategic buildup plans, President Clinton was in Moscow. It was September 1998. He failed even to mention the Russian military programs. Worse, the president went out of his way to present a false picture of U.S.-Russian relations. In a speech to Moscow University students, Clinton said: "Look what our partnership has already produced. We reversed the dangerous buildup of nuclear weapons. We're two years ahead of schedule in cutting nuclear arsenals under START I. START II, which still awaits ratification in the Duma, will reduce our nuclear forces by two-thirds from Cold War levels. President Yeltsin and I already have agreed on a framework for START III to cut our nuclear arsenals even further."

For Clinton, arms control agreements that are long on symbolism and short on substance are the most important element in maintaining national security, even if only one side—the United States—takes its treaty commitments seriously, and the other side—Russia—has a track record of broken promises, deception, and cheating. Clinton also announced that "we've reached an important agreement" to share warning information on worldwide launches of ballistic missiles or space launchers. "This will reduce the possibility of nuclear war by mistake or accident," the president said. What the president neglected to add was that the agreement amounted to a series of discussions among U.S. and Russian officials and that, in the words of Robert Bell of the National Security Council, "there are many details that experts will still need to agree upon in the coming months."

And the "agreement"? It promises Russia's Strategic Rocket Forces a windfall of extremely valuable intelligence on American missile detection and warning systems, which could be used to make Russia's strategic missiles harder to detect.

SUITCASE BOMBS

Another serious Russian problem was identified by General Alexander Lebed, who for a short time was chairman of the Russian Security Council and Boris Yeltsin's senior national security adviser. Lebed revealed in 1997 that Russia had built small, portable nuclear bombs called "Special Atomic Demolition Munitions" that are designed for sabotage. The bombs are truly "first strike" weapons that would be used at the outbreak of nuclear war by saboteurs. They would set the bombs off in order to block communications with the electromagnetic pulse of their small nuclear blast; in addition, of course, the bombs' explosive power can do extensive damage. The threat posed by these weapons is not theoretical. The U.S. Army operates a Special Forces unit devoted to finding these small nuclear munitions before any saboteurs can use them at the outbreak of a war. The danger, according to Lebed, is that some of the one-kiloton–sized bombs—the equivalent of 1,000 tons of TNT—are missing. During his short time in power, Lebed ordered the Russian military to make an accounting of the weapons. But before it could be completed, Lebed was fired by Yeltsin. According to Lebed, "more than a hundred" of the bombs are missing. "I am saying that more than a hundred of the weapons out of the supposed number of 250 are not under the control of the armed forces of Russia," Lebed said in an interview with CBS's *60 Minutes* broadcast on September 7, 1997. Lebed added, "I don't know their location. I don't know whether they have been destroyed or whether they are stored or whether they've been sold or stolen. I don't know."

Lebed said that the weapons, the size of a suitcase, could be set off in twenty or thirty minutes and that security codes held by military or civilian leaders were not needed to use them. "Can you imagine what would happen psychologically, morally, if this weapon is detonated in a big city? No government would want to see such a situation. About 50,000 to 70,000, up to 100,000 people would be killed."

The general, who is credited with ending the war in Chechnya, knows what he is talking about. He was in charge of tactical nuclear weapons as a ground forces commander.

As if by reflex, the Clinton administration's response was to play down the alarming claims. Once again, the White House did not want to paint Russia in a dangerous light because of its efforts to woo Moscow and pretend that post-Soviet Russia had become an ally. It was more of the naive policies of a president who had convinced himself there were no dangers in the world. A White House National Security Council official was quick to say the general's statements were exaggerated, and repeated that the president and his national security aides believe current Russian leaders when they say all nuclear weapons are under control. "Lebed did not have responsibility in this area so his knowledge is not current," the National Security Council official said, a statement that was flatly and obviously untrue. Behind the denials was the obsessive desire of the president to negotiate arms agreements with Russia.

Lebed said the Russian military's response to his concerns about the missing nuclear weapons was "an ostrich reaction." Yeltsin showed no concern for the threat posed by the suitcase weapons, he added. Former CIA Director R. James Woolsey, the first of several CIA directors during the Clinton administration, said the Lebed allegations should not be ignored and that they warranted a detailed intelligence examination.

Lebed testified flat out before the U.S. Congress in March 1998 that Russia was dangerous. "The principal threats to Russia's security come from within," Lebed said. "They include political instability, economic crisis, corruption and crime, separatists...." Russian armed forces have not been paid regularly for years, and have been forced to work outside jobs. "They serve as guards, they work as porters," he said, noting that the military is consistently humiliated and degraded.

THE THREATS MOUNT

If Russia, a former superpower, had the potential to become a rogue nuclear state because of its internal instability, what about other states that are potentially even more hostile? What about other nations, like North Korea and Iraq, that pose a direct threat to U.S. troops stationed abroad?

Iraq, indeed, had already proven the lethality of its missiles during the Persian Gulf War.

CHAPTER FOUR
Nuclear Nightmare (Part Two)

"The threat to the United States posed by these emerging [foreign missile] capabilities is broader, more mature and evolving more rapidly than has been reported in estimates and reports by the intelligence community. Under some plausible scenarios, the United States might well have little or no warning time before operational deployment."

—Executive Summary, Report of the Commission to Assess the Ballistic Missile Threat to the United States, July 15, 1998

T he missile crew drove the launcher out from beneath a highway overpass in southern Iraq. The Iraqis had spent the day hiding from U.S. fighter bombers. It was shortly after dark on February 25, 1991, and the ground phase of the Persian Gulf War had been under way for two days. Thousands of U.S. and allied tanks and armored vehicles, backed by hundreds of attack helicopters, were pouring into Iraq in a pincer movement aimed at forcing Saddam Hussein to withdraw his forces from occupied Kuwait. The Iraqi flatbed-truck launcher moved into position in a culvert, set its brakes, and put its hydraulic stabilizers into the ground, as the erector bearing the missile slowly elevated the gray Al Abbas rocket into an upright position. The missile was a homemade version of the Soviet Scud missile, with a range of about 300 miles. Calculations were made to aim the missile at Dhahran, Saudi Arabia—about 200 miles to the south and the major hub for some of the 500,000 troops that had massed in the region since Iraq's August 1990 invasion of Kuwait. A few seconds later, the rocket blasted off with a deafening roar—a huge fireball that lit up the nighttime sky for miles around. The missile quickly reached a speed of 1,670 meters per second.

Half a world away, in a dimly lit command center at the U.S. Air Force's Space Command in Colorado, the missile appeared as a blip on an airman's green display screen. He recognized an Iraqi Scud heading for Saudi Arabia and immediately alerted the U.S. Central Command. The information was sent to the Patriot air defense batteries deployed around Dhahran. Patriots are truck-mounted supersonic missile interceptors adapted to kill Scuds, although they were originally designed to provide anti-aircraft support for infantry forces.

Five minutes after its launch, the Scud slammed into a makeshift barracks in Dhahran. Although it had a primitive guidance system, the missile scored a direct hit. Among the immediate casualties were scores of reservists of the U.S. Army's Fourteenth Quartermaster Detachment, who only weeks earlier had been whisked from their jobs and deployed to the Gulf. The weapon hit as the soldiers, many of them from the same small town of Greensburg, Pennsylvania, sat eating their field-ration dinners. The blast killed twenty-eight soldiers and wounded ninety-eight others—more casualties than the allies suffered in any other engagement in the war.

The question was, what went wrong? Why couldn't the Patriot intercept the Scud, as it had been designed to do?

The computers that operated the Patriot missile units had been running non-stop for more than a hundred hours, and the extended combat operations exposed a fatal flaw. The software glitch, which the Army was trying to fix, prevented the Patriot's tracking system from detecting the incoming Iraqi missile until two minutes before impact. By then it was too late.

The Dhahran missile attack showed that guided missile combat is no longer solely the province of advanced nations. The attack and the shortcomings of the Patriot energized the Pentagon to step up work on newer and better missile defenses. But years later the U.S. military has still failed to deploy a single missile defense system designed specifically to shoot down short-range missiles. And President

Clinton is largely to blame because of his stubborn belief that arms control diplomacy should be America's first line of defense.

THE GRAND SCHEME

On his election, President Clinton for the most part passed arms control policy over to Vice President Al Gore. Gore, in turn, tapped Robert Bell, the top arms control aide to Senator Sam Nunn, then chairman of the Senate Armed Services Committee, to become the White House National Security Council's key official in charge of "defense and arms control policy." While many Democrats believed all money spent on missile defense research was just another Pentagon boondoggle, others went further and actually claimed that missile defenses endangered world peace by undermining the 1972 Anti-Ballistic Missile Treaty. This belief persisted even though the Soviets had been violating the treaty since

The Iraqi missile attack on Saudi Arabia showed that guided missile combat is no longer solely the province of advanced nations.

the early 1970s. But for die-hard arms controllers like Bell and others who joined the Clinton administration, the Anti-Ballistic Missile Treaty became an end in itself, even though it was outdated. For one thing, there had been tremendous technical advances in long-range missiles. For another, the treaty was signed with the now-defunct Soviet Union. And finally, other nations were seeking their own long-range missile systems with no regard for the U.S.-Russian agreement.

The Bush administration had engaged Russia in serious negotiations to update the Anti-Ballistic Missile Treaty by adapting it to modern technical realities and broadening it to allow the sides to deploy limited nationwide missile defenses. The negotiations were still under way when the Clinton administration took over in January 1993.

In early 1993 Bell wrote, and President Clinton signed, Presidential Review Directive 31, which launched a major U.S. government review of U.S. policy on ballistic missile defense, with specific emphasis on the "future of the Anti-Ballistic Missile Treaty." That secret document led to Clinton's 1993 Presidential Decision Directive 17, which declared that the Clinton administration would regard the Anti-Ballistic Missile Treaty as "the cornerstone" of not only U.S. strategic policy but also U.S.-Russian strategic relations. The directive was the work of Bell, who in the secret review document outlined what he called a "comprehensive grand bargain."

The deal was this: The United States would agree to expand the membership of the Anti-Ballistic Missile Treaty to include Russia as well as Ukraine, Belarus, Kazakhstan, and other countries, effectively diluting American influence in negotiations on how the treaty is interpreted or modified. As part of the "bargain," the United States would "defer indefinitely" any discussion of changing the treaty to allow national missile defenses beyond the limited single-site system outlined in the treaty. Russia would agree to "clarifications" covering "theater," or regional, missile defenses. One American military officer told me, "This was no grand bargain; it was a grand sell-out" of American defenses, and he was not the only one to think so.

Any leverage Bell's grand scheme might have created instantly evaporated when the administration gave the non-Russian states seats at the table as full treaty parties, allowing them an equal say in the negotiations regarding regional missile defenses.

The Clinton administration betrayed its awareness of the political sensitivity of the negotiations by stamping documents related to the talks "Secret/Prose." "Prose" was a code word concocted by the National Security Council to hide the negotiations from public and congressional scrutiny. The code, later replaced by "Meteor," was described variously within the administration as a security "compartment," an ultra-secret "special access program," an intelligence agency "distribution list," and a top-secret "communications channel." But none of these classifications was permitted under federal secrecy rules. Although special access programs may be established to protect extremely sensitive national security information or intelligence sources and methods, federal law prohibits their use to conceal information that is merely politically sensitive, which is how the administration used "Prose" and "Meteor." The bogus code words were used so haphazardly that during some interagency meetings, officials from different executive agencies would show up with identical documents, some marked "Secret/Prose," some just "Secret," and some not classified at all.

Clinton administration efforts to defend the Anti-Ballistic Missile Treaty at all costs led to the death of President Reagan's Strategic Defense Initiative (SDI)—the revolutionary concept of shifting the reliance on mutual offensive nuclear annihilation to adopting strategic defense against long-range nuclear missiles. Defense Secretary Les Aspin killed what was left of the SDI program as part of a strategic review of U.S. forces. "We are here to observe another point of passage," a gloating Aspin announced in May 1993, "which is the end of the Star Wars era." The

> **The Clinton administration in essence gave the Russians a blank check to stymie development of American missile defenses.**

defense secretary said, "Ten years later we find that we have a different need for ballistic missile defense, not the massive program of space-based weapons that Ronald Reagan envisioned.... Saddam Hussein and the Scud missiles showed us that we needed ballistic missile defense for our forces in the field. That threat is here and now."

Yet according to Bell, the very first U.S. missile defense system designed specifically to knock out short-range Scud missiles, the Theater High-Altitude Area Defense (THAAD), was not legal under the Anti-Ballistic Missile Treaty because it could theoretically intercept strategic missiles. In 1993, when THAAD was still on the drawing board, Congress had directed the administration to determine whether the system was permitted by the treaty. Using computer models of the system's projected performance, the administration determined that under some circumstances, when THAAD's radar was assisted by high-quality tracking data from space-based early warning satellites, the system had a "theoretical" chance of intercepting the least capable Russian submarine-launched ballistic missiles.

The space-based tracking data could "cue" the radar, telling it where to expect an incoming missile to appear. By focusing its radar energy only on that section of sky where the missile was expected, the radar could detect the missile at greater distances, much as a narrowly focused flashlight beam can illuminate objects at greater distances than a wide angle beam.

Officials at the Pentagon protested, saying the theoretical analysis was arbitrary, self-imposed, and fashioned largely by a group of inter-agency lawyers with no expertise in weapons development. Moreover, the computer analysis ignored evidence that it was impossible to use THAAD to intercept strategic ballistic missiles; in fact, Lieutenant General Malcolm O'Neill, director of the Ballistic Missile Defense Organization, told Congress that THAAD could not be used as an anti-ballistic missile system, even though it was declared noncompli-ant under the administration's novel interpretation of the Anti-Ballistic Missile Treaty.

For the Clinton administration, even theoretical or potential viola-tions of the Anti-Ballistic Missile Treaty could not be tolerated. Preserving the pact was more important than building defenses that could defend American troops or cities. At Bell's urging, Clinton decided THAAD "could not be field-tested or deployed... without vio-lating the Anti-Ballistic Missile Treaty," according to a secret memo-randum. One problem with this decision was that the language of the treaty is ambiguous on this point; it states only that neither country can give missiles, launchers, or radar "capabilities to counter strategic ballistic missiles." The treaty provides no guidance for determining what the term "capabilities to counter" means. For decades the United States and the Soviet Union were free to determine the mean-ing for themselves—that is, until the Clinton administration decided that the term must be clarified with Russia at the "Standing Consultative Commission" in Geneva. Thus THAAD faced an impass-able roadblock—put in place by the Clinton administration, remov-able only by the Russians. Ironically, only the U.S. government charged that THAAD was noncompliant; the Russians never voiced any concern about the system.

Bell also succeeded in getting Clinton to assert that "the administration... will adhere to the traditional or 'narrow' interpretation of the Anti-Ballistic Missile Treaty. The United States will not seek amendments to the Anti-Ballistic Missile Treaty to permit (1) expansion of the number of anti-ballistic missile sites and ground-based interceptors beyond those currently permitted [1 and 100, respectively], and (2) development, testing, or deployment of space-based sensors for direct battle management, or (3) development, testing, or deployment of space-based interceptors." Clinton said such options could be looked at in the future if a national missile defense were to be built and deployed. But secretly, President Clinton, at the urging of Bob Bell, made sure that U.S. negotiators would be involved in talks that would ultimately make the Anti-Ballistic Missile Treaty more restrictive of U.S. short-range missile defenses, systems that the treaty was never intended to limit.

The grand bargain had become a grand scheme. Instead of continuing the Bush administration's effort to cooperate with Russia on developing missile defenses through the Defense and Space Talks, the new administration first abandoned those talks and then in essence gave the Russians a blank check to stymie development of American missile defenses.

The presidential directive proved to be a prescription for a national security disaster. Russian negotiators welcomed the talks and proceeded, in Soviet-style fashion, to use them as a diplomatic means to limit the effectiveness of U.S. regional defenses, at the same time selling Russia's SA-10 and SA-12 anti-missile air defense systems to other countries.

The negotiations began in late 1993. The opening U.S. proposal, and its accompanying logic, were simple: Theater missile defense systems would not be deemed to have "capabilities to counter strategic ballistic missiles" so long as they were never tested against ballistic missiles traveling faster than 5 kilometers per second, the speed of the most capable missile that U.S. theater defense systems were designed to intercept. The logic was that neither side could ever be confident of a weapon's capability if that capability had not been tested; thus neither side could be confident its theater defenses would be effective against strategic missiles, and strategic stability—the ability to annihilate each other—would be preserved.

The Russians agreed—and then asked for more. They demanded that the range of target missiles—which is closely associated with the missile's speed—be restricted as well, to 3,500 kilometers. That concession secured, they demanded that the capability of the *interceptor missile* also be restricted. Russian negotiators were particularly insistent that the United States not have missile defenses capable of shooting down Russian submarine-launched nuclear missiles. In June 1994 the administration agreed to Russia's interceptor speed limits, despite opposition from many in the Pentagon who viewed the concession as a prescription for "dumbing down" U.S. missile defenses.

The author broke the story on July 1, 1994, in the *Washington Times*, with an article bearing the headline "U.S. accepts Russian speed limits on interceptors."

A confidential June 16, 1994, memorandum to General John Shalikashvili, the chairman of the Joint Chiefs of Staff, from Admiral Jeremy Boorda, the chief of naval operations, and General Merrill A. McPeak, the Air Force chief of staff, laid out the reasons why accepting speed limits was a bad idea. "Accepting such limits could have the effect of locking us into our current defensive technology, while offensive threats continue to evolve," they wrote. "We urge continued JCS [Joint Chiefs of Staff] opposition to performance limits."

"Shali," as the chairman was known, at first stood firm against the speed limits. But Deputy Defense Secretary John Deutch assured him and the military chiefs that the speed limits would be "temporary." "The problem is, 'temporary' is not defined," said an official involved in the debate. "This is going to kill future Navy and Air Force programs."

Predictably, the conciliatory U.S. negotiating tactics prompted the Russians to ask once again for even greater concessions, which stiffened General Shalikashvili's spine. "During the recent Standing Consultative Commission, Russia rejected the U.S. proposal and countered with additional, unacceptable limits," Shalikashvili noted.

"Clearly the United States should make no further concessions. It may even be time to start thinking about rolling back the U.S. negotiating position. At a minimum, we should take a broader approach."

"The United States has made important concessions in advance of each SCC [Standing Consultative Commission]," Shalikashvili wrote. "The Department of Defense should make it clear to the interagency that we can make no further such adjustments without seriously undermining our ability to field needed TMD [Theater Missile Defense] capabilities." Any more Russian obstruction of U.S. proposals should result in a "top-to-bottom reevaluation of the entire U.S. approach" and a "rollback" to the position that strategic systems are designated by tests and nothing else.

The Joint Staff also heard from Lieutenant General Malcolm O'Neill, director of the Ballistic Missile Defense Organization, in a secret memorandum on November 9, 1994. "This negotiation has been a history of U.S. concessions to Russian demands," he said. "Each concession was supposed to bring about the breakthrough; instead each has invited more concessions." The talks in Geneva were effectively "dead" because of Moscow's unreasonable demands. "The Anti-Ballistic Missile Treaty is a treaty which *is not* based on performance limitations," O'Neill wrote. Worse, O'Neill said, by engaging Moscow in the negotiations at the anti-ballistic missile commission, "we are discussing new obligations."

By November 1994 the military leadership felt it was time to bail out of the Geneva talks. Admiral William Owens, vice chairman of the Joint Chiefs of Staff, said in a handwritten note to "Shali" on November 10: "I believe we should: 1) Take our time and not get locked into a written agreement now; 2) *Build* a cooperative U.S./Russian TMD approach (FOR REAL)." He suggested scrapping the Geneva forum and creating a "board of directors" with senior U.S. and Russian defense officials, telling the Russians "we intend to continue testing/deployment of THAAD" without interceptor speed limits. Whatever negotiations took place in Geneva, the United States should continue "working toward [the] long-term goal of protecting our capability at *any* interceptor speed."

A month later Shalikashvili wrote to the director of the Joint Staff: "I want to send a letter from me to John Deutch outlining a) that some months ago when I agreed to go along w/Deutch formula on this, we had an understanding that if the Russians wouldn't bite, we would withdraw our offer and go back to the drawing board; b) Therefore I want to start over along the lines outlined by VCJCS [Vice Chairman of the Joint Chiefs of Staff Admiral Owens]; c) Recommend therefore our staffs work out details and inform interagency—JS."

The Pentagon put together a damning assessment of the U.S. position on missile defense. The early U.S. concessions set the pattern for the negotiations, in which U.S. compromises and openness—intended as inducements and signs of good faith—generated more demands by the Russians and their allies in Geneva. By the fall of 1994 the Russian negotiators had worked over their American counterparts and succeeded in attaching a host of restrictions, including interceptor speed limits, where and in what numbers the systems could be fielded, and numerous other restrictions that many in the Pentagon thought would stymie effective U.S. missile defense development.

MISSILE DEFENSELESS

Meanwhile, events were intruding on this "delicate ballet," as chief negotiator Stanley Riveles liked to describe the Standing Consultative Commission negotiations. The first flight test of the THAAD system was approaching, and the Pentagon was growing impatient with negotiations that were standing in the way of its test program. Bell stated in a "Secret/Prose" memorandum of December 8, 1994, that with the first flight test of THAAD two months away, the administration had to decide whether to go ahead without a U.S.-Russian Anti-Ballistic Missile Treaty clarification. Although the White House regarded THAAD testing as contrary to the treaty, a legal review by the Pentagon in November had determined that THAAD testing would be allowed if the software was altered so that it blocked "external cueing data." Thus began the "dumbing down" of the THAAD system to make sure it was less effective at its job—killing enemy missiles.

Bell agreed that any "significant delay in THAAD testing" would delay deployment, and time was running out. Bell conceded that the "theater-range missile threat continues to grow, as underscored by continued North Korean development of a family of No Dong ballistic missiles." So THAAD testing was allowed to go forward, with President Clinton approving the test on December 22, 1994. Still, Bell fretted about the Russian reaction.

Things became more difficult for Bell after November 8, 1994, when the Republicans took control of the House and Senate, winning seats by promoting a "Contract with America" that called for, among other things, building missile defenses. With the Russians playing games in Geneva, Bell felt that his beloved Anti-Ballistic Missile Treaty might be thrown into the ash can of history.

In January 1995 Bell wrote an "eyes only," "Secret/Prose" memorandum to members of the Interagency Working Group Principals—the top arms control officials from the State Department, Office of the Secretary of Defense, Department of Energy, CIA, Joint Chiefs of Staff, Arms Control and Disarmament Agency, and Office of Science and Technology Policy. It outlined a post-election strategy for another

> **President Clinton bargained away the most effective missile defense system the United States could develop.**

grand bargain to save the Anti-Ballistic Missile Treaty. The document was headlined "ABM/TMD Demarcation Game Plan."

Bell had no intention of giving up on the Geneva talks, as the military leadership was suggesting. Instead, he determined to defeat Shalikashvili's plan in the interagency group. The plan rested on a dubious presumption: The United States could "convince" Russian leaders that U.S. regional missile defenses "pose no threat" to Russian strategic missiles. The Russians would be told, "absent an agreement on demarcation, the Anti-Ballistic Missile Treaty will be threatened by those who view it [as] a barrier to legitimate theater missile defenses," Bell wrote. "Put differently, critics of our handling of this issue will argue that the 'demarcation impasse' threatens the very existence of the treaty. Failure to resolve this issue will lead to domestic pressure to abandon the Anti-Ballistic Missile Treaty in order to provide for effective theater defenses. Thus the best way to ensure that the Anti-Ballistic Missile Treaty regime continues in place is to resolve the demarcation issue."

The endgame plan was to reach a "demarcation framework" that would avoid the difficult constitutional requirement of Senate ratification of treaties. The goal was to finish the framework agreement for the May 1995 summit meeting between Clinton and Yeltsin, a deadline that gave the Russians leverage to wring out further concessions. The White House offered the Russians an initial enticement of up to $30 million in technology for missile defenses, and a commitment to share early missile launch warning data with the Russian military.

But Bell's strategy seemed doomed, for the Russians continued their intransigence at the Geneva talks and responded to the THAAD testing with warnings that ratification of START II could be "easily derailed."

As the talks dragged on, a group of sixteen Senate Republicans wrote a stinging letter to Defense Secretary William Perry in late December 1995, chastising the administration for its failure to move ahead with missile defense. "American troops now deploying to Bosnia... are as vulnerable to the threat of ballistic missiles today as they were during Desert Storm, when 28 soldiers died from a ballistic missile attack on their barracks in Dhahran," the senators wrote. "We are not willing to depend upon luck the next time Americans in uniform are called upon to risk their lives abroad."

On the Geneva missile talks, the senators said: "[W]e are hopeful that you will work with us to ensure that five years from now we will not be lamenting the passage of another five years since the end of Desert Storm without the deployment of effective theater missile defenses to protect our troops and interests abroad." The letter was signed by all the Senate GOP leadership, including Majority Leader Bob Dole of Kansas, Majority Whip Trent Lott of Mississippi, Republican Conference Chairman Thad Cochran of Mississippi, and Ted Stevens of Alaska, chairman of the Appropriations subcommittee on defense.

The missile talks continued for another two years, in the course of which the Clinton administration intentionally misled the Joint

Chiefs of Staff. During a briefing in the Pentagon's secure room known as "the tank," a White House official told the military leaders that during President Clinton's April 1996 summit meeting with Boris Yeltsin there would be no discussion of missile defense negotiations, only a proposed nuclear test ban treaty and revisions to the treaty on conventional forces in Europe.

"That briefing was part of a deliberate deception plan on the part of the White House," said one Pentagon official. "The only conclusion we could come to was that the White House negotiated with the Russians against its own military." What the White House had been hiding from the Pentagon was its new concessions to the Russians—the U.S. agreed to Russia's long-sought demands to ban all space-based regional defenses and to allow nuclear-armed regional defenses.

President Clinton held a press conference on April 22, 1996, announcing that "real progress" had been made on the missile defense issue he had assured the Joint Chiefs of Staff would not be discussed. "I'm convinced that if we do this in an open way that has a lot of integrity, I think we'll all be just fine on this and I think it will work out very well," Clinton said of the missile defense talks.

But rather than negotiating with "integrity," Moscow again stonewalled, knowing that its S-300 missile defense systems, which are comparable to the Patriot, would soon be competing on the international market.

The CIA, however, was well aware of Moscow's motivations. In May the National Reconnaissance Office obtained satellite intelligence photographs of a Russian manufacturing plant at Verkhnaya Salda, about 650 miles southeast of Moscow. The photos showed that Russia had restarted production of at least thirty-eight SA-12 short-range missile defense systems. The CIA revealed in its "National Intelligence Daily" report that Russia had concluded several contracts in early 1996 to sell the advanced defense systems—the first such exports outside of Eastern Europe. Since Russia had all the air defense systems it needed, the CIA concluded, "Any surge in production is probably intended for export." Among the potential buyers were India, Finland, China, the United Arab Emirates, and Cyprus.

Missile defense expert Keith Payne said Russia clearly sought to curb U.S. theater missile defenses in order to boost the sales potential of SA-10s and SA-12s. "The Russians themselves have said that one of the reasons for trying to limit U.S. TMD systems is so their own TMD systems would be more marketable," said Payne, president of the National Institute for Public Policy near Washington, D.C.

Congressman Curt Weldon of Pennsylvania believes the Clinton administration's approach to missile defense seriously damaged efforts to build urgently needed defenses. Weldon is chairman of the House Armed Services subcommittee on research and development and is one of the few members of Congress who took an active interest in the missile defense talks. Weldon, who speaks Russian, traveled to Geneva to see firsthand what was going on. There he met with the chief Russian negotiator, General Victor Koltunov. Weldon uncovered an alarming fact about the talks in Geneva. It wasn't the Russians who wanted to add three new signatories to the treaty—Belarus, Ukraine, and Kazakhstan—it was Clinton. "I asked Koltunov, 'Why are you so adamant on multilateralizing the treaty with nations that aren't interested in missile defense?' And he said, 'You're asking the question to the wrong person. The person you should be asking is sitting next to you.'" That person was Stanley Riveles, the chief U.S. negotiator.

The congressman said he also could not understand why the United States and Russia were seeking to impose "artificial" limits on theater missile defenses. The reason became clear after he read a foreign news report in May 1998 indicating the Russians had begun marketing a new missile defense called the Antei-2500 system, which Moscow claims is the most advanced anti-missile defense system on the market. "They were negotiating with us to limit our systems so they could sell theirs," Weldon said. The Russian manufacturer Antei Concern announced in June 1998 that the Antei-2500 system is "beyond competition on the world weapons market." The state-of-the-art system is designed to "protect important state, military, and industrial objectives and Army groups from attacks" by ballistic and cruise missiles.

Weldon said that, after learning about the system, he immediately called the CIA and was given a briefing on it. Unsurprisingly, the system characteristics fit the Russian negotiating positions at the Geneva missile talks. The Russians were negotiating to protect their new Antei-2500 from treaty constraints and knew it would be years before the United States could put its missile defenses on the world market.

Weldon said Clinton should have never engaged in trying to expand the Anti-Ballistic Missile Treaty to cover theater missile defenses. "Theater systems were never intended to be part of that treaty," he insisted.

The missile defense talks got little attention in the media, outside of reporting by the author and some coverage in the trade press, and senior Pentagon officials refused to discuss the talks on the grounds that the negotiations were secret. One of the few voices to be heard on the matter was that of General Ronald Fogleman, the Air Force chief of staff, who worried that future U.S. missile defense capabilities were being negotiated away in Geneva. "All the chiefs have great concerns about this," Fogleman said in an interview in April 1997. "I would hate to see us negotiate away any kind of advantage we might have in space-based sensors, or in the airborne laser or anything like that."

The final agreement negotiated in Geneva was signed in September 1997 and contained two "agreed statements." The first stated that "low-velocity" missile interceptors could be tested only against targets that were obviously not stand-ins for strategic ballistic missiles. The second statement *prohibited* testing higher-speed regional missile defenses—such as the Navy's new Theater Wide Defense system—against target missiles with velocities greater than 5 kilometers per second or ranges beyond 3,500 kilometers, but did not conclude whether these faster interceptor missiles were legal even if they complied with the restrictions. Thus the years of talks had failed to resolve the most important issue—whether theater missile defenses are legal if they can theoretically hit long-range missiles.

The second agreed statement, however, *did* ban altogether, and for the first time, space-based interceptors or lasers for regional defenses. Space-based defenses offer probably the most promising way of stopping missiles early in flight; President Clinton thus bargained away potentially the most effective missile defense system the United States could develop.

In addition, a so-called "confidence building measure" agreement was signed, requiring missile defense launch notifications and data sharing, though the Russians were allowed to exempt their widely deployed SA-10.

The administration attempted to circumvent the Senate's advise and consent role for the U.S.-Russian Anti-Ballistic Missile demarcation agreement, but the Senate forced the White House to submit it for ratification by adding language in other treaty resolutions of ratification. By 1999 the White House had not sent the agreement to Capitol Hill, fearing it would be rejected. According to administration officials, Bell's White House strategy is to try to attach the Anti-Ballistic Missile demarcation agreement to a separate modification accord to START II, with the hope that linking the two will have a better chance of surviving a Senate ratification vote. The Russians, meanwhile, are continuing to toy with the United States by repeatedly threatening to reject parliamentary ratification of the START II treaty. The treaty was again withdrawn from Duma consideration in December 1998 as an expression of Russian anger over U.S. military strikes against Iraq.

NATIONWIDE VULNERABILITY

If President Clinton's achievements on theater missile defenses were negligible, his position on strategic missile defenses verges on the irresponsible.

More than once he has vetoed or used Democrats in Congress to filibuster and defeat legislation that calls for deploying limited defenses against long-range missile attack. The White House spin is that, while not fielding a defense, the Clinton administration will continue its multibillion-dollar "research" program. Yet in 1997 Pentagon documents revealed that the so-called national missile defense program was underfunded by an astonishing 100 percent. A single testing failure in 1997 had set the program back for an entire year. The reason? The Pentagon had not thought to produce a back-up test missile in case the test failed. And why was that? Most likely because the Clinton administration is uninterested in the program and failed to make building successful systems a top priority. And if the president keeps saying there are no missiles pointed at America's children, can missile defense for the nation be important?

The administration excused its failure to act on deploying national missile defenses by simply denying the existence of a ballistic missile threat to American soil. But that excuse was shattered by the report of the Commission to Assess the Ballistic Missile Threat to the United States. The commission, mandated by Congress in 1997, was headed by Donald Rumsfeld, President Gerald Ford's secretary of defense, and included promi-

> **The Rumsfeld Commission disclosed once and for all the truth that the Clinton administration had refused to acknowledge—the growing missile threat.**

nent defense and national security experts with diverse views, including Dr. Richard L. Garwin, a physicist with the Council on Foreign Relations who is one of the most outspoken opponents of SDI.

The Rumsfeld Commission looked into the potential of existing and emerging world powers to arm themselves with missiles tipped with warheads of mass destruction. Unlike most U.S. government analysts, who do not see all aspects of intelligence, the commission was given free access to all intelligence. The unfettered access was the key reason the commissioners came up with unanimous and comprehensive judgments about the dangers of developing missiles.

The final 307-page report was labeled "Top Secret," but even the relatively brief unclassified executive summary was stark:

> We unanimously recommend that U.S. analyses, practices and policies that depend on expectations of extended warning of deployment be reviewed and, as appropriate, revised to reflect the reality of an environment in which there may be little or no warning....
>
> We began this study with different views about how to respond to ballistic missile threats, and we continue to have differences.

Nevertheless, as a result of our intensive study over the last six months we are unanimous in our assessment of the threat, an assessment which differs from published intelligence estimates.

Whether short or long range, a successfully launched ballistic missile has a high probability of delivering its payload to its target compared to other means of delivery. Emerging powers therefore see ballistic missiles as highly effective deterrent weapons and as an effective means of coercing or intimidating adversaries, including the United States.

The commission noted that a "number of countries with regional ambitions do not welcome the U.S. role as a stabilizing power in their regions and have not accepted it passively. Because of their ambitions, they want to place restraints on the U.S. capability to project power or influence into their regions. They see the acquisition of missile and WMD [weapons of mass destruction] technology as a way of doing so."

As for Russia, the commission reported, "In the context of a crisis growing out of civil strife, present early warning and command and control (C2) weaknesses could pose a risk of unauthorized or inadvertent launch of missiles against the United States." And unlike the Clinton administration, which refused to recognize publicly the important role Moscow played in Iran's missile program, the commission noted that "Russian assistance has greatly accelerated Iran's ballistic missile program."

The commission also abandoned the self-deluding views of the Clinton administration on China, noting that China's uncertain future poses new dangers. "China is modernizing its long-range missiles and nuclear weapons in ways that will make it a more threatening power in the event of a crisis," the report said.

Moreover, "The extraordinary level of resources North Korea and Iran are now devoting to developing their own ballistic missile capabilities poses a substantial and immediate danger to the United States, its vital interests and its allies." The report added: "While these nations' missile programs may presently be aimed primarily at regional adversaries, they inevitably and inescapably engage the vital interests of the U.S. as well. Their targeted adversaries include key U.S. friends and allies. United States deployed forces are already at risk from these nations' growing arsenals. Each of these nations places a high priority on threatening U.S. territory, and each is even now pursuing advanced ballistic missile capabilities that pose a direct threat to U.S. territory."

North Korea posed a particular threat, since it had had to test-fire its No Dong missile only one time in 1993 before the missile was successfully deployed. When asked about it in 1998, Defense Secretary William Cohen would not admit it. Instead, Cohen said only that the missile had "completed development." The answer was a deception. Military commanders in South Korea knew it had already deployed and had acknowledged privately that the missile could be used against U.S. troops. The secretary apparently was hiding the fact that U.S. forces in Korea and Japan were vulnerable to No Dong missile attacks.

"The Commission judges that the No Dong was operationally deployed long before the U.S. government recognized that fact," the report continued. "There is ample evidence that North Korea has created a sizable missile production infrastructure, and therefore it is highly likely that considerable numbers of No Dongs have been produced."

Because of the intelligence community's failure to assess both the scope and pace of the No Dong development, the commission warned that "the United States may have very little warning prior to deployment of the Taepo Dong-2"—the missile that can target the United States.

As for Iran, according to the commission, it is making an extraordinary effort to build missiles capable of carrying nuclear, chemical, or biological weapons, and its missile-building capabilities are greater than those of the world's premier missile exporter, North Korea. The commission warned that Iran's new Shahab-3 medium-range missile would be tested soon and "deployed soon thereafter." Within weeks of the prediction, Iran fired off its first Shahab-3.

As for longer-range missiles, the report warned, "We judge that Iran now has the technical capability and resources to demonstrate an ICBM-range ballistic missile similar to the Taepo Dong-2 (based on scaled-up Scud technology) within five years of a decision to proceed—whether that decision has been already made or is yet to be made.... A 10,000 km-range Iranian missile could hold the U.S. at risk in an arc extending northeast of a line from Philadelphia, Pennsylvania, to St. Paul, Minnesota."

The commission also came to a startling conclusion: Because of "significant gaps" in U.S. intelligence agencies' knowledge of Iran's nuclear weapons program, the United States is "unlikely" to learn whether Tehran possesses nuclear weapons until after the fact. And even though Iran is building nuclear power plants under International Atomic Energy Agency safeguards, the materials Iran acquires for its nuclear power stations could be used as a source of nuclear weapons fuel to "construct a small number of weapons within the next ten years" simply by violating the safeguards. That was the course followed in the early 1990s by North Korea, which joined the International Atomic Energy Agency and then proceeded to build nuclear weapons.

The commission's findings about Iraq's missile program were also sobering. Despite nearly a decade of intrusive United Nations weapons inspections designed to identify and destroy all of Iraq's medium- and long-range missiles, Baghdad is developing new short-range missiles and in doing so is maintaining the engineering and industrial skills needed for long-range systems.

"Once U.N.-imposed controls are lifted, Iraq could mount a determined effort to acquire needed plants and equipment, whether directly or indirectly," the report said. "Such an effort would allow Iraq to pose an ICBM threat to the United States within 10 years. Iraq could develop a shorter range, covert, ship-launched missile threat that could threaten the United States in a very short time."

Although the intelligence community and the Pentagon's Joint Chiefs of Staff continue to assert they will have ample warning of new missile threats, the commission said the danger of new threats is increasing. "Precise forecasts of the growth in ballistic missile capabilities over the next two decades—tests by year, production rates, weapons deployed by year, weapon characteristics by system type and circular error probable (CEP)—cannot be provided with confidence. Deception and denial efforts are intense and often successful, and U.S. collection and analysis assets are limited. Together they create a high risk of continued surprise.

"The question is not simply whether we will have warning of an emerging capability, but whether the nature and magnitude of a particular threat will be perceived with sufficient clarity in time to take appropriate action."

The commission concluded its summary by stating flatly: "Ballistic missiles armed with weapons of mass destruction payloads pose a strategic threat to the United States. This is not a distant threat. Characterizing foreign assistance as a wild card is both incorrect and misleading. Foreign assistance is pervasive, enabling and often the preferred path to ballistic missile and weapons of mass destruction capability."

The Rumsfeld Commission disclosed once and for all the truth that the Clinton administration had refused to acknowledge—the growing missile threat. And the point was hammered home six weeks after the commission issued its final report.

NORTH KOREA'S NUCLEAR REACH

On August 31, at a remote missile facility in North Korea, the first Taepo Dong missile was fired. The missile accelerated quickly and traveled over northern Japan. Despite monitoring by U.S. and Japanese ships, airborne surveillance aircraft, and space sensors, the initial reaction from the U.S. government was that the missile was a two-stage rocket, nothing more. But after the North Koreans announced that their rocket had launched into orbit a satellite that was playing patriotic songs to the people of North Korea, the assessment was reviewed. On September 15 Pentagon spokesman Ken Bacon came out with this statement: "We believe that North Korea attempted to launch a satellite and failed."

"There are at least two significant revelations from this effort," Bacon told reporters. "The first is that they launched a multistage missile, and they were able to get the stages to separate. And the second is that the third stage of the missile apparently was a solid-fuel missile." The other two stages were older, lower-technology, liquid-fuel missiles, used in the North Korean Scud and No Dong missiles. "So they have some solid-fuel capability," Bacon said. "That's what we have learned from this latest test.

"When you add those two factors up, it means that they were experimenting with missiles," he added. "They have gone some way down toward developing a missile with a much longer-range capability. Now this is worrisome, and we have stated that many times. It shows that they are attempting to develop missiles that would give them a longer-range strike capability.... We're talking something that could be approaching intercontinental ballistic missile range." In short, North Korea had taken a quantum leap in its relatively primitive missile program, which had been based on 1950s Scud missile technology.

Inside the Pentagon, the news was explosive. U.S. intelligence agencies analyzed the trajectory of the debris from the satellite and concluded the new North Korean missile had a range roughly between 2,500 miles and 3,700 miles. According to a chart produced by the Pentagon in 1997, a missile with a range of 3,700 miles would be enough to hit almost all of Alaska and would reach the northernmost part of the Hawaiian Islands chain.

The communist regime in Pyongyang had achieved a major missile breakthrough. With a huge arsenal of chemical weapons and a secret nuclear program, could a warhead containing a weapon of mass destruction be far behind? The long-range missile threat to the United States was here and now. Robert Walpole, CIA national intelligence officer for strategic and nuclear programs, admitted that the CIA had been caught by surprise. "Although the launch of the Taepo Dong-1 as a missile was expected for some time, its use as a space launch vehicle with a third stage was not. The existence of a third stage concerns us; we had not anticipated it," Walpole said in a speech some two weeks after the missile test.

At the Pentagon, spokesman Ken Bacon refused to say whether the missile had been designated a Taepo Dong-1 or a Taepo Dong-2. "I think I don't want to get into the semantics of it here, because I'm not sure that we know at this stage. But it was a Taepo Dong." But the distinction was important, because intelligence agencies believed the North Koreans were developing a longer-range Taepo Dong-2. Many analysts feared that a Taepo Dong with a third stage would have even greater range, and perhaps could lob chemical or biological weapons not just on Alaska and Hawaii, but on some of the western United States as well. But Bacon, in the best tradition of a Clinton spin doctor, said that despite the test—and despite the CIA's being caught flat-footed—the North Koreans obviously had problems and were not ready to deploy. Other Pentagon officials, however, confessed to me that with even just one more test, the North Koreans could achieve something few other nations had done: develop an ICBM.

Would this new threat change the Pentagon's plans not to deploy a missile defense? Bacon would not answer directly. "You know, making decisions and reaching decisions about things is an organic process, it's not something we just do in the month of September," he said. "We monitor stuff all the time and adjust our conclusions according to the evidence. So far, we are still looking at aspects of this launch. We're still sort of combing through the radar and other information that we collected to figure out what happened."

The White House added its own spin to the alarming development. Since the North Koreans had failed to orbit a satellite, there was no worry, according to the political line emanating from the White House. North Korea still had to "master the unique and fairly daunting challenges of returning a reentry vehicle back to land, reentering the earth's atmosphere to hit a target without burning up," said White House spokesman Michael McCurry. "And given what they attempted to do, we don't think that that's something that was in the scope or parameters of the current program."

The president's response was not to speed up or deploy a national missile defense. It was to "aggressively pursue concerns we have... as we continue the bilateral dialogue" with the North Koreans, McCurry said. That is, a bilateral dialogue with a communist regime that still considers itself at war with the United States.

Once again the secret agenda was related not to North Korea but to Russia. The president was wedded to the Anti-Ballistic Missile Treaty, and missile threats would undermine the treaty's viability. The North Korean long-range missile test notwithstanding, the Clinton administration has maintained its almost religious commitment to the Anti-Ballistic Missile Treaty. On September 9, 1998, the Senate failed by a single vote to end a Democratic filibuster blocking legislation calling for deployment of a national missile defense capable of hitting missiles like the Taepo Dong. Senator Joseph Biden, Delaware Democrat and ranking member of the Senate Foreign Relations Committee, typified the inflammatory level of the debate when he took to the floor saying, "This bill will destroy the Anti-Ballistic Missile Treaty." Moreover, deploying a national missile defense would cause Russia and China to adopt "launch-on-warning" nuclear stances that, according to Biden, would make "nuclear war closer." But all Biden had done was to revive the Cold War doctrine of Mutual Assured Destruction, a doctrine irrelevant in dealing with rogue states like North Korea.

Henry Sokolski, a Pentagon official who specialized in foreign weapons development during the Bush administration, described the North Korean missile for what it was: "This is a totally new threat, and it looks like they leapfrogged beyond our expectation of a two-stage missile. They said, 'Hey, we're moving on to three stages.' What shouldn't amaze us is that the third stage failed. What is amazing is that up to now we never knew they had a third stage capability. It's alarming that they are working on a third stage at all."

Several months after the North Korean test launch, the Pentagon was shocked by new intelligence indicating China and North Korea were cooperating on a program to develop space launchers and satellites. Would the Chinese provide the North Koreans with their newly developed smart-dispenser satellite launcher that with a few modifications could become a multiple-warhead dispenser? When the National Security Agency intercepted communications between China and North Korea indicating that scientists from China were helping North Korea's satellite program, the White House again ignored the danger. An administration official told me, yes, there were exchanges of scientists working on the North Korean satellite but not on the Taepo Dong missile program. The Pentagon, however, was not fooled. Satellite and space technology is virtually identical to the know-how needed for building long-range missiles and their warheads. "I think the Chinese are helping them with the missile program, not just with satellites," said one senior Defense official. "The two are so closely intertwined, there is no way you can separate them."

The threats were mounting. About a month before the North Korean Taepo Dong test, Iran had test-fired its first medium-range missile, the Shahab-3, with a range of eight hundred miles, and Pakistan had test-fired a medium-range missile that had come off-the-shelf from North Korea. The tests showed that the missile danger—both to U.S. troops in the field and to the American homeland—was accelerating. And yet the Clinton administration's response once again was to dither.

By the end of 1998, the growing long-range missile threat became too great for the president to continue to ignore. In January 1999 Defense Secretary William Cohen announced with great fanfare that the Pentagon would begin budgeting, but not actually spending, $6.6 billion over the next six years for deployment of a national missile defense. While no money would actually be spent during the Clinton administration, still, for the first time the Pentagon admitted that it was wrong to think that no long-range missile threats would emerge until 2010. The threat could no longer be dismissed as a distant possibility; it was a reality. Nevertheless, Cohen asserted that no decision would be made to actually deploy a system because he was not sure the technology was available to make a missile defense system work. A deployment decision would not be made until June 2000, or even later.

Asked by the author what the United States would do if the Anti-Ballistic Missile Treaty could not be modified to permit a future U.S. national missile defense system, Cohen said the United States would pull out of the treaty should amending it fail. The secretary had committed arms control heresy. To rectify the damage, the president sent Bell out the next day to address a White House press conference. Bell told reporters that the United States was not going to pull out of the treaty and that the administration remained "committed" to its strategic vulnerability provisions. Clinton had planned to announce the added funds for missile defense during his 1999 State of the Union address before Congress, but he backed off when Russia's Duma refused to consider the START II arms treaty in response to the U.S. "Desert Fox" military operation against Iraq the previous month. To many observers, the administration's ploy appeared to be a political effort to nullify missile defense as a political issue for Republicans in the coming presidential campaign.

Congressman Curt Weldon believes the solution to this vital national security problem is not to expand the Anti-Ballistic Missile Treaty, but rather to deploy a limited national missile defense. Instead of reinforcing the Anti-Ballistic Missile Treaty, talks with the Russians should focus on developing a new strategy that includes not just offensive nuclear weapons, but a combination of offenses and defenses that would be mutually beneficial to both the United States and Russia. "We need to convince the Russians that it is time to move away from the antiquated MAD [Mutual Assured Destruction] theory," Weldon said.

Development and deployment of effective theater missile defenses, he argues, urgently need speeding up. No agreement with the Russians should be allowed to stand in the way of this urgent national security requirement. The danger of delays and restrictions is real, he believes. "In the end it is going to cost American lives," Weldon said. "Here we are seven years after Desert Storm and we still don't have a system than can defend troops against missile attack. That's unacceptable. This administration simply doesn't believe in missile defense."

In March 1999 Congress endorsed Weldon's stance on missile defenses when both the House and the Senate passed a bill declaring that it is the policy of the United States to deploy a national missile defense. The bill won wide bipartisan support, so much so that President Clinton could not veto it. Nevertheless, in private the White House remained opposed to deployment. And the Pentagon said in response to the legislation that it would not alter its plan to decide in June 2000 whether to field a national system.

So, as the 1990s came to a close, U.S. citizens and soldiers were still undefended against a missile attack because of the arms control policies of President Clinton. In the president's view, having an agreement limiting arms takes precedence over building systems that could defend against the growing threat of long-range missiles, whether from rogue states like North Korea and Iran, or from nuclear powers like Russia or China. Our lack of missile defenses is a fundamental failure of the most important tenets of government, the constitutional requirement to provide for the common defense. It is a betrayal that could be brought home to Americans in the coming years should a rogue state successfully reach United States soil with a long-range missile armed with a nuclear, chemical, or biological weapon warhead. Unfortunately, there is good reason to fear such an attack—as weapons development efforts in China show.

CHAPTER FIVE

The Long March Forward

"There are no more nuclear missiles pointed at any children in the United States. I'm proud of that."

—President Clinton, remarks at a fundraising dinner in New York City, February 15, 1996

"Thirteen of China's 18 long-range intercontinental ballistic missiles are targeted on the United States."

—CIA's "National Intelligence Daily," 1998

*B*ill Clinton campaigned for president in 1992 with promises to end George Bush's alleged "coddling" of the dictators in Beijing who in 1989 ordered People's Liberation Army troops to fire on unarmed pro-democracy demonstrators in Tiananmen Square. But once in office, the president formed an unusual alliance with American high-technology industrialists. As a result, the United States turned a blind eye to dangerous Chinese weapons and technology sales around the world and treated China with kid gloves; at the same time, national security export controls were loosened to benefit key political supporters and industries. Within a few years of the changes, the small but growing force of Chinese strategic nuclear missiles had become more reliable—thanks to American high-technology. This betrayal has been called treason by some. At the very least, it was a policy rife with deception. Apparently, highly effective Chinese political influence and intelligence operations against the United States had led the president and his advisers to try to fool the American people into believing China poses no threat.

On March 8, 1996, Chinese military forces launched one of the largest and most provocative exercises in the communist regime's history. The exercise kicked off with test firings of M-9 short-range mobile missiles into "impact areas" north and south of the island of Taiwan. Exercise Strait 961 lasted for seventeen more days. "This was the latest and largest of what the Office of Naval Intelligence (ONI) assesses to be a series of rehearsals of a contingency scenario for the invasion of Taiwan," the ONI said in a report on the maneuvers. "Strait 961 actually began with the launching of three M-9 short-range ballistic missiles into two closure areas situated provocatively close to the major Taiwanese ports of Kaohsiung and Chilung." The ONI warned that Chinese actions "aroused the suspicion that China might conduct some limited military action using the exercise as cover: assaulting one of Taiwan's offshore islands would serve to underscore its seriousness over the issue of reunification."

What the ONI report failed to mention, however, is that the show of force by China's People's Liberation Army nearly resulted in a direct military conflict with the United States. Two U.S. aircraft carriers were dispatched to the region in response to China's attempted military intimidation. The carrier deployments—which included cruisers armed with long-range, precision-strike cruise missiles; submarines; and other warships—made a deep impact on Chinese leaders. Since the Taiwan Straits crisis China has undertaken a steady military buildup that is directly aimed at fighting a future war with the United States, both conventionally on the seas and with strategic nuclear arms.

During the events of March 1996, the Pentagon and the U.S. Pacific Command, the military headquarters for any war in the area, dusted off war preparation plans kept locked in a vault since the early 1970s. Defense officials say war with China would follow the strategy of the 1991 Persian Gulf War: Form a coalition of area states, apply America's most modern and high-technology weapons, use massive aircraft and cruise missile strikes, and dominate the battlefield through superior intelligence and communications capabilities. And, for the first time since the 1970s, the Pentagon placed targets in China back into its nuclear war-fighting plans. In all areas American forces are superior. But China knows its weaknesses and vulnerabilities and is moving quickly—often with U.S. assistance—to improve its capabilities.

China's military modernization is deceptive and measured in order to avoid arousing international attention. But China's secret goal is to drive the United States out of Asia and become the dominant regional power.

Since 1997 Pentagon strategy reports have referred to the three million–strong People's Liberation Army as a "near peer competitor" of the United States. Within fifteen years, in fact, China will be a major military power, according to the Pentagon. But since coming into office in 1993, the Clinton administration has played down the danger of China's growing political and military power and has expanded business ties with China, at the cost of undermining U.S. national security.

China's military buildup is directly aimed at fighting a future war with the United States, both conventionally on the seas and with strategic nuclear arms.

In a revealing September 15, 1993, letter to Silicon Graphics chief executive officer Edward McCracken, President Clinton stated that, although he believed in the need for "strong controls" on U.S. exports of militarily-useful goods, "we also need to make long overdue reforms." "One reason I ran for president," Clinton wrote, "was to tailor export controls to the realities of a post–Cold War world." And in the post–Cold War world, Commerce Secretary Ron Brown was Clinton's point man, responsible for drumming up foreign business, even with potentially hostile states.

Clinton's reforms loosened export controls on computers, telecommunications products, and other high-technology goods that directly benefited China's military. Clinton created a new mercantilism. Many of his most senior officials involved in the policy were eager to do business, literally, with Chinese government- and military-owned companies. Defense Secretary William Perry was linked to Chinese People's Liberation Army General Ding Henggao, head of the weapons technology acquisition bureaucracy until 1997. His successor, Defense Secretary William Cohen, had set up an international business consulting firm that was seeking trade with China at the time he was tapped for the post. In short, United States "engagement" with China became, under Clinton, appeasement.

Within a few years, the liberalization of defense trade controls had reaped disastrous results for U.S. security. In April 1998 Congressman Dana Rohrabacher, a California Republican, disclosed alarming information about how U.S. aerospace companies had helped China improve its strategic nuclear missiles as part of a major ICBM modernization effort. He identified companies such as Loral Space & Communications, Ltd., Hughes Electronics, and Motorola as supplying the Chinese with space launch know-how that China used to improve the reliability and thus the lethality of its nuclear missiles.

"There is ample evidence that American technology was transferred to this hostile potential enemy of the United States, and that the vast experience of some of our best aerospace engineers provided the Communist Chinese the guidance needed to upgrade and perfect highly sophisticated weapons systems, increasing the reliability and capability of Communist Chinese rockets," Rohrabacher said, after being approached about the problem by aerospace workers in his home district in Southern California. "This has given what anyone has to admit is at least a potential enemy of the United States, a better ability to deliver nuclear warheads to our country, to American cities, to incinerate millions of our people."

It would soon be revealed that the chairman of Loral Space & Communications, Bernard Schwartz, had been a major contributor to the Democratic Party, giving some $1.1 million to Democrats and President Clinton between 1992 and 1998. In exchange, Schwartz was allowed to travel to China with Commerce Secretary Brown, and won favorable treatment from the administration in getting controls loosened so that Loral could launch its satellites on inexpensive Chinese booster rockets, which are nearly identical to the Chinese strategic missiles that would benefit greatly from U.S. technology transfers. Another key player in China's missile improvement was

C. Michael Armstrong, who as chairman of Hughes Electronics successfully lobbied Clinton into relaxing controls on exports of sensitive technology. According to internal White House memos, Armstrong pressured the administration into easing trade restrictions on China by threatening to launch a major publicity campaign against the White House.

IMPROVING CHINA'S ARSENAL

On February 15, 1996, a Chinese rocket exploded on its launch pad, killing six people and injuring fifty-seven others, with the fire destroying about eighty homes. As later revealed, the launch failure ended up seriously damaging U.S. national security. After the Long March rocket explosion, a team of scientists from Hughes and Loral was formed to find out what happened.

American "engagement" with China became, under Clinton, appeasement.

Their conclusion: An electrical problem in the flight guidance system caused a malfunction. The report also identified other problems with the new Long March booster. Without informing the U.S. government, the team gave the results of its accident report to Great Wall Industry, part of the Chinese government consortium known as China Aerospace Corporation. The data must have brought smiles to the Chinese missile makers' faces. It not only helped the Chinese company improve its commercial space launchers but also helped make China's nuclear-tipped missiles more reliable as ICBMs.

The Pentagon investigated the transfer of know-how to China by Hughes Electronics resulting from a January 1995 Chinese rocket launch explosion. In helping the Chinese rocket/missile manufacturers find the cause of the failure, the company provided militarily-useful technology. The Pentagon's bottom line, from a classified report of December 1998, was that "the Chinese were provided with technical data and assistance from Hughes' failure investigation that enabled the Chinese launch manufacturer and launch service provider to make design and/or operational launch vehicle reliability."

As Congressman Rohrabacher later noted, "Chinese missiles blowing up on launch is a good thing. We should not be making their missiles better." The Air Force's National Air Intelligence Center agreed, concluding in a secret report that "U.S. national security has been harmed" by the assistance that engineers from Loral and Hughes provided to the Chinese after the 1996 launch failure.

In February 1999 the Clinton administration—in the face of intense pressure from congressional Republicans—finally acted and blocked an export license for a Hughes communications satellite to be sold to the Chinese. According to Pentagon officials, the Chinese military would have benefited directly from the sale and deployment of the satellite, which would provide them with important command and control capabilities, including the capability to direct multiple warheads to distant targets. Additionally, launch of the Hughes satellites would have required the Chinese to closely scrutinize the satellites' maneuvering rockets, which would have given away important military know-how.

A special House committee formed in 1998 to look into the missile technology transfers uncovered a twenty-year intelligence and espionage effort by the Chinese government to acquire weapons technology. The bipartisan report of the Select Committee on U.S. National Security and Military/Commercial Concerns with the People's Republic of China determined that serious damage had resulted as a consequence. The report was kept secret. But the chairman of the panel, Congressman Christopher Cox of California, offered this stark conclusion: "We have found that national security harm did occur." Among the panel's findings, contained in the seven hundred pages of highly classified information:

- During the late 1980s, Chinese intelligence operatives infiltrated the Lawrence Livermore National Laboratory and obtained secret design data on the U.S. enhanced radiation nuclear warhead. The so-called neutron bomb kills by spreading deadly radiation, not by a large blast. According to officials familiar with the report, although the United States never tested its neutron bomb due to political pressure, the Chinese conducted five tests of the bomb, indicating they are ready to use the weapon.

- Chinese espionage agents penetrated the Los Alamos National Laboratory in New Mexico and obtained design data from an American scientist on the W-88 nuclear warhead, which is used on Trident II submarine-launched ballistic missiles. The W-88 is the most advanced U.S. warhead in the nuclear arsenal. The compromise took place in the late 1980s and was discovered only in 1995. The warhead data loss was one of the most damaging incidents in the twenty-year Chinese espionage spree outlined in the report. The Chinese tested a small warhead similar to the W-88 in the mid-1990s and are believed to have saved between two and ten years in development time by acquiring the U.S. data.

- The United States shipped high-performance computers to China by the hundreds—through waivers issued by the president. The Chinese had none of these ultra-high-speed computers as recently as 1996, but as of 1999 they had some 350 of the computers, which U.S. intelligence agencies believe are being used by the People's Liberation Army for nuclear weapons design and nuclear testing simulation.

- As a result of President Clinton's decision to loosen export controls on satellites, China was able to obtain very valuable high-technology information from U.S. companies, particularly Hughes Electronics and Loral Space & Communications, Ltd. Lax controls allowed the Chinese government to improve the reliability of its space launchers and, consequently, its strategic missiles. "They clearly went overboard [in cooperating with Chinese space entities], and they circumvented the law," said a U.S. government official close to the Cox Committee. "And they knew what they were doing."

- Launch failure investigations, such as those involving Hughes and Loral on two Chinese rocket failures in 1995 and 1996, were found to be woefully inadequate in protecting militarily-useful data from being lost to the Chinese government.

- Security in China before launches of U.S. satellites on Chinese rockets was lax. In some cases, China would have been able to gain access to militarily-useful technology on U.S. satellites and satellite launchers that were left unattended.

- A U.S. military colonel who worked in the Pentagon's Defense Technology Security Administration, and who was involved in overseeing Chinese launches of U.S. satellites, retired from the military and went to work for Loral. The arrangement raised questions among some Cox Committee members about the security problems related to satellite exports.

- Evidence indicated that Chinese space technicians and scientists were assisting North Korea's space and missile program.

The committee had set out to find out how U.S. satellite technology had helped make Chinese missiles more reliable, but it came to an even more startling conclusion: Chinese spies had stolen nuclear design secrets from the Los Alamos National Laboratory, achieving a major leap in China's nuclear technology—miniaturizing nuclear warheads. Paul Redmond, the CIA spycatcher who unmasked turncoat Aldrich Ames, told the *New York Times* that the nuclear warhead spying was on par with that of Julius and Ethel Rosenberg, who at the start of the nuclear age had given Moscow nuclear weapons secrets from the same laboratory. "This is going to be just as bad as the Rosenbergs," Redmond said of the case.

The case was discovered in 1996, but the White House kept it secret from both Congress and the American public because the administration feared the affairs would upset its pro-Beijing engagement policy. The espionage was also kept secret because of the ongoing investigations into Democratic Party fundraising, which showed that extensive funds from the Chinese government were funnelled into President Clinton's 1996 reelection campaign.

The panel recommended that the administration step up efforts to counter Chinese intelligence operations targeted at U.S. weapons technology, after Chinese agents in the late 1980s had obtained the critical design information on U.S. nuclear warheads. One recommendation called on the Energy Department, which runs the nuclear weapons laboratories, to "implement as quickly as possible and then sustain an effective counterintelligence program" as an "urgent priority." The panel also called for a comprehensive damage assessment to be carried out on past Chinese activities, and on whether nuclear weapons laboratory cooperation with China is too risky. In addition, the panel called for stricter Defense Department controls on satellite launches in China: "The Department of Defense monitors shall maintain logs of all information authorized for transmission to the [People's Republic of China], including copies of any documents authorized for transmittal, and reports on launch-related activities." It also recommended that all laws and regulations on export controls be "applied in full" to satellite manufacturers "including... communications after launch failure"—a recommendation clearly directed at the illicit sharing of technology with China.

Moreover, the Select Committee recommended a comprehensive review of the administration's loosening of export controls on high-speed computers to China. It called on China to set up an open system that would allow U.S. inspectors to check on whether U.S. supercomputers are being used to boost the Chinese military—monitoring that Beijing has so far refused to allow.

AMERICA IN THE CROSSHAIRS

In April 1998 the CIA circulated its premier intelligence publication, the top-secret "National Intelligence Daily," to the usual customers: Secretary of State Madeleine Albright, Defense Secretary William Cohen, National Security Adviser Samuel Berger, and several hundred deputies and aides. In preparation for a visit to China by Secretary of State Albright, the NID, as it is called, carried a brief article on the status of China's small arsenal of long-range nuclear missiles. Its conclusion: Thirteen of China's eighteen ICBMs are targeted on the United States. The CIA analyst who wrote the report unknowingly contradicted one of President Clinton's favorite political quotes, one used frequently in his political campaign rhetoric and fundraising speeches. In boasting of what he claimed were notable achievements of his administration's record on controlling nuclear arms, Clinton said to an audience of Democrats at a dinner in New York City: "There are no more nuclear missiles pointed at any children in the United States. I'm proud of that." Clinton made the statement on February 15, 1996—the very same day the Chinese booster exploded with the U.S. satellite, an event that would eventually lead to improvements in Chinese strategic missiles.

What the president was praising was the 1994 agreement with Russian President Boris Yeltsin to "detarget" U.S. and Russian nuclear missiles on each other's territory. A similar agreement was reached with the Chinese during a summit meeting in Beijing in 1998. The trouble with detargeting, of course, is that it cannot be verified and has no real-world military effect. A classified Pentagon report to Congress stated in 1997 that the detargeting was largely symbolic and could be quickly reversed, literally in minutes.

Peter Rodman, a senior White House National Security Council defense specialist during the Reagan administration, dismisses detargeting as not only hollow, but actually harmful. "It is the kind of agreement that brings arms control into discredit; it is unverifiable and, even if complied with, is reversible within fifteen minutes."

But for the president, detargeting was a prime example of the feel-good approach to national security, something that could not be challenged by any subordinate: There are no threats and most of all there are no missile threats because he has said so.

China claims it will use its nuclear arsenal only in retaliation against a nuclear attack. But the hollowness of China's promise was exposed when in October 1995 a Chinese general threatened to fire a nuclear missile at Los Angeles if the United States did not better accommodate an increasingly aggressive China. The tension started after the United States granted a visa to Taiwan's President Lee Tenghui to attend a class reunion at Cornell University in New York in June 1995. China responded by holding missile exercises near Taiwan in July and August, and two U.S. military officers were expelled from China for monitoring the missile maneuvers in southern China.

During a discussion in Beijing, People's Liberation Army General Xiong Guangkai, the deputy chief of staff for intelligence, told Charles

Freeman, a former assistant secretary of defense, that Taiwan was "a matter of vital interest to us. It is a matter of national unity. We are ready to sacrifice a million people for Taiwan." Moreover, General Xiong (pronounced "Shwong") said, given American inaction in Somalia and Bosnia, it was obvious the United States would not intervene to protect Taiwan. General Xiong then recalled U.S. threats to use nuclear weapons against China and North Korea during the Korean War. "You could do that then because you knew we couldn't retaliate," said the general, a rising star in the People's Liberation Army. "Now we can. In the end, you care a lot more about Los Angeles than you do about Taipei."

But even this thinly veiled threat, which Freeman reported to the White House, was dismissed by State Department spokesman Glyn Davies, who said, "There is no outstanding nuclear threat against the United States from China, and it's silly to build this up into anything more than it is, which is some low-level official saying something that could perhaps have been interpreted that way, and that was irresponsible to begin with." That "low-level official," General Xiong, just happened to be one of China's most important military leaders in charge of intelligence and the officer in charge of dealing with Pentagon officials.

"ENGAGEMENT" AND THE NUCLEAR BUILDUP

U.S. intelligence agencies reported in July 1998 that China's military is undergoing a major reorganization of its ICBM production facilities. This led to a surge in production of the CSS-4 Mod 2 strategic missiles. By the end of 1998 China had closed its sole ICBM production facility at Wanyuan in central China. Satellite reconnaissance and intercepts revealed that the Chinese were constructing a new ICBM production facility near Chengdu. "Closing hinterland underground production complexes like the Wanyuan facility are part of an effort to restructure and relocate defense industries to economic hubs like Chengdu," a Defense Intelligence Agency report stated. "Wanyuan's associated ICBM component factory completed a multi-year relocation to Chengdu in December."

"The decision to relocate the factory has led to complete production of the CSS-4 Mod 2 ICBM silo-based ICBM," the report continued. "Wanyuan delivered six of the missiles during the first four months of this year and will soon deliver the final two."

The production surge greatly increased the number of deployed ICBMs; only months earlier the CIA had concluded that only eighteen Chinese ICBMs had been deployed. The CSS-4 is the mainstay of the Chinese long-range nuclear missile force, but the system is being replaced with two new mobile ICBMs that will give China a highly survivable strategic force.

Wanyuan is part of what China calls its "rocket city," located in a highland region that was once a hunting ground for Chinese emperors. Before the relocation, it had thirteen research institutes, seven factories, and employed some 27,000 engineers and technicians. Wanyuan is also where China manufactures the Long March space launchers that benefited from the technical assistance of Loral and Hughes in 1996.

The similarities between China's space boosters and ICBMs were revealed in a chart produced by the CIA for the Senate Governmental Affairs subcommittee on international security, proliferation, and federal services. The CIA said booster stages used to launch satellites into orbit "could generally be used to develop an ICBM" and noted that "booster staging technology would be the same." Also, missile guidance and control systems, such as accelerometers, rate gyros, and guidance computers, are similar for both systems, although software and programming features would be different.

A secret report by the National Air Intelligence Center also stated that, under a multimillion-dollar contract with the American high-tech communications company Motorola, China was required to develop a special satellite dispenser that, with few modifications, would provide a rudimentary carrier for multiple-warhead missiles. Multiple warheads vastly increase the lethality of nuclear missiles. When MIRVs, as they are called, came on the scene during the 1970s, it was the most dangerous new development of the Cold War because a single missile now could double, triple, or quadruple its killing power. U.S. and Russian nuclear missiles today can carry up to ten warheads on a single missile, and a prime target of U.S.-Russian arms control talks is reducing the number of multiple-warhead missiles.

Motorola insists no vital U.S. technology was transferred to China under the contract between Motorola and China's space launch/missile industry. In any event, the Clinton administration approved an export license for the Motorola contract and appeared unconcerned about the consequences of China's missile warhead development. The administration even tried to deny that satellite dispensers could be converted into multiple-warhead launchers, ignoring the fact that the United States developed its ten-warhead bombs from similar space technology.

What did surprise the administration and the CIA was North Korea's August 1998 launch of a missile with a solid-fuel satellite launcher as its third stage. The missile came within minutes of putting a satellite into orbit. Intelligence agencies could not directly link the surprise North Korean satellite capability to China. But in addition to the findings of the Cox Committee, sensitive intelligence reports disclosed

Under Clinton, weapons proliferation was allowed to flourish so long as business was served—especially the business of key Democratic supporters.

to the author from the fall of 1998 provided clear evidence that China is covertly cooperating with North Korea on missile and space development.

China's interest in obtaining ICBM technology was disclosed by the Pentagon in 1996. On January 24, 1996, the "Military Intelligence Digest," the Defense Intelligence Agency's premier daily intelligence report to policymakers, revealed that China was trying to buy advanced technology related to Russia's SS-18 ICBM. Liu Huaqing, chairman of China's Central Military Commission, visited Moscow in December 1995 and "expressed great interest in purchasing SS-18 ICBM components," the report said. According to East European diplomats in Beijing, "the Chinese reportedly claimed they were only interested in using SS-18 boosters for their civilian space launch programs." The Chinese were also seeking "a possible SS-18 purchase" from Ukraine, which manufactures the giant ten-warhead missiles, the report added.

"China's interest in using SS-18 boosters in its civilian space program seems odd because the SS-18 engine characteristics may be incompatible with many sensitive satellite payloads," the report said. China's interest in the SS-18 "has military implications" because the communist regime "is updating its strategic missile forces."

"Beijing is working on an improved version of the CSS-4 ICBM and seems to be planning to incorporate MIRV technology into its missile force," the report went on. "China's interest in Russian SS-18 military technology probably is linked to Beijing's strategic force modernization, particularly the areas of missile guidance, accuracy, rocket engines, and warhead improvements. Incorporating SS-18–related military guidance and warhead technologies into China's strategic missile forces would greatly improve Beijing's ability to threaten targets in the United States."

Defense Secretary William Perry said in a 1996 interview that the report prompted the Clinton administration to send diplomatic protest notes to both Moscow and the Ukrainian government in Kiev. "We are aware that the Chinese have requested some components of SS-18 technology," Perry said. "We think that is a very bad idea. We vigorously oppose and have vigorously opposed such transfers.... I will assure you that there have been communications at high levels both to the Russian and Ukrainian governments. The demarche [official protest note] to the Russians and the Ukrainians was very specific on action they might take" on SS-18 technology transfers. Protests made to China over the attempts to buy the technology were "more general," he added.

The Chinese wanted the SS-18 technology to assist their two new ICBMs, called the DF-31 and DF-41. According to a National Air Intelligence Center report in November 1996, the DF-31, when deployed around the year 2000, "will give China a major strike capability that will be difficult to counterattack at any stage of its operation." The report warned that the DF-31 "will be a significant threat not only to U.S. forces deployed in the Pacific theater, but to portions of the continental United States and to many of our allies." The DF-31 will have a range of about 5,000 miles, and the DF-41 will be able to hit targets up to 7,500 miles away.

Another U.S. intelligence report in late 1998 reported that China was making progress on its DF-31 program. Satellite photographs had revealed preparations at the Wuzhai Missile and Space Test Center, located about 250 miles southwest of Beijing, for an "ejection test" of the new mobile missile—a special firing of the missile outside its launch tube before its engine fires. Ejection is the first stage of mobile or submarine launch. The first flight test, the report said, was set for December 1998, and deployment is expected around 2002, with each missile carrying an advanced thermonuclear warhead with a yield of about 500 kilotons—the explosive equivalent of 500,000 tons of TNT. With its range of about 5,000 miles, the DF-31 will be able to strike targets as far away as the northwestern United States. The deployments will make China only the second nation, after Russia, to deploy mobile long-range missiles, systems that are very difficult to track and harder to destroy in a conflict. The intelligence report confirmed that the longer-range DF-41 is also being developed.

According to the Air Force intelligence report, China has been focusing on improving the accuracy and ability to defeat missile defenses of its new ballistic missiles. "The Chinese gave evidence of this intent by testing two probable endoatmospheric reentry decoys on each of their two most recent ballistic missile R & D flight tests," the report said, referring to tests conducted on November 10, 1995, and January 10, 1996. "The decoys are designed to survive harsh atmospheric reentry conditions, and to simulate characteristics of the actual RV [reentry vehicle, or warhead]."

As if to send a message to President Clinton during his June 1998 summit meeting in China, the People's Liberation Army conducted a rocket motor test of the DF-31 at that time. The July 1 test was detected by U.S. satellites and other monitoring equipment at the Wuzhai Missile and Space Test Center. Highly classified intelligence reports on the test were sent to Secretary of State Madeleine Albright in China as she accompanied the president.

The White House and State Department reaction to these Chinese actions was typical. They sought to play down the significance of the increase in ICBM production and the missile motor test. The rocket test was "way down in the minutiae of what we know is an effort by the Chinese military to modernize their military forces," presidential spokesman Michael McCurry said. "The fact that they tested a rocket motor is not surprising. It is consistent with their overall effort to modernize their military." As it had in the past, the White House did everything possible to downplay China's growing military might and the threat it poses to the United States.

The president was quite simply protecting his alliance with the high-technology industrialists whose business would be harmed if the dangers of Chinese military development were publicized.

State Department spokesman James P. Rubin had earlier affirmed that the surge in Chinese ICBM production was not a concern and that it would not affect Washington's effort to develop a "strategic partnership" with China. "The U.S. and China are building a cooperative security relationship, as symbolized by the agreement of the two presidents not to target strategic nuclear missiles at each other," Rubin said. "At the same time, we are aware that China continues its limited efforts to modernize its nuclear forces."

Under White House instructions as part of the "engagement" policy with China, nothing was to be said by official spokesmen about the menacing buildup. The public was not to be told about Chinese weapons development, and, should unofficial leaks and other public revelations occur, the plan was to minimize the impact by disparaging or playing down the issue. With few exceptions, the press went along with the deception and never challenged the official view.

Clinton's engagement policy with China is based on the notion that if the United States "engages" China with trade and discussions, Beijing's communist rulers will respond in kind. The opposite has been the case. The more the administration looks the other way on dangerous activities and development by China, the more brazen the Chinese leaders have become in their efforts to reduce American influence in Asia and to crack down internally on those in China seeking basic freedoms and democracy.

A case in point was a Pentagon report on Chinese weapons developments. The report was turned over to the House National Security Committee, but never made public until Richard Fisher, a military analyst at the Heritage Foundation in Washington, discovered it. The report revealed that China was building lasers for use against satellites in space. China was also buying high-technology equipment including laser radar for this purpose. "China already may possess the capability to damage, under specific conditions, optical sensors on satellites that are very vulnerable to damage by lasers," the report said. "However, given China's current level of interest in laser technology, it is reasonable to assume that Beijing would develop a weapon that could destroy satellites in space."

After the story appeared in the *Washington Times*, a Pentagon spokesman, Navy Captain Michael Doubleday, denied it. He said there was "no evidence" for it and claimed the report was based on Pentagon "speculation" about future Chinese weapons development. But when pressed about China's current capabilities, Doubleday admitted that under some conditions Beijing's lasers could blind U.S. satellites. Army Colonel Richard Bridges, another Pentagon spokesman, also denied that China was building laser weapons. The importance of laser weapons—and perhaps the reason their development by the Chinese was denied—is that they strike at the primary advantage U.S. military forces have over adversaries: space-based surveillance, reconnaissance, intelligence, and communications. If it became public that this advantage had been betrayed by the administration's pro-business policy toward China, there could be profound political consequences.

Business interests have dominated Clinton's policies toward China since he first came into office and created the Economic Security Council parallel to the National Security Council. The creation of the office highlighted Clinton's desire to put trade on a par with defense and national security affairs. As a result, the president adopted policies that made sure no economic penalties were imposed on Beijing for covert sales of nuclear weapons technology to rogue states and proliferators. And he loosened export controls on satellite technology and supercomputers with little or no regard for the consequences to national security. When his intelligence agencies brought to his attention growing evidence of the weapons dangers, each new revelation was dismissed as inconclusive and ignored. U.S. business interests were treated as of paramount importance, and weapons proliferation was allowed to flourish so long as business was served.

CHINA'S BEST FRIEND

As it turned out, the scandal that emerged when the missile technology transfers to China were uncovered helped derail another potentially damaging Clinton administration plan to sign a formal agreement that would actually increase the flow of missile-related technology to China.

In preparation for Clinton's June 1998 summit meeting in China, National Security Council proliferation specialist Gary Samore drew up a plan that was secret until it was leaked to the author. On the cover note of the proposal, Samore said the following paper "proposes the elements of a missile deal with China, to be presented during Undersecretary [of State John] Holum's trip to China March 25–26." The plan noted, "In essence, we would offer to expand commercial and scientific space cooperation with China (in limited areas) if China meets our conditions for joining the MTCR [Missile Technology Control Regime, an international export-control agreement] and controlling its missile-related exports to Iran, Pakistan, etc." Despite Chinese promises and Clinton administration public assurances, these exports had not ceased.

Under the heading "Elements of the China Missile Deal," Samore outlined a proposal "to be announced during the president's trip to China later this year." China would be required to establish "effective" missile export controls, including controls on technology and components with missile applications. Samore also proposed having the Chinese agree again to something Beijing had said it would do since

1988: stop selling missiles that violate the missile technology control agreement. Under the Samore deal, China "does not transfer" missile equipment and technology to banned countries "including Egypt, Indonesia, Iran, Libya, Pakistan, Syria, Turkey, etc." A third requirement for China would be to agree "not to assist ground-to-ground missile programs in Iran."

Under the section labeled "what the U.S. does," Samore said the administration was prepared to support China's membership in the MTCR: "This would provide China with political prestige, the ability to shape future MTCR decisions, substantial protection from future U.S. missile sanctions, and would expedite somewhat the consideration of MTCR-controlled U.S. exports to China."

This remarkable statement captures the essence of the dangerous, misguided proliferation policies of the Clinton administration. Not only did the White House go to great lengths to ignore and cover up Chinese violations of international agreements that should have triggered economic sanctions, it also offered more concessions and a way to avoid U.S. missile sanctions. It would, that is, be rewarding China for selling dangerous weapons and technology around the world.

The Samore plan also offered China a new agreement on "scientific cooperation." The United States would issue a "blanket presidential waiver of Tiananmen Square sanctions to cover all future commercial satellite launches."

In addition, the United States would agree to increase the number of U.S. satellites that could be launched on Chinese boosters. "We would amend the existing commercial space launch agreement to increase the launch quota. We would also make clear to the Chinese that, as a practical matter, a lack of progress on the missile issue would prevent us from increasing launch quotas and could even endanger the existing quota."

The reference to "lack of progress" was telling. For months, the administration had been praising the "progress" made by the Chinese government in curbing dangerous proliferation activities, which ran the gamut from missiles and related technology to chemical and biological weapons materials and equipment.

Chinese reaction to the proposal was swift and negative. It is not clear why the Chinese rejected the plan, but White House officials said the fact that its presentation coincided with fresh newspaper reports about illicit missile technology transfers to China made it politically difficult to move ahead with it. Upon his return from Beijing, John Holum, the director of the U.S. Arms Control and Disarmament Agency, said, "I suspect it will be some time before the Chinese are interested in joining the Missile Technology Control Regime." He continued to insist, however, that China had made "enormous progress" in stemming its dangerous missile and weapons sales.

This was obviously untrue, and it overlooked the greater threat China was posing to the United States. As China specialists Richard Bernstein and Ross H. Munro noted in their 1997 book *The Coming Conflict with China*, Beijing's goal is to replace U.S. power and influence in Asia with its own. "No matter what happens in China, American policy toward that country should be guided by a clear and firm sense of American national interests. Today, that is not the case." Instead, the Clinton administration has combined a policy that is pro-business, pro–diplomatic appeasement, and, as a consequence, opposed to America's national security interests. With the growth in Chinese military power, Bernstein and Munro warn, "China could use even the vaguest threats of nuclear attack to preempt decisive American action in a matter... such as coming to the aid of Taiwan in the event of a Chinese invasion."

According to an ONI analyst, China's military strategy is provocative and alarming. Based on a 1985 Chinese security assessment, China shifted the focus of its defenses from its inland borders to its coastal areas, and is expanding its military reach not only to Taiwan but also to Japan and even the Philippines. "With this kind of strategy they have to modernize their Navy," the naval intelligence official said.

"We expect them to have more nuclear subs, we expect them to have major surface combatants, and we expect them to have a ship that is at least one generation ahead of what they have now, and we feel that they will have assets that can give them greater strategic depth to be able to go out to the second island chain to be able to defend that area and if possible beyond that," the analyst added. The purpose of this strategy is to have "better defense against attack against the homeland."

The Clinton administration has a much more benign view of China than China has of the United States. According to Pentagon official Michael Pillsbury, a China specialist and senior defense policymaker during the Reagan administration, "Numerous Chinese books and articles suggest an active research program has been under way for several years to examine how China should develop future military capabilities to defeat the United States by exploiting the Revolution in Military Affairs more effectively and more rapidly than the United States, particularly by tailoring new technology to 'defeat the superior with the inferior' with a strategy of asymmetric warfare." China's weapons of choice could include exotic power microwave weapons, information warfare, and antisatellite weapons that would be the most relevant for use against the United States.

President Clinton and his advisers have done everything in their power to downplay the threat China poses to American security.

China, contrary to its official statements, is also taking action to set up strategic bases in the center of one of the world's most important trading routes, the South China Sea. The Chinese military is stepping up construction of bases on two sets of small islands, the Paracel Islands and the Spratly Islands. The Paracels are also claimed by Vietnam and Taiwan, and the Spratlys are claimed by the Philippines and several other Southeast Asian nations. Vast gas and oil deposits are believed to be underneath the chain of small islets and reefs. On Woody Island in the Paracels, a National Reconnaissance Office spy satellite in January 1999 photographed new fuel storage facilities being built; the Pentagon believes these will be used as a base for China's new Su-27 fighter bombers, which it purchased from Russia. On Mischief Reef, some 150 miles from the Philippines, China is building a military base and is keeping several warships in a move that has heightened tensions with Manila.

Senior Clinton administration officials have refused even to mention the disputes in public, apparently to avoid upsetting the Chinese government. The most they would say is that the United States supports freedom of navigation in the region.

The Pentagon detected another alarming development in November 1998. At that time, Chinese military forces conducted a large-scale missile exercise along the Pacific Coast that included mock missile firings against Taiwan—and for the first time demonstrated simulated nuclear missile attacks against the thousands of U.S. troops based in Japan and South Korea. The exercise began in late November and ended in early December, according to a secret Defense Intelligence Agency report of December 2, 1998. Truck-mounted CSS-5 medium-range missiles and older CSS-2 missiles were prepared for launch and maneuvered in elaborate exercises that included the use of "obscurants"—special particle-filled clouds that are used to disrupt the laser designators used on American high-technology bombs and missiles. "Both weapons had never been pointed our way before," a senior administration official told me. The targeting of U.S. forces had also contradicted the pledge made by Chinese President Jiang Zemin only months earlier, during his summit with President Clinton, when he had promised that China would not target nuclear missiles at the United States.

On February 23, 1999, Congress released a Pentagon report on the military balance in the Taiwan Strait. The report was required under legislation and revealed that China's buildup of new missiles and other high-technology weaponry was shifting the balance of power in favor of Beijing and away from Taiwan. The report said China's military strategy is focusing on "preparing for military contingencies along its southeastern flank, especially in the Taiwan Strait and the South China Sea." Additionally, the Chinese strategy included a military buildup that is designed to fight regional conflicts with precision weapons, primarily missiles, against better-equipped adversaries. "By 2005, the [People's Liberation Army] will possess the capability to attack Taiwan with air and missile strikes which would degrade key military facilities and damage the island's economic infrastructure," the report said. Regarding China's formidable submarine power, the report said, "China will retain the capability to interdict Taiwan's [sea lanes of communications] and blockade the island's principal maritime ports." New weapons being considered for future warfare include laser guns that can kill or cripple satellites and "information warfare" weapons—the capability to cripple computer- and telecommunications-based infrastructures.

According to the ONI, the Pentagon, and other U.S. intelligence officials, China's new conventional and nuclear weapons program is comprehensive:

- It comprises at least six tactical aircraft, including three modern fighters: the license-built Russian Su-27 air superiority fighter, the indigenous F-10 multirole fighter, due out in 2005, and an aircraft carrier–deployed jet (possibly a derivative of the F-10). China currently has more than 50 Su-27s purchased from Russia and by 2012 will have built or purchased more than 250 of the fighters equipped with advanced radar and AA-11 radar-guided missiles capable of hitting targets beyond visual range. The Chinese are also designing an advanced fighter with radar-evading stealth characteristics known as the XXJ, along with a new FB-7 light strike aircraft, an improved F-8 interceptor, and the FC-1, a light fighter based on the MiG-21 that the Chinese will export.
- By 2010 the Chinese will field at least one aircraft carrier with a displacement of more than 40,000 tons.
- Beijing recently concluded a deal with Russia to buy two Sovremenny-class destroyers that will be armed with SS-N-22 Sunburn cruise missiles that were designed specifically to attack U.S. Aegis-class ships, like those that accompanied U.S. aircraft carriers during the Taiwan Strait crisis in 1996. Pentagon officials said the Russian destroyer purchase, part of a weapons purchase worth between $8 billion and $10 billion, was a direct response to the deployment of U.S. aircraft carriers.

- China is building a new version of an 8,000-mile–range CSS-4 nuclear missile. In 1995 China conducted the first test of a new road-mobile ICBM believed to be similar in design to the Russian SS-25. The test confirmed that China will be only the second nation in the world to field hard-to-find road-mobile nuclear missiles.

- China's strategic force also includes more than seventy medium-range nuclear missiles and one Xia-class ballistic missile submarine with twelve CSS-N-3 nuclear missiles. The DF-31, with a range of 5,000 miles, will be deployed on mobile launchers and submarines. Another new missile, the DF-41, will be deployed around the year 2000 and will have a range of up to 7,500 miles.

- In addition to the Russian-made destroyers, which will be used to enhance Chinese naval technology, China is focusing vast resources on building several new types of surface warships, notably adding to the two Luhu-class guided-missile destroyers and five Jiangwei-class guided-missile frigates now in its fleet.

- The conversion of five B-6 bombers into aerial refueling tankers was described in one Pentagon intelligence report as part of an effort to extend the range of Chinese aircraft over large areas of the Pacific. "By 1997, Chinese tanker and receiver aircraft probably will be able to perform some long-range escort, air-to-air, and ground attack missions over the South China Sea or elsewhere in the region," the report stated.

- China is developing new nuclear submarines to replace its diesel submarines. The first is a new attack submarine called the "Type 093" that is expected soon after the year 2000, according to the ONI. The submarine will use advanced quieting, weapons, and sensors, and will be equipped with torpedoes, anti-submarine warfare missiles, and a submarine-launched anti-ship cruise missile based on an advanced version of China's C801. China is also building a new ballistic missile submarine that the Navy believes is part of China's "announced long term national goal of attaining a survivable nuclear retaliatory force." The Type 094 submarine will be built early in the next century and will be the largest Chinese submarine. It is expected to be armed with sixteen JL-2 missiles, each with a range of 4,000 miles. "When deployed in the next decade, this missile will allow Chinese SSBNs [ballistic missile submarines] to target portions of the United States for the first time from operating areas located near the Chinese coast," the ONI report states. The ONI estimates that by 2010 China will have ten nuclear submarines, including three new ballistic missile submarines and three new attack submarines. Its diesel submarine force will number about forty-five boats, including several submarines of a new type.

- China has purchased four new Kilo-class submarines from Russia, upgraded to be among the quietest diesel submarines in the world. In addition, they will have a weapons package that includes both wake-homing and wire-guided acoustic homing torpedoes. The Russian wake-homing torpedo is described by the ONI as highly effective and designed to ignore acoustic ship defenses and evasive maneuvers.

- China's military is also actively acquiring Western and U.S. military technology. For example, a Chinese company last year obtained sophisticated U.S. power transmission devices used in airborne missile guidance, fire-control radar, targeting systems, and navigation pods. China is investing in advanced Russian and Western surface-to-air missile systems, including up to one hundred of Russia's long-range SA-10s, which will project major government and industrial centers. Beijing is producing new shoulder-fired anti-aircraft missiles copied from Russia's SA-7. And China is developing defenses against radar-evading stealth aircraft and cruise missiles—systems owned exclusively by the United States.

- A secret Pentagon intelligence report in January 1999 estimated that China will dramatically step up production of short-range M-9 and new CSS-X-7 missiles and that most of them are aimed at Taiwan. The total number of the mobile missiles is expected to increase from 150 deployed in 1998 to 600 in 2005.

- Finally, China is purchasing ten Il-76 aircraft transports, twenty-four Mi-17 assault helicopters, and some fifty T-72 tanks from Russia.

According to the ONI, China is acquiring technology for its aircraft and missile programs via "reverse-engineering" or direct design assistance from Russia, Israel, and the United States. Intelligence officials said the F-10 fighter jet is based on U.S. technology illicitly supplied to China by Israel from its cancelled Lavi fighter program.

"The United States clearly fits in the category of a potential competitor of China for regional dominance," said a senior military official and specialist on the region. "And probably we fit into the category of a possible adversary over Taiwan. It's clear that in the past we have committed military force toward the Taiwan Straits in the event China might not get our true meaning, might mistake our message. But the issue of portraying it as a trend line upon which… possible conflict is inevitable is something we're all working against, and we'd like to portray it in the most positive way we can." CIA Director George Tenet tried to offer the same positive spin by saying, during a Senate hearing, that while Beijing's goal is to become East Asia's major power and a world economic power equal to the United States by 2050, "it is too soon to say what this portends," whether China will be an aggressive or benign power. "There is no doubt that China has the potential to affect our security posture in Asia, but the extent to which its ambitions and growing capabilities represent a challenge or threat to U.S. interests is still an open question."

James Lilley, who served as ambassador to China and as assistant secretary of defense for international security affairs during the Bush administration, believes the Clinton administration has badly misjudged China. "Their whole approach," Lilley said, "is designed to soften the image of China, because the administration fundamentally has decided that they want a good relationship with China, they want to bill it as a foreign policy success, therefore they had to sell China." To divert attention from Chinese threats to the United States, the administration chose to limit all criticism of China to a single area: Beijing's poor human rights record. All other threats were ignored or dismissed with hollow statements of concern.

"It's a diversion," Lilley told me. "It's a diversion from very bad things to a bad thing. It's a lesser of two evils."

"What is hardest for the administration to explain," Lilley continued, "is the Chinese steady and relentless pursuit of weapons of mass destruction, their expansion of their influence in Asia, the modernization of their armed forces and the specific goals and objectives that they themselves spell out in their writings." China is systematically undermining U.S. interests in Asia.

According to Lilley, the message to China should be: "You want a good relationship, get this proliferation thing under control. You get illegal campaign contributions under control. These are spoilers."

President Clinton and his advisers have done everything in their power to minimize the threat China poses to American security. From ignoring dangerous weapons proliferation activities to explaining away threats by Beijing to use nuclear weapons against the United States, the Clinton administration has dismissed the Chinese threat and lulled many Americans into thinking China's communist rulers are harmless autocrats. The danger, however, is that unless steps are taken to reduce the Chinese threat, the United States could find itself in a real conflict with the world's most populous state in the next ten years. Clinton has increased the danger that American men and women could face in an Asian war instead of protecting long-term national security interests by seeking to reduce the dangers posed by China.

In the end, the Chinese are banking on the fact that the United States is a shrinking world power, with a dwindling ability to project military might, including U.S. plans to remove its 100,000 troops from the Pacific region. The Chinese take the long view and might easily regard Bill Clinton as the best friend the communist regime has ever had in its long march forward to surpass the United States as the chief power in the Pacific.

CHAPTER SIX
Flashpoint Korea

*"Our diplomacy backed with force persuaded
North Korea to freeze its nuclear program."*

—President Clinton, February 17, 1996, Rochester, New York

*"We have suspicions that North Korea has engaged
in construction activities that could constitute
a violation of its commitment to freeze its nuclear-
related facilities under the Agreed Framework."*

—Secretary of State Madeleine Albright, February 25, 1999,
House International Relations Committee

In the spring of 1997, U.S. intelligence agencies came to a startling conclusion. North Korea had been building a huge underground complex analysts believed would house a nuclear reactor that could be used for one thing only: making plutonium—the highly radioactive material potent and compact enough to use as the pit of a nuclear missile warhead. The construction, which had been monitored for months, was unwelcome news to President Clinton. It meant that the "freeze" on North Korea's nuclear weapons, which the administration had negotiated and the president had hailed as a great arms control achievement, was an illusion. And the illusion could be deadly. North Korea already boasts the third-largest chemical weapons stockpile in the world. With nuclear-capable long-range missiles, currently under development by the North Koreans, or other agents of mass destruction, the specter was raised of nerve gas raining on American cities in Alaska, Hawaii, and even California. With as little as a single additional flight test, the North Koreans would have the long-range missile capability they needed.

The "freeze" the Clinton administration negotiated in 1994 had proven to be nothing but a deadly diplomatic ploy whereby the North Koreans had taken advantage of the Clinton administration's pattern of diplomacy. "Threat, followed by retreat, followed by renewed threat has characterized Mr. Clinton's foreign policy style to the point where leaders of many foreign countries are uncertain about his intentions and resolve," said diplomatic historian and former intelligence analyst William Goldcamp. "This waffling is most dangerous where nuclear and strategic weapons non-proliferation are at issue. The 'agreed framework' arranged with North Korea was a negotiation to cover retreat, not to protect U.S. long-term interests, and was deliberately structured" as a "framework" rather than a treaty "to avoid the Senate ratification process"—another tactic typical of the Clinton administration, which has consistently sought to conduct foreign policy in the shadows, away from congressional oversight.

The Clinton administration was so embarrassed by the intelligence about North Korean nuclear developments that the report was given a level of secrecy normally reserved for the Pentagon's most secret weapons, like the Stealth bomber, as part of a "special access program" (SAP). SAPs are so secret that officials allowed "into" the Pentagon compartments are authorized to lie about their very existence.

In this case, the deception might in part have been driven by the administration's 1993 announcement that it was almost obligated by its non-proliferation policies to go to war with North Korea rather than permit it to develop nuclear weapons.

"For those out to salvage this much-touted diplomatic accomplishment"—North Korea's supposed nuclear freeze—"the experience of dealing with the North from 1991 to 1994 should be a warning," said former CIA Asia specialist Kent Harrington. "At every step that led to the nuclear framework agreement, the North Koreans lied, hid their weapons work, and tried to frustrate the United States, its allies, and international inspectors. We would be foolish to assume that the challenge is anything less today."

Harrington added, "It is fair to assume that the North did not begin planning its newly discovered nuclear site yesterday. And if that is so, then it is reasonable to believe that other aspects of the 'frozen' nuclear effort—weapons design and fabrication work, for instance—also have thawed. Indeed, if the intelligence is accurate, the analysts' findings raise troubling questions, not the least of which is whether at other secret sites the North's program was ever frozen at all."

The CIA came close to that conclusion in early 1999. CIA Director George Tenet followed the official administration political line during a Senate hearing, noting that the 1994 nuclear agreement had frozen the plutonium facility at Yongbyon. "But," he added, "we are deeply concerned that North Korea has a covert [nuclear] program. The key target for us to watch is the underground construction project at Kumchangni, which is large enough to house a plutonium production facility and perhaps a reprocessing plant as well."

> **North Korea's nuclear weapons and long-range missiles put it on a par with the world's superpowers, despite the nation's significant internal problems.**

Top-secret satellite photographs taken in the spring of 1997 showed fifteen thousand workers building the underground facility in Kumchangni, an area some twenty-five miles northeast of Yongbyon—the original North Korean nuclear facility whose construction was supposed to have been frozen by the 1994 agreement. The intelligence photographs revealed that a three thousand–volt, high-tension electronic wire had been constructed around an artificial lake and an artificial island, according to officials who have seen them. Military forces were deployed in the surrounding regions to provide security. There was no other conclusion the analysts could reach: North Korea was building a new secret facility for a graphite-moderated reactor—an excellent source for producing plutonium. Since the United States, Japan, and South Korea had already agreed to provide North Korea with two other reactors that were not graphite-controlled, the only real use of the new facility was for nuclear weapons. The North Koreans could build the two "light-water" reactors for electrical power generation, but still use the facility at Kumchangni to transform the "communist hermit kingdom" into a regional and even global nuclear power.

In early 1999 the U.S. Department of Energy intelligence office, which monitors foreign nuclear programs, stated in a secret report that a North Korean trading company was seeking gas centrifuge technology—equipment used in enriching uranium to make fuel for first-generation nuclear weapons. The report was a smoking gun, revealing that the North Koreans had jettisoned the 1994 agreement with the United States and were pursuing new weapons technology that was a departure from earlier efforts to extract plutonium from nuclear reactors. The report said the North Korean Daesong Yashin Trading Company was trying to buy "frequency converters" from a Japanese company in order to power gas centrifuges linked together in a cascade—the same technology that, as we will see in Chapter 7, Pakistan acquired from China. The report concluded that North Korea "probably is in the early stages of a uranium enrichment capability." "On the basis of Pakistan's progress with a similar technology, we estimate that the DPRK [Democratic People's Republic of Korea, or North Korea] is at least six years from the production of HEU [highly enriched uranium], even if it has a viable centrifuge design," the report said. "On the other hand, with significant technical support from other countries, such as Pakistan, the time frame would be decreased by several years." In another section, the Energy report concluded, "Islamabad may well have lent some level of assistance on uranium assistance." It was clear the North Koreans were seeking the capability to produce uranium as part of a covert nuclear weapons program.

The final assessment among the intelligence analysts: The North Korean facility at Kumchangni, approximately 400,000 cubic meters in size, was likely being built to house a 200-megawatt graphite-moderated reactor—possibly the same Yongbyon reactor.

The North Koreans realized their communist system, based on the ideology of "*juche*" or self-reliance, had failed. But they also knew that nuclear weapons and long-range missiles would put North Korea on a par with the world's superpowers. In December 1998 the Korean Central News Agency, the government's official organ, warned the United States that more missile launches, like the test firing of North Korea's first long-range Taepo Dong missile in August 1997, could be expected. The agency noted that it was "foolish" for the United States to expect any change in North Korean government attitudes. After the United States warned North Korea not to undertake further "destabilizing" missile tests, the North Koreans blustered: "We will

> **The North Koreans revealed how easy it was to subvert international safeguards as part of a calculated effort to build a nuclear bomb.**

never be frightened by the U.S. warning. The U.S. still knows little about the DPRK." On that point they were right.

One failure of understanding was the Clinton administration's assumption that the North Koreans could be bribed to comply with the freeze. The administration had offered to help replace North Korea's graphite reactors with two light-water reactors, which the White House considered more "proliferation-resistant"—less likely to be used in building nuclear bombs, more focused on producing nuclear energy for electrical power that would help the North Korean economy. The deal, worth $4.6 billion, included a promise from South Korea to pay 70 percent of the costs of dismantling the graphite reactors, or about $3.2 billion, while Japan agreed to provide $1 billion. As part of the arrangement, North Korea would also receive 500,000 tons of heavy fuel oil as a form of compensation to make up for the electrical power temporarily lost from agreeing to switch reactors.

Yet from the start, there were concerns in Congress that the fuel oil would be diverted from civilian use in order to help North Korea's one million–man armed forces. In fact, in late 1998, according to one government official, the State Department had evidence that ten thousand metric tons of the imported fuel oil had been diverted to China, probably as part of a barter arrangement between the communist countries.

Moreover, it was clear from the beginning of the Clinton administration that the North Koreans had no intention of limiting its nuclear program to producing electrical power. In February 1993 North Korean technicians at Yongbyon, north of the capital of Pyongyang, reprocessed spent fuel from a nuclear reactor to create plutonium out of the fuel rods used in the reactor. The North Koreans claimed they produced only one hundred grams of plutonium, but it became obvious to nuclear experts working for International Atomic Energy Agency Director Hans Blix that the North Koreans had at least the eight kilograms necessary for one nuclear warhead, and probably had more. It seemed that the agency could do little about North Korea's plutonium. Blix reported in 1994 that the North Koreans raised major suspicions about their sincerity during inspections carried out in March and May of 1994. At Yongbyon inspectors spotted a second reprocessing facility in an advanced state of construction that had never been inspected, and the North Koreans refused to let the inspectors into the second site. The two reactors are part of seven sites under international inspection that became the focus of a crisis in mid-1994, a crisis in which Clinton blinked.

APPEASEMENT

On May 12, 1994, North Korea began discharging eight hundred bundles of fuel rods, each bundle containing ten rods, before international inspectors could determine how much plutonium had been produced by the reactor. The North Koreans were violating this vital safeguard in an obvious attempt to cover up the fact that they were extracting plutonium for nuclear weapons. By June, Hans Blix was convinced the North Koreans had amassed enough plutonium to make nuclear weapons. "North Korea has more plutonium than it has reported," Blix said bluntly.

In July 1994 Blix said his agency could not make an accurate assessment of the amount of plutonium produced by the North Koreans. Blix noted that the reactor rods, which were needed for conducting measurements, were unavailable and that the North Koreans would not provide—and perhaps did not have—records for the International Atomic Energy Agency.

The United States responded to North Korea's nuclear projects by seeking to impose economic sanctions through the United Nations Security Council. North Korea replied that any sanctions would be considered an act of war.

On June 13 North Korean Foreign Minister Kim Yong Nam sent a diplomatic note to Secretary of State Warren Christopher, announcing that the International Atomic Energy Agency "has jeopardized the supreme interests of the DPRK, flagrantly encroached upon its sovereign rights and dignity, and created such a circumstance which makes it impossible for the DPRK to maintain normal relations with the IAEA [International Atomic Energy Agency] any longer.... I have been authorized to inform... the Government of the United States of America, the depository government, that the Government of the Democratic People's Republic of Korea decided to withdraw from the International Atomic Energy Agency as of June 13, 1994."

The withdrawal exposed the weakness of the international system of providing nuclear power to any nation as long as it promised to agree to safeguards. The North Koreans revealed how easy it was to subvert the process as part of a calculated effort to build a nuclear bomb.

President Clinton's response was an attempt to appease the North Koreans with negotiations in Geneva, which began in the summer of 1994 and eventually resulted in the "Agreed Framework" and North Korea's return to the International Atomic Energy Agency. The agreement gave the North Koreans ten years to dismantle their weapons program and five years to turn over the existing stockpile of plutonium. For Clinton and his aides, the arms control agreement and the mere promise by North Korea to abide by it was all that mattered. As with other arms accords, compliance was secondary, and the seemingly inevitable violations of agreements were explained away or ignored.

When the agreement was nearing completion, Clinton was asked by a reporter if it was possible to know "with full confidence" whether the

North Koreans had actually stopped work on their nuclear program as promised. "We believe we would be able to know, based on the representations that were apparently made today whether they have, in fact, frozen their program while talks continue." But as his later reaction to the intelligence on the underground facility at Kumchangni showed, the intelligence was minimized and shrugged off. U.S. spy agencies had first spotted the facility in early 1997, but it was kept hidden from Congress, despite a statutory requirement to inform lawmakers about nuclear weapons–related developments like Kumchangni.

The negotiations, however, were nearly scuttled at the last minute by former President Jimmy Carter. Carter—in his role as a self-styled international peacemaker—launched his own private diplomatic mission to Pyongyang and began making promises for the U.S. government, such as claiming the United States would not seek sanctions against North Korea over the nuclear program. Asked if the president was willing to put off sanctions, as Carter had promised, an angry Clinton snapped at reporters, "No, I gave my position yesterday." The United States would not forgo sanctions until there was an acceptable agreement from the North Koreans.

"What is President Carter talking about?" he was then asked.

"None of us have talked directly with President Carter," Clinton said. "We don't know what he said."

President Clinton had done nothing to stop a former president from conducting his own foreign policy without even consulting the White House. The incident revealed the president and his advisers to be amateurs. The president had (1) been threatening to go to war with North Korea over the nuclear problem, posing great risks to the lives of thousands of soldiers and millions of civilians, and (2) allowed former President Carter to meddle in important matters of state without authorization.

THE TRUTH ABOUT NORTH KOREA

The real story of what was going on inside North Korea rarely became public, though the author was able to help shed light on many of the details as a conduit for leaks from frustrated U.S. intelligence officials who had been ignored by Clinton political appointees. For instance, in 1996 a top-secret U.S. intelligence report obtained from South Korea's Defense Security Command revealed what widespread famine in North Korea had wrought; according to the report, three cases of cannibalism had prompted North Korea's paranoid communist ruler, Kim Jong-il, to order a crackdown on the practice and a nationwide investigation. More important, however, was the information gleaned when communist party official Hwang Jang-yop, the chief ideologist for the ruling Korean Worker's Party, defected by walking into the South Korean embassy in Beijing on February 12, 1996, setting off a major diplomatic confrontation in the Chinese capital that lasted several weeks.

As a member of the ruling inner circle in North Korea, Hwang had unprecedented access to what was going on, and he revealed that the North Koreans planned to turn South Korea into a "sea of flames." Hwang stated in a letter that, even if some thought he had gone mad with his defection, two enemies, North and South Korea, that seek to destroy each other in the name of unification could not be considered sane.

Hwang had another startling revelation for the West that was not made public either by the South Koreans or by the Clinton administration, and only became known when a secret U.S. intelligence report based on Hwang's testimony was disclosed by the author on June 5, 1997. In the April 1996 debriefings in South Korea, Hwang disclosed that North Korea already possessed nuclear weapons and had planned to conduct an underground nuclear test—the final step in nuclear weapons development. According to Hwang, the North Korean Foreign Ministry had argued against the provocative action in order to avoid arousing new suspicions about the secret nuclear weapons program, because a test of a nuclear device would end all speculation about the covert effort by Pyongyang. The intelligence tip, once exposed, prompted further investigations into the North Korean nuclear program, which helped uncover the secret underground facility at Kumchangni several months later.

Hwang also revealed new information about North Korea's huge chemical and biological weapons arsenal, describing the chemicals as "high grade" deadly poisons, including nerve agents, blistering agents, and blood agents.

Other military defectors helped U.S. intelligence agencies expose North Korean duplicity about its weapons programs and the most worrying secret underground nuclear site. Former North Korean Army Colonel Choi Joo-hwai told a Senate subcommittee in 1997 that North Korea had no intention of living up to any obligations under the Agreed Framework. "I believe the important facilities are underground... and these underground facilities will never be opened up to anyone from outside the country," Choi said. Choi, who defected in 1995 and had been directly involved in procuring technology for the North Korean nuclear weapons program while posted as a military attaché in Czechoslovakia, stated in an interview that the covert weapons effort began actively during the 1970s and continues today. Moreover, Choi said, most North Koreans believe the government had built two or three nuclear devices before ever concluding the Agreed Framework.

Another North Korean defector, former diplomat Young-Hwan Ko, backed the assertion that the North Koreans had nuclear weapons. "Like Colonel Choi, I am not 100 percent sure North Korea already has a nuclear bomb, but what is a fact is that North Korea has tried for a long time to acquire the necessary technology and develop their capability for nuclear bombs," Ko said. Both men now work in Seoul, South Korea, watching events and the political situation in North Korea. According to Ko, North Korea's withdrawal from the nuclear Non-Proliferation Treaty in 1993 was a clear sign Pyongyang had some level of nuclear weapons capability. And, he added, the agreement to build the two light-water reactors for the North Koreans under the Agreed Framework will not in the least affect the North's drive to develop nuclear bombs and warheads.

Colonel Choi, for his part, reported that North Korean forces are currently prepared to launch a war despite the harsh economic conditions in the country. "Their readiness is unquestioned. The key question is when they will choose to wage war," he said. If a war breaks out on the Korean Peninsula, the North's main target will be the 37,000 U.S. troops based in the South and 47,000 based in Japan. To meet that strategy, Pyongyang is working furiously to build several long-range missiles. Unlike U.S. missiles, North Korean missiles are not built for surgical precision, Colonel Choi said, so their missile program does not need extensive flight testing. "They require only that they impact on a target region," he explained. The North Korean military strategy, he added, is to inflict more than 20,000 American casualties in the region as quickly as possible after the onset of fighting.

According to the defectors, North Korea has also set up several secret missile factories, with such cover names as the "Pyongyang Pig Factory" and "January 18 Machinery Factory." Ko said he learned about the missile programs from his brother, who was employed as part of the military industry that builds missiles. The missile program began from redesigns of Soviet Frog-7 surface-to-surface missiles, and later from Scuds that were built up and developed. As a result, North Korea is now on the verge of deploying ICBMs. The North Koreans also acquired French Exocet anti-ship missiles. And from Afghanistan they procured U.S.-made Stinger shoulder-fired anti-aircraft missiles.

The Clinton administration has asked for more talks with a regime that has shown no commitment to abiding by its commitments.

But the hardware isn't just coming in. North Korea has earned up to $1 billion a year from missile sales to countries such as Iran, Syria, Egypt, and Libya. "Exporting missiles is crucial to North Korea's economy," Ko said. Ko's analysis was confirmed in 1998, when Pyongyang's official news agency revealed for the first time that it was in the business of exporting missiles for cash.

Senator Thad Cochran, chairman of the Senate Governmental Affairs subcommittee on international security, proliferation, and federal services, who hosted the defectors' Senate testimony, said the revelations were more than a "wake-up call" about the dangers of North Korean military activities. "This ought to be a call to general quarters," he said. But the Clinton administration, as it had done in the past with military threats and dangerous weapons developments, played down the defectors' warnings and, once again, touted its diplomacy. The State Department, meanwhile, did its best to convince the nation that the North Koreans had not negotiated in bad faith.

"The objective in the nuclear case several years ago was to convince North Korea that they had more to gain by giving up their nuclear capability and engaging in a dialogue with the outside world that has led to this watershed nuclear agreement with the North Koreans," State Department spokesman James Rubin said. "We are now engaged in a similar exercise to try to convince them of the wisdom, for their own interests, of discussing with us limitations on medium- and longer-range missile systems. Hopefully, some day soon, we will get those talks back on track and be able to have as much success in the missile area as we had in the nuclear area." In other words, the Clinton administration wants more talks with a regime that has shown no commitment to abiding by its commitments.

It was typical of the strategy followed in other cases, whether Russia's sale of missile technology to Iran or China's transfers of weapons know-how to rogue states. "The administration foolishly believes that by talking to these governments and trying to explain that it is in their interest not to help develop foreign weapons that they can prevent their development," said a frustrated former military officer now involved in proliferation policy. "But it's like talking to a wall."

The Pentagon, too, sought to play down the developments. Asked if the North Koreans posed a "clear and present danger" to the United States and the world, Pentagon spokesman Ken Bacon said: "We're very aware of what the threat is, and we believe we're taking prudent actions to counter those threats. We believe that although the North Korean force is large and stationed close to the border; although they're working on new missiles, we know that; we believe that our force is extremely potent, is extremely well trained, is extremely well equipped, and we hope that neither force will be used. But we think we have a force that is very adequate to the challenge that it could possibly face on the Korean Peninsula."

On the nuclear issues, Bacon said, "We persuaded them to stop through negotiations, which led to the Framework Agreement. It is generally believed that the North Korean nuclear program is frozen, although there can be no absolute assurance that it does not already possess a small number of nuclear weapons."

But Colonel Choi told me that North Korea's commitment to its weapons program is so strong that military production is continuing despite the stories of starvation and cannibalism. "No matter what happens on the economic side…, as long as South Korea and the United States allow the situation to remain as it is, the military side of North Korea will continue to expand and become stronger and stronger," Choi said. He urged the United States to press North Korea to become more open about its nuclear and chemical weapons and missile programs, rather than focusing on dealing with humanitarian problems, such as the famine that has devastated the nation.

The Clinton administration finally admitted what U.S. intelligence had known for years: North Korea was engaged in a covert nuclear weapons program.

The U.S. Arms Control and Disarmament Agency, which under the direction of Clinton associate John Holum has become the least credible and one of the most politicized national security agencies in the administration, has stated that the Agreed Framework was Clinton's move to "aggressively… reduce the threat posed by nuclear weapons to all Americans." The agency declared in a statement posted on its Internet web site that "North Korea's nuclear program, under international inspection, has been frozen and is to be dismantled under the U.S.-DPRK Agreed Framework."

Few in the administration bothered to pose questions about the fate of the plutonium the North Koreans had already extracted from their reactors prior to the agreement. Former Defense Secretary William Perry estimated that by April 1994 the North Koreans could have had enough plutonium for four or five nuclear bombs. That plutonium remains unaccounted for and is rarely mentioned in connection with the nuclear agreement. Perry was called back into government service in 1998 as a special presidential envoy to deal with the new North Korean crisis. His solution was to offer concessions to the North Koreans, and, if that did not produce changes in Pyongyang's behavior, then the policy would revert to containing the communist regime until it collapsed. "We can't really afford to ignore Pyongyang if they persist in building nukes and ICBMs," Perry told the *Wall Street Journal*.

In August 1997 Stephen W. Bosworth, a senior U.S. diplomat who would become ambassador to South Korea, gave no hint of the secret North Korean construction project at Kumchangni. In an article in the magazine *Arms Control Today*, Bosworth was quoted as saying that the North Koreans were abiding by the Agreed Framework. Asked about Pyongyang's compliance, Bosworth said, "All I can say is that I look at what they have done. They have, in fact, complied quite assiduously with the commitments that they made under the Agreed Framework.... I draw from that the inference that they remain satisfied with the agreement, but, beyond that, I really can't speculate."

The remark was misleading because Bosworth had more than likely been made aware of reports about the secret underground construction that would become public in an article in the *New York Times* just three days after he made the statement.

DECEPTION

U.S. intelligence officials confirmed that the Kumchangni construction project could have only one purpose: secret nuclear weapons production. Thus, despite specific legal requirements to inform Congress of all significant developments related to nuclear weapons proliferation, the president never notified or informed Congress about the Kumchangni construction; that is, the intelligence was suppressed. It wasn't until more than a year later, at a closed-door hearing on July 28, 1998, that a group of senators and staff was briefed on the Kumchangni nuclear project. According to officials present, the evidence presented was stark; there was little room for doubt about the nature of the project and its usefulness to the North Korean nuclear weapons program.

"In the spring of 1997 senior Clinton administration policymakers were alerted that the North Korean nuclear weapons program was not frozen," said a government official who was angered by the fact that Congress had been kept in the dark. "And Madeleine Albright lied to the Senate about it."

On July 8, 1998, before the Senate Finance Committee, Albright testified that the nuclear accord has "frozen North Korea's dangerous nuclear weapons program." But that was not all; she had fed this line to Congress several times previously. As far back as February 12, 1997, Albright had said this to the House Appropriations Committee: "The Framework Agreement is one of the best things the administration has done because it stopped a nuclear weapons program in North Korea." Later, on February 10, 1998, she defended the request for $35 million to fund the agreement's implementation organization, stating that the funds were needed to "secure continued DPRK compliance with its non-proliferation obligations." And on March 4, 1998, she told the House Foreign Operations Appropriations Committee that the agreement "has succeeded in freezing North Korea's dangerous nuclear program."

When, in August 1998, Albright was confronted by angry senators who questioned her about the new intelligence on Kumchangni, she said that she had not learned about the new evidence until July. Sitting in the room with her was Army Lieutenant General Patrick Hughes, director of the Defense Intelligence Agency in charge of the special access program to monitor North Korean nuclear weapons development. Hughes politely interrupted her. "Madame Secretary, that is incorrect," Hughes said. The Defense Intelligence Agency had reached its conclusions that North Korea was still building a new underground nuclear facility some eighteen months before and had provided the information to Albright's office. Albright was silent.

Finally, in late February 1999, Albright admitted what had been obvious to the U.S. intelligence community for years: North Korea was engaged in a covert nuclear weapons program outside of its supposedly frozen program. "We have suspicions that North Korea has engaged in construction activities that could constitute a violation of its commitment to freeze its nuclear-related facilities under the Agreed Framework," she told the House International Relations Committee. She for the first time admitted that North Korea, with its missiles and unfrozen nuclear program, had become "a huge problem."

CIA Director George Tenet, a close political ally of the president, provided cover for Albright. He explained in testimony before the Senate Armed Services Committee in February 1999, that, yes, the Yongbyon program was still frozen, "but we are deeply concerned that North Korea has a covert program." In short, the administration hid behind its statement that the nuclear program at Yongbyon *alone* was frozen, even if Pyongyang's overall designs on building nuclear bombs had not been halted. In this situation, the administration had followed the perverted parsing of language that defined its president—the man who responded to a prosecutor's question about having sexual relations with an intern by answering, "It depends on what the meaning of the word 'is' is."

The deception about the North Korean weapons program was also put forward with statements by James Rubin, the assistant secretary of state for public affairs and one of Albright's closest advisers. "The freeze, in our view, is still in effect," Rubin told reporters in July 1998. "We have frozen and stopped the North Korean nuclear program from moving in a direction that would have threatened the world—and that freeze is still being monitored and we believe it is still in effect."

Rubin was responding to a report released the same month by the General Accounting Office (GAO), which concluded that the problem of determining how much plutonium the North Koreans had diverted was "far worse now" than when the International Atomic Energy Agency sounded the alarm in July 1994. The measurements needed by the atomic agency "are not likely to occur in the near future and therefore will be even more difficult and expensive to perform," the GAO said. The report also noted that the administration's Agreed

Framework contained a major loophole that "allows North Korea to continue operating certain nuclear facilities not covered by the freeze." The facilities were not identified, but the report said they were "smaller and generally less significant to North Korea's nuclear program than the facilities under the freeze." The report made no mention of the secret underground construction at Kumchangni.

The Arms Control and Disarmament Agency's 1998 report was typical of the political spin Clinton political appointees like John Holum, a lawyer who worked with Clinton on Senator George McGovern's 1972 presidential campaign, would use to describe President Clinton's policies. One section of it sounded excessively conciliatory when it stated that in 1991, "North Korea began to take steps to convince the world that its nuclear program was peaceful." How was that done? By concluding the safeguards agreement. And then the fact that North Korea lied about its plutonium production was described in the most flattering terms: "North Korea appeared to be attempting to conceal two possible nuclear waste sites"—the sites were declared off-limits to inspectors. Holum was typical of the liberal arms control advocates who dominated all national security policies. Another was Deputy Secretary of State Strobe Talbott, a former *Time* magazine columnist and college roommate of Clinton who became famous during the Cold War for attacking Ronald Reagan's arms control policies as insufficiently pro-Soviet.

The arms agency claimed in its report that the agreement with North Korea "does not rely on trust" because "all of its steps will be verifiable"—but how they were to be verified is not mentioned. Worse, the arms agency gushed over the false claim that "North Korea has halted construction and operation activities at its reactors."

The safety factor in the agreement as Clinton envisioned it was supposed to be that no critical components for the 1,000-megawatt "proliferation-resistant" reactors would be provided until North Korea lived up to its International Atomic Energy Agency commitments, something that has not taken place and appears less likely to happen as more information about underground nuclear facilities is revealed. In the meantime, nuclear weapons work is continuing secretly inside North Korea.

The CIA had no illusions about North Korea's adherence to the accord. "Our reading of reporting from public and clandestine information on North Korea's approach to the framework suggests that the best that can be hoped for is uneven implementation," the CIA stated in a secret National Intelligence Estimate in 1995. "Clandestine reporting indicates that some North Korean officials expect disagreements over interpretation of the framework and an increase in tensions with the United States." Worse, the CIA said that a "variety" of intelligence reports suggested the North would follow through with refueling the Yongbyon reactor, which would produce more plutonium for weapons. "Even if the North refuels the reactor it would not necessarily perceive the Agreed Framework has lapsed."

Intelligence agencies, however, were divided on key questions about Pyongyang's approach to the framework, including "whether the leadership believes it faces a military threat from the United States."

The CIA report said it was not clear why North Korea accepted the agreement, but that it could have been driven by the possibility of improving relations with the United States and expanded economic ties, along with "the ability to retain ambiguity about its nuclear weapons program."

The secret report made it clear, however, that North Korea was unlikely to give up its nuclear arms project. "The United States and countries in the region want this issue resolved, but, according to clandestine reporting and public statements, the North calculates that this issue will diminish over time with progress on the framework. Based on these sources, the [intelligence] community agrees that at this stage the North does not intend to provide a full accounting of previous activities."

The bottom line for the CIA was that North Korea would give up its nuclear weapons program under the framework only if it could continue building nuclear bombs in other ways. "Based on North Korea's past behavior, the [intelligence] community agrees it would dismantle its known program, if it had covertly developed another source of fissile material," the 1995 report said, in a remarkable forecast of the covert underground facility at Kumchangni.

CRISIS LOOMS

When Larry Robinson, a key State Department North Korea watcher, retired in 1998, his outgoing classified assessment provided a dire picture of Kim Jong-il. Robinson's secret report, entitled "Through a Glass Darkly: Reflections on North Korea," concluded that North Korea is run by a weak and psychologically unbalanced leader. The report stated that the Korean People's Army blindly follows Kim's orders and is the "bulwark" of his rule, but it also revealed that "there is extensive evidence [of] a major coup attempt by elements of the VI Corps in 1995, which appears to have been crushed only with some difficulty.... [R]ecent defectors consistently assert that military discipline has eroded, and that gangs of soldiers... prey on civilians."

Robinson warned that the situation in North Korea is explosive. His report questioned Kim's power, since the leader "(unlike most of the male population) never spent a day in uniform until his appointment as marshal...." Moreover, Robinson wrote, Kim's penchant for promoting officers and lavishing "cars and other expensive presents on field commanders" may "be interpreted as an attempt to buy off an establishment whose loyalty is vital to the regime's survival, but of which he is not confident."

Worse, the report said, there is little evidence that the North Korean government is functioning at all, noting that the party central committee and the government have not met since 1994. The standing committee of the politburo, the ultimate ruling authority, has only one member—Kim—and "can be considered in session whenever Kim Jong-il is awake." The country's economic structure is a "planned economy without a plan" and appears similar to China during the tumultuous Cultural Revolution.

Factories are idle, and, in some plants, equipment has been stripped and sold in China. International attention has focused on North Korea's famine—what Robinson described as "one of the most lethal famines of the century." Several independent sources, including Hwang Jong-yop and other defectors, and government and non-government agencies, estimated two million to three million North Koreans—a staggering 10 percent to 15 percent of the population—have died from starvation since 1995, making it twice as bad as the Chinese famine of 1959 to 1962. "But famine is only one aspect of the overall economic collapse," Robinson wrote. "North Korea is woefully short of almost everything." A black market has developed in the country that is now providing 50 percent to 80 percent of daily needs, even though private markets are illegal.

The bottom line, according to Robinson's secret report, is that North Korea is gradually disintegrating as a nation, with increasing numbers of high-level defectors and a loss of faith in the ruling communists and Kim Jong-il. Robinson makes only scant reference to the Agreed Framework—that it came about as part of an effort by North Korea to find help outside the traditional and diminishing support from Russia and China. Kim Jong-il's tactical successes were the nuclear power plants, fuel oil from the framework, and some $10 million from South Korea's auto conglomerate Hyundai. "In strategic terms, however, this has been about as significant as adding a few lifeboats to the *Titanic*'s complement."

Nevertheless, the secret report said, those who had predicted the collapse of North Korea in the past had been embarrassed, and, "There are simply too many unknown variables—the resilience of the North Korean people, the coercive power of the regime, the level of outside aid—to make forecasts of North Korea's future anything but a game for fools." North Korea could reform into a relatively stable state, as China and Vietnam have done, but "it is dangerous to rule out the possibility of a quixotic invasion of the south, should Kim conclude that the odds against military success are no longer than those for other alternatives," Robinson said. A likely outcome: collapse and revolution. But, he warned, "The North Korean collapse into revolution would be a humanitarian disaster at best, a grave security threat to the region at worst," and all efforts should be taken to avert it.

Robinson warned that following the example of the Agreed Framework is a mistake in dealing with the growing threat of North Korean collapse due to Kim's weakened position, because "the agreed framework already stretched the limits of what is politically doable in the U.S., ROK [the Republic of Korea] and Japan." Any U.S. proposals would be viewed by the North Koreans with "profound suspicion— particularly if it required Pyongyang to give up the only thing that makes it of interest to the rest of the world—its ability to cause trouble." The bottom line: U.S. diplomacy toward the North Koreans will not produce satisfactory results. Instead, the United States and South Korea must be prepared for a collapse, and prepared to wage war. The United States should prod the Seoul government to "continue quiet but intensive collapse planning, even as we work together to avert that outcome."

Robinson's dire end-of-tour reflection made no mention of the looming crisis over Kumchangni, but during a November 1998 visit to South Korea, Charles Kartman, the State Department's expert on North Korea, said that there was "compelling evidence" the Kumchangni facility was related to nuclear weapons development, though he declined to explain why. Within a day, and under pressure from the White House, the U.S. embassy in Seoul issued a "clarification," backing away from Kartman's use of the term "compelling evidence": "There is strong information that makes us suspicious, but we lack conclusive evidence that the intended purpose of the underground site is nuclear related and, if so, what type of nuclear facility it might be. We, therefore, require full access to this site to determine whether this site is nuclear related." If the embassy was pressed to make what was, apparently, a statement of political cover, it is perhaps no surprise that President Clinton went so far as to give a false certification to Congress about North Korean cooperation with the nuclear accord. On March 19, 1997, Clinton issued a formal declaration that North Korea "is complying" with the Agreed Framework while "not significantly" diverting U.S. fuel oil for purposes outside the agreement. It is not known whether the president was aware of the first intelligence reports about Kumchangni, or whether he was alerted later. But no matter what, Clinton's chief priority was to maintain the fiction that the agreement was holding, since anything less would reflect poorly on his arms control "achievements."

NORTH KOREA'S ACCOMPLICE: THE CLINTON ADMINISTRATION

Suspicions were also raised about the administration's culpability in covering for North Korea when Henry Sokolski, a Pentagon arms control policymaker during the Bush administration and now the executive director of the Non-Proliferation Policy Education Center, caught the Clinton administration in what appeared to be a quiet effort to approve a controversial export license for the North Koreans.

On December 23, 1997, the nuclear power manufacturer ABB Combustion Engineering Nuclear Systems, based in Connecticut, notified the Nuclear Regulatory Commission that it wanted an export license under the Clinton administration's Agreed Framework with North Korea. The license would last through 2040, covering the supply of components of nuclear reactors—including reactor vessels, steam generators, pressurizers, reactor internals, reactor coolant pumps, reactor control rods systems, reactor instrumentation, monitoring and control equipment, and more—all of which could be used to build nuclear weapons. The company expected the total value of the contracts to be "millions of U.S. dollars." Along with the request, the company included a check for $8,100, to cover the fee for the license.

As required by federal rules, on January 28, 1998, the Nuclear Regulatory Commission made a quiet announcement in the *Federal Register*, stating that Combustion Engineering was seeking a license to help build two 1,000-megawatt reactors for North Korea. Anyone who opposed the license could request a public hearing, and Sokolski saw the notice and recognized something was not right. "It looked like an effort to avoid having the North Koreans conclude a 'nuclear cooperation agreement,'" as required by the Nuclear Non-Proliferation Treaty, Sokolski said. "They were trying to end-run the licensing process." Sokolski took the initiative as a public citizen and filed a notice to the Nuclear Regulatory Commission seeking a hearing. Within days he was called by the White House's top proliferation official, Gary Samore, who assured him any license would be premature. "The license will never see the light of day," Samore said.

But Sokolski knew from his experience in the Pentagon that the intricacies of federal licensing could be manipulated. So he put his concerns in writing. "Is there a reasonable assurance that the facility can be safeguarded in view of North Korea's noncompliance with the inspections requirements of the Non-Proliferation Treaty?" he asked. "Can the export take place in view of the possibility that North Korean may be engaged in illicit nuclear weapons–related activities?"

Both Samore and the State Department's proliferation official, Robert Einhorn, denied to Sokolski that they were trying to pull a fast one by short-circuiting the license process. But it is unlikely the company would have spent $8,100 to cover the license fee unless it had been led to believe that approval was likely.

Sokolski believes that the U.S. government should follow the letter of the anti-proliferation law and apply sanctions on states like North Korea and China. "The White House is currently allowing North Korea to put off proving what nuclear weapons material it has produced and dismantling its weapons material production facilities until the first of the two promised U.S. reactors is nearly complete," he said. "This may be convenient for North Koreans, who also plainly enjoy blackmailing us, but it strains U.S. nuclear non-proliferation laws that prohibit extending nuclear assistance to probable proliferators." Instead, the United States should make Pyongyang prove its "nuclear innocence" before any reactor is provided. The administration should also "stop subsidizing proliferators" with technology transfers. And it should "stop making the most vicious proliferators seem legitimate by continuing negotiating non-proliferation deals with them," Sokolski added. "Like it or not, the United States has created special relationships with Iraq and North Korea, two vicious, tyrannical states that either have, or are but a screwdriver's twist away from, possessing weapons of mass destruction."

President Clinton is guilty of hypocrisy when he condemns arms proliferation and then proceeds to practice a policy of "engagement" with proven proliferators.

By 1999 the Clinton administration's efforts to prevent North Korea from becoming a nuclear power were failing, and the much-touted Agreed Framework was near collapse. The North Koreans appeared to have duped the president and his arms control–obsessed advisers into believing the nuclear arms race on the strategic peninsula had been stopped. In reality, the North Koreans were given more time to secretly develop their nuclear weapons—and the delivery systems that were getting dangerously closer to being able to target those weapons directly on the United States. The response was more of the same: negotiations and discussions.

"There is no substitute for non-proliferation strategies with clear, country-specific objectives," Sokolski says. "Flailing about on the global threat that proliferation presents, as this administration is prone to do, may be great theater.... But a host of initiatives that raise global expectations but rarely deliver any benefits makes for lousy non-proliferation policy. We know what works: orchestrating persistent, tailored, leveraging actions... that move better governments toward the right choices and keep the worst from making the wrong ones." But for the Clinton administration, the "right choices" appear to be driven by short-term political gain—touting nonexistent freezes—rather than by a clear-eyed, long-term strategy.

PART III

Deadly Dealing

CHAPTER SEVEN

Missile Deception

*"If you're not satisfied with the intelligence
on this, you will never be satisfied with
any intelligence on anything else."*

—CIA Director John Deutch at a White House cabinet meeting
on China's sale of nuclear technology to Pakistan

For at least a decade, China has routinely carried out covert
weapons and technology sales to the Middle East and
South Asia, despite hollow promises to the contrary. For
instance, China sold Pakistan equipment to develop fuel for nuclear
weapons, and it sold Iran cruise missiles, missile guidance systems,
machine tools, and long-range missile test equipment. In nearly every
case, however, the Clinton administration insisted it could make "no
determination" about violations of U.S. proliferation laws.

When President Clinton ignored and covered up China's dangerous
weapons and technology transfers, he circumvented U.S. laws that
required the imposition of economic sanctions against China and
other nations engaged in selling nuclear, chemical, and biological
weapons materials and missile delivery systems. When the evidence of
sanctionable activity could not be ignored, only the mildest sanctions
were imposed, and even then they were quickly lifted. The reason was
simple: Clinton had promised American businesses not to punish
weapons proliferators with sanctions so as not to interrupt trade with
those nations.

In short, China was allowed to get away scot-free with major missile
and nuclear weapons technology transfers, and was emboldened to
make further dangerous sales that ultimately harmed U.S. national
security by making the world more dangerous.

At a White House speech in 1998, Clinton told a group of visitors that legislation automatically triggering sanctions to punish dangerous arms sales forced the administration to "fudge" the facts about those sales. Enter the "fudge factor" in American national security policy, the deliberate ignoring of unwelcome intelligence about foreign weapons developments.

On May 29, 1998, the ground shook in a remote region of southwestern Pakistan. The underground nuclear test marked the culmination of a covert weapons development program that had begun in the early 1970s. It was the beginning of a new arms race in Southwest Asia, and it could have happened only because the Clinton administration chose to ignore China's sales of nuclear weapons technology to Islamabad. Clinton administration policymakers, presented with solid intelligence information of a dangerous sale of nuclear technology, closed their eyes to the evidence and lied to protect the Chinese from the consequences of blatantly violating the Nuclear Non-Proliferation Treaty, which bars signatories from exporting nuclear weapons–related know-how.

The largest of the nuclear tests registered a magnitude 4.9 on seismic monitors at the U.S. Geological Survey station in Golden, Colorado. But the political shockwaves are being felt to this day. Pakistan is the first developing nation in two decades to test a nuclear weapon and, in so doing, to become a nuclear power. Tensions with India, which had set off its own nuclear test blasts weeks earlier, remain high, and clashes have broken out in the disputed northern border region of Kashmir that threaten to trigger the first nuclear warfare since the atomic bomb was dropped on Japan in 1945. Pakistan's "Islamic Bomb" is also an inspiration to Iran. Run by radical Shiite Muslims, Tehran's government is aggressively working to develop a nuclear weapon. Its nuclear missile delivery systems are already well advanced.

Hours before the underground blast in 1998, a small group of Pakistani officials and scientists involved in the twenty-three–year nuclear weapons development program gathered at the site to pray.

Among them was Abdul Qadir Khan, head of the nuclear program and director of the laboratory that bears his name, the A. Q. Khan Research Laboratory in Kahuta. Khan said that the blasts were tests of warhead-sized devices—not the huge bombs like those first developed by the United States in the 1940s and 1950s.

"Our nuclear bombs are more precise, advanced, and guaranteed," Khan said, comparing Pakistan's weapons to India's. "This is due to the technology that we used in making these bombs. We used enriched uranium, which is more guaranteed and less expensive but is also difficult to work with. This technology, which is considered the most advanced in the world, is possessed only by a few countries."

The nuclear arms race on the Indian subcontinent is a direct result of the Clinton administration's ignoring Chinese weapons deals.

More ominous, Pakistan test-fired a new medium-range missile called the Ghauri only weeks before its nuclear tests. The missile will soon be nuclear-tipped, increasing the threat of a nuclear exchange in one of the most volatile regions of the world.

On the day of the tests, Pakistanis took to the streets in several cities in wild celebration, shooting guns into the air and setting off fireworks. Pakistani Prime Minister Nawaz Sharif was defiant. The tests, he said, had answered India and showed the more populous neighbor that Pakistan had demonstrated its capability to use weapons of mass destruction. "Today, we have settled the score with India," Sharif said. "We have matched India with five tests of our own."

The United States, the sole remaining superpower since the end of the Cold War, had made a last ditch effort to convince the Pakistanis not to test. At midnight the evening before the test, President Clinton called Sharif and urged him not to go ahead. "Two wrongs don't make a right," Clinton told the Pakistani leader. But Sharif, though facing the prospect of international sanctions and condemnation, rang off unconvinced. President Clinton was left looking impotent.

The U.S. president would later declare how important it was for both India and Pakistan to renounce further tests and sign the

Comprehensive Test Ban Treaty, an arms control treaty that was pending before the Senate. The tests, however, appeared to doom any prospect that Republicans in the Senate would bring the pact to a vote. It died quietly with the end of the session in October 1998. Ratification of this treaty would become a top priority for Clinton in 1999.

The president's call for arms control was ironic. His administration's approach to the spread of dangerous weapons is characterized by a naive reliance on agreements and diplomacy, while ignoring the cold hard facts about violations of agreements, treaties, and U.S. law brought to his attention over the past six years in highly detailed classified intelligence reports. The intelligence was ignored, downplayed, or dismissed by political appointees concerned more with promoting U.S. business interests around the world and concluding arms control agreements than with preventing the spread of deadly weapons. The policy is driven by Clinton aides who do not understand the international security environment, many of them liberal political appointees who grew up during the Cold War as true believers in arms control diplomacy—reaching agreements for agreements' sake—but never worrying about violations and noncompliance.

The emerging nuclear arms race on the Indian subcontinent is a direct result of ominous weapons deals that the Clinton administration ignored in the interest of protecting China from economic sanctions. Beginning in December 1994, China sold some five thousand ring magnets to Pakistan's A. Q. Khan nuclear facility. The magnets are key components in making the fuel needed for nuclear bombs. The ring-shaped high-technology magnetic bearings are made of a special alloy known as samarium-cobolt and must be precision manufactured to withstand the high speeds of the gas centrifuges that are part of the process for making nuclear bomb fuel. China is the world leader in producing the components.

But instead of punishing China for helping Pakistan develop nuclear weapons, President Clinton looked the other way. Intelligence reports exposing the transfer were ignored until word leaked out. China had violated its international obligation not to transfer technology for nuclear weapons to nations that do not have them, but that too was ignored. For a few months, the Clinton administration held up U.S. government loan guarantees to American businesses seeking trade in China while the sale was "investigated." But the probe was a ruse. The State Department asked the Chinese government if the sale had occurred, and when Beijing officials professed ignorance, the loan ban was dropped. Several U.S. corporations, including Boeing and Honeywell, lobbied against sanctions. To the business community, nuclear weapons transfers should not be allowed to disrupt the flow of trade. Commerce Secretary Ron Brown led the fight against punishing China for its weapons transfers. U.S. national security interests, he asserted, should not be a higher priority than trade. "I happened to think the best chance for us to have an impact in those other areas is through being engaged with China," Brown said.

By pursuing this policy of "engagement," the Clinton administration overlooked real dangers. The ring magnets were part of a major program at the Khan Research Laboratory to upgrade several thousand centrifuges, which spin at supersonic speeds and in the process create enriched uranium—that is, nuclear weapons fuel. The material is not suitable for making fuel to run civilian nuclear power reactors. The ring magnets deal thus enabled the Pakistanis to develop the radioactive fuel that provides nuclear bombs their explosive power— power that has to be measured in its equivalent in thousands of tons of conventional TNT.

China has played a pivotal role in Pakistan's nuclear program, having supplied nuclear weapons design material and several reactors. But this aid to Pakistan's uranium enrichment process is the most blatant example of Beijing's weapons proliferation activities. In fact, China's role in Pakistan's uranium development goes back as far as the 1970s. A secret State Department memorandum of January 30, 1976, stated that Pakistan's efforts to acquire equipment to produce nuclear weapons fuel was part of a "crash program to develop weapons." In 1983 another secret memorandum stated that "there is unambiguous evidence that Pakistan is actively pursuing a nuclear weapons development program."

IGNORING ALARMS

On a cold December day in 1995, alarm bells went off at the head-quarters of the supersecret National Security Agency. The National Security Agency, located inside an Army base at Fort Meade, Maryland, is the United States intelligence community's ears around the world, picking up millions of communications, ranging from coded military radio conversations to the cell phone discussions of weapons dealers in Kazakhstan.

The December intercept picked up by National Security Agency listeners got the immediate attention of Vice Admiral J. Michael McConnell, the agency's director and the former intelligence chief on the Joint Staff. In 1995 he had become the nation's premier electronic spymaster known as the DIRNSA, the intelligence community's name for Director, National Security Agency. The intercept that crossed his desk that day revealed that in December 1994 China had completed a $70,000 deal with Pakistan to sell five thousand custom-made ring magnets produced by the China Nuclear Energy Industry Corporation (CNEIC), an arm of the Chinese government's China National Nuclear Corporation. The intelligence report noted how the ring magnets could be used to produce fuel for nuclear weapons.

The National Security Agency immediately sent out the cable under Admiral McConnell's title to the head of the CIA's Non-Proliferation Center, and to senior officials at the Pentagon, White House, and State Department, notifying them of the shipment. It was labeled "Top Secret" with several code words following it, including "Gamma," the highest classification. It also contained the notice, "Warning: this report contains Gamma Commint of an extremely sensitive nature."

The intelligence report created a furor within the administration over whether China had helped Pakistan to upgrade its ability to make nuclear weapons fuel for its nuclear arsenal, estimated to be about ten to fifteen unassembled nuclear devices. At the State Department, Robert Einhorn, deputy assistant secretary of state for political-military affairs, recognized the problem immediately. He had been assigned the task of looking into how a complex set of laws passed by Congress, aimed at putting teeth into U.S. policies to halt the spread of weapons of mass destruction, might apply to various international weapons activities. The ring magnets triggered a provision of American law related to U.S. business loans. Einhorn called the U.S. Export-Import Bank and notified officials there about the intelligence reports that could trigger the 1994 Nuclear Proliferation Prevention Act. The act requires the secretary of state to notify the bank if any nation is caught assisting foreign nuclear weapons development. The State Department said the bank could be required to hold up all new loan guarantees for projects sought by American businesses in China because of the ring magnets deal.

The Commerce Department, headed by former Democratic National Committee Chairman Ron Brown, was soon leading the charge to block sanctions. Sanctions against China had been imposed in 1993 for selling M-11 missile components but were lifted after Brown and the chairman of satellite maker Hughes Electronics, C. Michael Armstrong, fought to have them nullified. They were removed in 1994. Armstrong wrote a tersely worded letter to Clinton on October 29, 1993, highlighting his support for the president's economic package, for his legislation in California, and for loosening export controls. "I am respectfully requesting your involvement to resolve the China sanctions," Armstrong wrote, noting that he had spoken to a Chinese official who informed him Beijing was "positive" about the idea.

But when Secretary of State Warren Christopher told the Chinese that the United States needed to see "some sign of movement" that China was curbing weapons proliferation, a National Security Council memorandum reported, "The Chinese were not forthcoming." The memorandum said that Armstrong and Hughes "lobbied aggressively" to allow satellites from the company to be sold to China. In 1995 Clinton named Armstrong to the influential Export Council, where he worked hard against national security trade controls. The council produced a lengthy paper that argued against imposing sanctions on foreign trading partners that engaged in illicit weapons sales.

Bernard Schwartz, chairman of Loral Space & Communications, Ltd., was also engaged in an aggressive lobbying campaign to ease restrictions on sales of satellites to China. Schwartz denied that the large donations he had made to the Democratic National Committee had been meant to influence President Clinton's satellite export policies.

A Senate investigation into illegal foreign political payments could not make a direct connection between the conciliatory policies of President Clinton toward China and illegal campaign payoffs. Both the White House and the Chinese government deny that Chinese cash influenced policies. But a 1998 Senate Governmental Affairs Committee report concluded: "It is clear that illegal foreign contributions were made to the DNC [Democratic National Committee] and that these contributions were facilitated by individuals with extensive ties to the PRC [People's Republic of China].... It is also clear that well before the 1996 elections, officials at the highest levels of the Chinese government approved of efforts to increase the PRC's involvement in the U.S. political process."

DENIALS AND HOLLOW PROMISES

Two years before the ring magnets deal, in March 1992, China signed the Nuclear Non-Proliferation Treaty. The 1970 agreement recognized five states—the United States, the Soviet Union, Britain, France, and China—as the only nuclear weapons powers and sought to prevent others from becoming nuclear-armed nations. The treaty was extended indefinitely in 1995 in what the Clinton administration has hailed as a major arms control victory. Because of China's aversion to joining international agreements like the Non-Proliferation Treaty, the action was welcomed as a major step forward by U.S. arms control advocates. The treaty forbids signatories from providing nuclear weapons components to non-nuclear states. The ring magnets sales clearly violated the treaty and should have triggered economic sanctions against Beijing and Islamabad. But the violations of the treaty were ignored.

The State Department's Bureau of Political-Military Affairs was in a quandary. China had failed its first test as an Non-Proliferation Treaty signatory. Selling ring magnets undermined years of work to keep states like Pakistan from building nuclear bombs. Pakistan's program to enrich uranium for weapons using gas centrifuges began in 1975. The Khan Research Laboratory is currently spinning out enriched uranium for nuclear weapons.

The enrichment program owed its early success to a Pakistani government agent who stole design plans for the centrifuges from a European manufacturer, according to a declassified State Department report of June 23, 1983. "The Engineering Research Laboratories (ERL), the organization responsible for Pakistan's unsafeguarded enrichment program, has long relied on an international network of procurement agents and front organizations to purchase equipment for use in their centrifuge program in these various countries, sometimes disguising their activities by providing false end-use statements information," the State Department report said. According to the report, the Pakistanis were having problems in 1983 in getting the European-design centrifuges to work. The machines were not producing significant quantities of enriched uranium. "Because of these operational problems, the Pakistanis in the recent past sought help from the Chinese," the memo said. "We do not know what the present status of that cooperation is."

The Chinese lied—and the State Department and White House National Security Council knew it.

But the report made clear what the consequences of solving the enrichment problems would be. "Once the operational difficulties are overcome, and [if] only part of the plant were put into sustained operation, it could produce sufficient fissile material for a single device within two to three years of startup," it said. "When completely operational, the plant could probably produce enough highly enriched uranium for several devices per year."

It took the Pakistanis eleven years to solve the centrifuge problems. The Chinese ring magnets did the job. With these superior ring magnets, the centrifuges at Kahuta were upgraded at a rate of between one thousand and two thousand machines a year. By 1998 all were spinning with Chinese magnetic suspension bearings.

The ring magnets transfer remained secret until the story was broken by the author on the front page of the *Washington Times* on February 5, 1996. In January, a month before the story became public, the State Department quietly approached the China National Nuclear Corporation about the sale, and the Chinese said there was "no information" about it. They lied. And the State Department and White House National Security Council knew it. The intelligence was solid. The National Security Agency had the intercept showing in great detail that the transfer had taken place.

How the nuclear technology reached Pakistan is a story of deceit. Both the Chinese and Pakistani governments to this day deny the ring magnet sale. But for $70,000, China gave Pakistan's nuclear weapons program a major boost.

The first reaction to reports of the magnet sale came from State Department spokesman Glyn Davies on February 5, 1996, the day the *Times* story broke. "The United States does have concerns about possible nuclear-related transfers between China and Pakistan," he said, refusing to comment directly on the transaction. The matter, he went on, had been raised at senior levels of the Chinese and Pakistani governments. But how the "concerns" were raised—and what the exact nature of those worries was—was never made public. They were secret, and the Clinton administration was never pressured to explain them, either by Congress or by the news media.

Ten days later, Chinese Foreign Ministry spokesman Shen Guofang denied to reporters in Beijing that any ring magnet sale had taken place. "China, a responsible state, has never transferred equipment or technology for producing nuclear weapons to any other country, nor will China do so in the future." Then he threatened that U.S. economic sanctions against China would cause "serious harm" to relations. "China hopes the U.S. side will not use rumors as the basis for making decisions," he said.

Rumors? The rumors were hard intelligence reports, most of them classified at the top-secret level and above. The CIA, however, did produce an unclassified report to Congress covering the period between July and December 1996. "During the last half of 1996, China was the most significant supplier of weapons of mass destruction goods and technology to foreign countries," the report said. "The Chinese provided a tremendous variety of assistance to both Iran's and Pakistan's ballistic missile programs. China also was the primary source of nuclear-related equipment and technology to Pakistan and a key supplier to Iran during this reporting period."

Back at the State Department, spokesman Davies droned on. "We'll continue to raise this issue at every opportunity, including in diplomatic discussions this week during the visit of Chinese Vice Foreign Minister Li Zhaoxing," he said. The issue came up during talks between Li and Deputy Secretary of State Strobe Talbott. Davies went on to state that the United States "objects to any transfers from China to Pakistan that would contravene China's obligations under the NPT [Non-Proliferation Treaty] and that could assist Pakistan to develop nuclear weapons." But, he noted, "we have not determined that China has violated the NPT or that it's done anything that would trigger sanctions under U.S. legislation. That is obviously an issue that's constantly under review by the United States government, and so we constantly reassess that."

The White House, however, made sure such a determination would never be made. The policy was that sanctions against China should be avoided; it would be bad for the business that Commerce Secretary Ron Brown was trying to drum up. "The lengths this administration went to ignore great dangers to U.S. national security in the name of promoting business were unprecedented," said a former military officer who worked in the White House and declined to be named.

Then, in a move aimed at keeping the dispute quiet, Secretary of State Warren Christopher wrote to the U.S. Export-Import Bank later in February, asking the bank to defer all loan approvals for American businessmen operating in China. The cutoff would have been worth about $10 billion in new loans if it had been kept in place. But the measure lasted only thirty days and did not affect loans that had already been approved. The bank began considering new loans after the thirty-day period lapsed in March 1996, without even waiting for an official go-ahead notice from the State Department. The president even considered waiving the thirty-day sanctions but backed off after Congress protested. Christopher broached the subject in his April 19 meeting with Chinese Foreign Minister Qian Qichen, who had a reputation as a hardline communist and vehement critic of the United States. Questioned by Christopher on the ring magnets sale, Qian lied: China had not violated its commitment to the Nuclear Non-Proliferation Treaty, and therefore there was no reason for China to commit itself to refraining from exporting nuclear materials to Pakistan in the future. But promises, however hollow, were all the United States was seeking—anything, it seemed, that would not interfere with business.

CHINA GETS OFF THE HOOK

The Christopher-Qian meeting revealed the administration's plan to avoid imposing sanctions on China. If China would just pledge not to transfer any more nuclear weapons technology, the United States would agree not to impose sanctions, even though they are required under U.S. anti-proliferation laws.

After months of secret U.S.-Chinese talks on the issue, State Department spokesman Nicholas Burns issued a carefully worded statement on May 10, 1996. The statement cleared China of any culpability in its sale of nuclear weapons technology to Pakistan. Burns said months of "intense" discussions, including the talks between Christopher and Qian, had led to new "clarifications and assurances" from China about its weapons-related sales. "Of particular significance, the Chinese assured us that China will not provide assistance to unsafeguarded nuclear facilities, and the Chinese will now confirm this in a public statement," Burns said. Unsafeguarded facilities are nuclear plants and support facilities that are not subject to inspection by the International Atomic Energy Agency, which monitors nuclear facilities around the world under the Nuclear Non-Proliferation Treaty.

"In addition," Burns declared, "senior Chinese officials have informed us that the government of China was unaware of any transfers of ring magnets by a Chinese entity, and they have confirmed our understanding that China's policy of not assisting unsafeguarded nuclear programs will preclude future transfers of ring magnets to unsafeguarded facilities."

The "official" Chinese response was reported by the Xinhua news agency, the communist government's official organ. It included the response of an unnamed Chinese foreign ministry spokesman about "the decision of the U.S. government not to impose sanctions on China."

"We have taken note of the above report," Xinhua quoted the Foreign Ministry spokesman as saying. "As a state party to the treaty on the Non-Proliferation of Nuclear Weapons, China strictly observes its obligations under the treaty, and is against the proliferation of nuclear weapons. China pursues the policy of not endorsing, encouraging, or engaging in the proliferation of nuclear weapons or assisting other countries in developing such weapons." Nuclear cooperation between Beijing and "the countries concerned is exclusively for peaceful purposes," it said, adding that "China will not provide assistance to unsafeguarded nuclear facilities. China stands for the strengthening of the international nuclear non-proliferation regime, including the strengthening of safeguards and export control measures." The statement, as we will see, was false. No mention was made of ring magnets, and no promises were offered on future sales.

The Chinese "assurance" fell short of the written guarantee that had been sought. In fact, Xinhua contradicted the claim Burns made at the Christopher-Qian meeting of April 19: "Foreign Minister Qian Qichen did not make any promise at the talks. He stressed that China has not violated the Treaty on Non-Proliferation of Nuclear Weapons. Hence, China deems it unnecessary to make a commitment on not exporting to Pakistan in the future materials which can be used to produce nuclear weapons."

Christopher's decision to clear China was based on "a close review of the evidence available in this case, and the clarifications and assurances provided by China regarding past transfers and Chinese nuclear export control policies." Thus, Burns said, there was "not a sufficient basis" to impose sanctions as required by the 1994 Nuclear Proliferation Prevention Act. Violating the act by way of "willful" transfer of nuclear weapons know-how would lead to a cut-off of Export-Import Bank credits.

The limitations of the U.S.-China understanding were highlighted by the fact that the U.S. statement was issued in the name of the State Department press spokesman, Burns, and not by Christopher himself.

China's public announcement of the accord said only that "China will not provide assistance to unsafeguarded nuclear facilities." The Clinton administration claimed this was a "significant public commitment." Yet it lacked any specificity about future transfers and made no mention of ring magnets or the nuclear weapons equipment, though the Clinton administration officially assumed these items were part of the agreement.

The agreement, according to Burns, would be subject to "verification" involving a "big American spotlight on some of the Chinese companies that have engaged in these practices in the past." "If we find that there are any violations," Burns said, "we'll be very quick to let the Chinese government know that, and of course we would accept nothing less. This significant step forward that we have taken with the Chinese comes with the understanding that the United States will be watching." Within a few weeks, the deal would be exposed as hollow.

In short, and with twisted logic, the State Department—in order to avoid declaring China in violation of the Nuclear Non-Proliferation Treaty, and to prevent having to impose economic sanctions opposed by some in the U.S. business community—first claimed Chinese leaders were ignorant of the ring magnets sale, and then accepted what it believed to be a new pledge not to commit any further violations of the Non-Proliferation Treaty.

Pressed to say whether the Chinese assurances were written or oral, Burns acknowledged they were only spoken assurances. Burns also said that if Christopher had decided to impose sanctions on the China National Nuclear Corporation for selling the ring magnets, "we subsequently would have had to have entered into a... political discussion with the Chinese government to undo the problem." He said the actual decision had put the department "in a better position" than if sanctions had been imposed.

The entire ring magnets fiasco drew only muted reaction on Capitol Hill, mostly in the form of statements and letters to the president seeking answers. "For some time now the intelligence community has been providing evidence that China is violating U.S. non-proliferation laws, but the State Department has avoided imposing sanctions by concluding that the evidence was not strong enough," said Congressman Benjamin Gilman, New York Republican and chairman of the House International Relations Committee, shortly after the ring magnets sale became public. Gilman spoke of the "overwhelming evidence" that China had violated its commitment to the Non-Proliferation Treaty. He said it was time for the administration to do something, adding, "It is obvious that Beijing believes that the administration is unwilling to confront them on these issues."

Even when the CIA revealed nuclear arms deals between China and Pakistan, the Clinton administration refused to acknowledge that China had violated its non-proliferation pledge.

Gilman continued, "The failure of the administration to address these issues head on, and in particular to enforce U.S. non-proliferation laws, can lead to further Chinese violations which not only will make a mockery of those laws but also threaten U.S. national security interests."

Congressman Floyd Spence, South Carolina Republican and chairman of the House National Security Committee, wrote to Clinton warning that the United States was losing credibility in halting the spread of dangerous weapons. "I believe there are no viable options but to respond to these violations by imposing sanctions against China in accordance with U.S. law," wrote Spence. "I fear that failure to do so will carry a heavy price in American credibility and demonstrate to the world that the U.S. commitment to non-proliferation is hollow."

Later, Spence would criticize the president for failing to sanction China for the ring magnets deal. "China's actions are only the latest in a continuing pattern of noncompliance with its international obligations," he said. The failure to sanction Beijing undermined the Non-Proliferation Treaty and encouraged China and other nations to disregard their non-proliferation obligations. "It is a further example of the administration looking the other way when the Chinese openly violated international law," Spence said.

In the Senate, Larry Pressler, South Dakota Republican, said: "I simply refuse to believe that the People's Republic of China was unaware of this massive transfer of illegal equipment to Pakistan. Let's get real. The government in Beijing has tight controls on the flow of any tangible resource, whether words, widgets, or weapons. So I find it amazing that the Clinton administration actually bought China's line that five thousand ring magnets left the country without one government official knowing about it." The failure to get tough "keeps our nation on the downward spiral of declining credibility regarding nuclear non-proliferation policy." The then-chairman of the Senate Intelligence Committee, Arlen Specter, Pennsylvania Republican, also challenged the administration: "The intelligence community has done an excellent job in identifying this violation, and now it is up to the executive branch, through presidential order, to carry out the tough sanctions as mandated by U.S. law."

It was a Democrat—a member of President Clinton's own party— who had some of the strongest words. "In exchange for no sanctions, the Chinese government will promise not to proliferate nuclear programs in non-safeguarded countries," Representative Nancy Pelosi of California said. "The Chinese government made that promise to the international community at least once already—when it signed the Nuclear Non-Proliferation Treaty." But the Chinese government was let off, as was the company that sold the magnets, she noted. "It is outrageous that the administration has now freed the Export-Import Bank to use taxpayer funds for loans to assist the China National Nuclear Corporation—the very company that sold the ring magnets to Pakistan." She noted that "when all is said and done, the Chinese proliferated nuclear weapons technology and got away with it, and Pakistan received essential nuclear weapons technology and was rewarded."

DANGEROUS DEAL

The National Security Agency unwittingly dashed any remaining hope the administration had that China was following the agreement. In August 1996—less than three months after Beijing's May 11 pledge—National Security Agency electronic eavesdropping picked up what could only be called a smoking gun: CNEIC, the arm of the Chinese government that had sold the ring magnets, agreed to sell additional illegal nuclear weapons equipment to Pakistan. This time the Chinese were supplying diagnostic equipment and a special furnace to unsafeguarded facilities in Pakistan. According to a highly classified intercept obtained by the National Security Agency, the furnace and diagnostic equipment were to be delivered to Pakistan on September 2. The furnace was special equipment that is used for all types of high-technology metals. It is a key component for manufacturing the equipment that is used to make nuclear weapons material. The diagnostic equipment was part of the deal and is believed to be used in similar high-technology weapons production equipment.

The intercept was unwelcome intelligence at the State Department, which wanted its past diplomacy on Chinese nuclear proliferation to be the end of the problem. But the information could not be ignored completely. It prompted the State Department to file a diplomatic demarche asking for an explanation of the equipment sale. It was delivered to the Chinese Foreign Ministry by a U.S. embassy official on August 30. In response, a Chinese official involved in the nuclear industry notified the U.S. embassy in Beijing on September 11 that the equipment had been sent in 1995 or early in 1996 to the Pakistani Atomic Energy Commission. He had no further information.

The National Security Agency intercept was one of the rare times when secret intelligence scores a direct hit. Had its consequences not been explained away in a diplomatic exchange by the White House and State Department, it would have been remembered as one of the most important intelligence coups in the area of international security in decades. The intercept showed conclusively how the Chinese and Pakistani governments conspired to deceive the United States about their collaboration on nuclear weapons and technology transfers.

The intercept prompted the CIA to lay out the conspiracy in a memorandum sent to top officials at the State Department, Pentagon, and White House National Security Council. Written by Ken Sichel and Ray Bogusz of the Office of Weapons Technology and Proliferation, with help from Ted Clark at the Office of East Asian Analysis, the September 14 memorandum was sent on a Saturday, showing its urgency, and was classified at the highest level used for data based on intercepted messages. It bore the markings "TOP SECRET UMBRA NOFORN ORCON GAMMA." UMBRA and GAMMA are code words designating special intelligence obtained from intercepted electronic communications. NOFORN means that "no foreign" nationals should be permitted to see it, and ORCON is the intelligence marking signaling that material contained is "originator controlled" and cannot be distributed further without the National Security Agency's permission. The fact that such a highly classified document was leaked shows the frustration felt by many in the U.S. intelligence community about the way the Clinton administration was ignoring important information about weapons sales.

According to the memorandum, officials from CNEIC met in early September with a Pakistani national in Beijing identified only as Kibria. He was the most important agent of Pakistan's nuclear and missile procurement office in Beijing, and he discussed the August 30 diplomatic note from the United States. Kibria told the officials that

Chinese nuclear technicians were already in Pakistan to install the equipment that had arrived September 2. The memorandum stated, "The Pakistanis' expectation of the 2 September delivery... indicates either that the Chinese shipment schedule in January did not occur or that it may have been only a partial shipment."

The memo continued, "In the aftermath of CNEIC's ring magnet sale to Pakistan and China's 11 May commitment not to provide assistance to unsafeguarded nuclear facilities, senior-level [Chinese] government approval probably was needed for this most recent assistance." In other words, this time the Clinton policymakers at State and the National Security Council could not claim Beijing was unaware of the nuclear technology transfer. But the most important evidence from the intercept was the reference to both governments' secretly planning to deceive the United States into thinking all Chinese nuclear assistance was for "peaceful" purposes and not for Islamabad's weapons program.

"The Chinese told Kibria," the memo added, that "they needed end-user certificates for the sale and all future dual-use shipments and other equipment for Pakistan's unsafeguarded facilities and vowed to discuss the certificates only with a 'third party'—apparently the United States—probably to demonstrate that Beijing is complying with its May commitment." End-user certificates are standard export documents used by customs officials around the world to find out what is contained in a shipment and where it is going. Dual-use products are objects that are under export controls because, while they are civilian in nature, the goods can be used for military products and weapons.

According to the CIA memorandum, Ishfaq Ahmed, chairman of the Pakistan Atomic Energy Commission, said that any decision to share the fake destination documents with other nations would "require the approval of Pakistan's president or prime minister."

Kibria, the Pakistani procurement agent working in China, "suggested possible language for the false end-user certificates to make it appear that one item—possibly the diagnostic equipment—was intended for the safeguarded Chasma nuclear power plant, which Chinese firms are building," the CIA memo said.

"The intercept indicates Kibria also suggested to the Chinese that all remaining contracts, apparently for unsafeguarded facilities, be cancelled and new ones drawn up naming unobjectionable end users," the memo added. "Kibria claimed the Chinese reacted positively to the idea, but added this kind of agreement is 'dangerous.' Such a subterfuge probably would require the approval of senior Chinese government leaders."

In addition, the Chinese told Kibria that the secret deal for the furnace and diagnostic equipment had "leaked" in Pakistan; in response, the Islamabad government ordered Kibria to stop using telephones and faxes. All future messages must be confined to diplomatic communiqués sent by protected pouch. The directive severely limited the National Security Agency's ability to learn more about the conspiracy involving "Chinese-Pakistani nuclear, and to a lesser extent, ballistic missile cooperation," the CIA said, noting that it would also slow down Pakistani government procurement efforts in those areas.

CIA analysts, having picked up unequivocal intelligence, concluded that the Chinese were fooling the United States about their support for Pakistan's nuclear weapons program. But hard facts notwithstanding, State Department spokesman Nicholas Burns responded to publication of the CIA's intelligence by saying, "Senior-level people in this government have looked at these specific charges, and based on the information available to us, we do not conclude that China has violated the commitment it made in its May 11th statement."

The State Department nevertheless continued to express "concerns" about Chinese proliferation activities. "This is a very serious issue which is one of the priorities of this administration," Burns said. "In July we had concerns.... In August we had concerns. In September we had concerns."

White House spokesman Michael McCurry noted that "China is selling what people are buying—high technology that raises proliferation concerns." Nevertheless, he refused to acknowledge the obvious, that China had violated its pledge not to transfer nuclear weapons–related technology to Pakistan. "Proliferation purists want no such transfers, but we're not living in a perfect world," McCurry said. The formulation was vintage spin. While closing its eyes to dangerous arms deals, the White House had turned the issue on its head: Since the world is not perfect, there can be no blame and no responsibility for looking the other way as the Chinese government lied to the United States.

More intelligence about the Pakistani nuclear program continued to find its way to the CIA. By 1998 it was clear the Pakistanis were well on their way to producing plutonium-based weapons for the new medium-range Ghauri missile.

According to an intelligence report produced in August 1998 by the Department of Energy, which is responsible for monitoring worldwide nuclear weapons developments, Pakistan was moving far beyond the technology for producing highly enriched uranium, which is the stuff of first-generation nuclear bombs; it was moving toward producing plutonium, the stuff of nuclear warheads for missiles. "Imagery analysis reveals the reprocessing plant in the New Labs area of the

> **In the Clinton administration, *all* national security policies have been subordinated to business interests.**

Rawalpindi Nuclear Research Center near Islamabad is being expanded and modified to handle irradiated fuel from the unsafeguarded plutonium production center at Khushab," the report said. "Given this reprocessing capability, with no major problems in Khushab production, Pakistan would begin receiving weapons-grade plutonium by 2000. When finally operational, the production reactor and the reprocessing plant can produce and recover sufficient weapons-grade plutonium for one nuclear weapon [each year]."

Despite winning control of the House and Senate in the 1994 elections, the Republicans showed little stomach for taking on the White House and exposing the cover-up of the nuclear technology sales to China. The only substantive legislation on the issue was introduced by the House National Security Committee, which won passage of an amendment to the fiscal 1997 Defense Authorization bill. It required the president to submit reports—in both secret and public versions—to Congress explaining why sanctions were not imposed on China for sales of nuclear weapons technology to China. The White House National Security Council report is the only official public record of what happened in the ring magnets deal. It makes no mention of the conspiracy by China and Pakistan to hide their nuclear trade from the United States.

In the law requiring the report, Congress noted, for the president's benefit, that the Chinese government–owned CNEIC "has knowingly transferred specially designed ring magnets to an unsafeguarded uranium enrichment facility" in Pakistan, and that the "ring magnets are identified on the Trigger List of the Nuclear Suppliers Group as a component of magnetic suspension bearings," which can be sold only to countries with facilities under International Atomic Energy Agency controls. "These ring magnets could contribute significantly to the ability of the Islamic Republic of Pakistan to produce additional unsafeguarded enriched uranium, a nuclear explosive material." Put another way, the sale violated China's Non-Proliferation Treaty obligations.

John Deutch, the CIA director at the time, sat in on a cabinet meeting in late 1996 to discuss the ring magnets case. In front of him was a loose-leaf binder with some five hundred pages of classified documents and reports showing that China had in fact sold the ring magnets. Deutch told the assembled officials, "If you're not satisfied with the intelligence on this, you will never be satisfied with any intelligence on anything else." The White House did nothing.

Not only that, but in the spring of 1998 President Clinton lifted a ban on U.S. nuclear technology sales to China and certified that China was not "proliferating" nuclear technology.

At a secret briefing for the Senate Foreign Relations Committee on March 12, 1998, Robert Einhorn, the deputy assistant secretary of state for proliferation, told the panel that China had discussed new nuclear technology sales to Pakistan, as well as Iran, earlier in the year. The administration contacted the Chinese and was told that the sale would not go through. "In the past few weeks we have encountered reports of a few potentially troubling contacts by Chinese entities or individuals with countries of concern," Einhorn said. "We raised these cases with the Chinese, pressed them to investigate and urged that they prevent any transactions inconsistent with their assurances. In part, we believe, because of the incentives promised by the implementation of the nuclear certification agreement, the Chinese government conducted investigations and responded promptly to each of the inquiries."

Despite new evidence of Chinese duplicity on nuclear sales, Congress did nothing to block the nuclear certification of China. Among those pushing for certification were companies such as Westinghouse, General Electric, and Bechtel, eager to do business with China using $800 million of taxpayer-supported loans from the Export-Import Bank. As would happen over and over again during the Clinton administration, big money proved it could make big changes in U.S. policy.

China's dangerous nuclear weapons–related sales continue. On January 3, 1999, the National Security Agency reported secretly within the U.S. government that discussions were under way between China and Iran, another burgeoning nuclear weapons power, for the sale of special zirconium alloy production. Zirconium sheaths are used on fuel rods in nuclear reactors. Later that same month, the National Security Agency also uncovered fresh intelligence revealing two cases of Chinese support for Iran's missile program. On January 20 the U.S. intelligence community reported to the White House and other national security policymakers that China was increasing its sales of weapons of mass destruction equipment and missile materials to Iran, including titanium alloy for missiles. The National Security Agency, in particular, revealed that a shipment of specialty steel used in the Iranian missile program had been shipped from China to Iran, aboard a North Korean freighter. The White House, in its typical fashion, ignored the intelligence, but everyone in the intelligence community knew that China had once again broken its promises to halt proliferation-related materials around the world.

THE PROLIFERATIONS CONTINUE

Another case in point was China's sale of M-11 missiles to Pakistan.

Daniel Poneman sat in his office at the Old Executive Office Building next to the White House listening to two senior CIA officials. As the White House National Security Council staff director in charge of weapons proliferation issues, Poneman was the top official responsible for figuring out whether weapons transfers violated U.S. anti-proliferation laws, and whether the president had to impose sanctions as a result. A holdover from the administration of President George Bush, Poneman was considered a lightweight who was in over his head on proliferation matters. But he was wise enough to know how to follow the dictates of his political masters, whether Republican or Democrat, since the Clinton administration had been kind enough to keep him on when it took over in 1993. It was now the summer of 1996. Presented with the latest top-secret intelligence showing conclusively that China had provided complete M-11 missiles to Pakistan, Poneman scoffed, "You're bringing me pennies; bring me some quarters." His point: The evidence was not strong enough. The real reason: The White House had adopted a pro-business approach to international security affairs and was being pressured by American business leaders to avoid sanctions on China.

The pennies remark was later recounted by a CIA officer who said Poneman was presented with a framed twenty-five–cent piece at his going-away party. On the bottom was an inscription: "In case of emergency, break glass." It was a lighthearted gesture, but it expressed the deep frustration of intelligence analysts who felt a highly politicized White House would do anything to avoid imposing legally mandated economic sanctions against China.

The M-11 transfer was not a new issue for Poneman. Twice before, two Chinese government–owned companies had been slapped with U.S. economic sanctions for selling M-11 components to Pakistan. But this time the issue was obscured to avoid new sanctions. The companies involved were the China Precision Machinery Import-Export Corporation, which produces a variety of missiles, and the

China Great Wall Industry Corporation, which produces both missiles and space launchers.

"It was a big Kabuki dance," said one frustrated CIA analyst. "Everyone knew the M-11s were there [in Pakistan], but the White House and State Department refused to act." The State Department, in the words of one CIA official, "kept moving the bar higher" of what was acceptable intelligence "every time new information came in."

Most details of the M-11 sales remain tightly guarded secrets. It wasn't until the summer of 1998 that the first official version of the transfers and the government cover-up was aired in glaring fashion. The facts were revealed in congressional testimony by Gordon Oehler on June 11, 1998. Oehler was the former director of the CIA's Non-Proliferation Center, which monitors the spread of nuclear, chemical, and biological weapons and ballistic missiles, with a clandestine operations wing that supports covert action against proliferators. In his testimony before the Senate Foreign Relations Committee, Oehler cited a 1997 CIA report that singled out China as "the most significant supplier of weapons of mass destruction–related goods and technology to foreign countries."

"Because I was involved in the production of this report, I have been asked to comment on the reasons for this strong statement," Oehler said. While some progress had been made in curbing Chinese weapons sales, "exports of materials and technologies with concern to Pakistan and Iran have not abated and some exports to other countries have continued as well," he continued.

Oehler disclosed that beginning in the early 1990s China had provided Pakistan with nuclear-capable ballistic missile technology and complete missiles. "In 1990, the intelligence community detected the transfer to Pakistan of a training M-11 ballistic missile, and associated transporter-erector launcher, indicating that operational missiles were not far behind. The intelligence community had evidence that the M-11 was covered by the so-called guidelines and parameters of the Missile Technology Control Regime, the MTCR." (By referring to the "so-called" guidelines, Oehler spoke to the fact that the MTCR, a voluntary arrangement, lacks an enforcement mechanism.)

Oehler testified that since 1992 China had changed strategies, and that instead of selling MTCR-covered missiles, Beijing's arms brokers had begun to concentrate on transferring production technology and components that would allow nations to build their own systems. "Production technologies and components are also covered under the MTCR, but they are easier to hide, or can be claimed to be for non-MTCR–related systems," he said. "One can argue, though, that the transfer of missile-related production technologies is a more serious infraction of the intent of the Missile Technology Control Regime."

China's missile transfers to Iran, for example, included guidance and control components, production technology, and testing jigs, Oehler added, noting that Beijing also provided chemical weapons materials and technologies. "But that's another story." Oehler went on:

> In sum, China has been for a long time a major proliferator of weapons of mass destruction materials and technologies. Moreover, the Chinese leaders have... a very poor record of living up to their commitments to the U.S., and in the name of national sovereignty they resisted U.S. efforts to put in place any means to verify their compliance with bilateral or international agreements.
>
> In my opinion, based on this past record, we need to base any future agreements with China on something more than the word of its leaders and make provisions for an easy out for the United States if they resist verification procedures in the agreement or simply if they choose to disregard their commitments to us.

The senators pressed Oehler on why China's M-11 sale to Pakistan had apparently been covered up with American complicity.

"The intelligence community knew that M-11s were going to be transferred sometime; at least, they had evidence [of] that," Oehler testified. "When the transfers took place, the evidence was quite strong at the time, and most agencies in the intelligence community agreed right away that the actual transfer of missiles had taken place. But it was not until accumulating evidence came in over the next year or two that finally... the unanimous view of the intelligence community, including the State Department's Bureau of Intelligence and Research, [was] that in fact the missiles—there was a high likelihood that the missiles themselves were transferred." And policymakers were informed about the intelligence at every step of the process, Oehler stated.

The chief policymaker at State on all sanctions issues was Undersecretary of State for International Security Lynn Davis. She had set the standard of proof so high that intelligence agencies would never be able to reach it, short of having the missiles taken out of their canisters and displayed in public. The intelligence equivalent actually happened when, in August 1996, a National Intelligence Estimate report—the consensus view of the CIA, the Defense Intelligence Agency, the National Security Agency, the National Reconnaissance Office, and the State Department Bureau of Intelligence and Research—concluded not only that M-11s had been sold, but also that China had provided Pakistan with an entire production facility for M-11–design missiles. The missile factory was located outside the northern city of Rawalpindi, near the capital of Islamabad. Within two years it would be able to produce all the components needed for assembling Chinese-design M-11s.

Construction began in 1995 and was photographed by U.S. spy satellites. The intelligence used to formulate the estimate was based on what is called "multiple sources," meaning that the reports were based on different types of intelligence. There were extremely sensitive reports from the several agents recruited by the CIA in the Southeast Asian region who were known only by their code names, such as "Foxfire." And there were electronic intercepts from the National Security Agency, including evidence of two visits by Chinese missile technicians to Pakistan's Sargodha missile facility in 1996 to train Pakistanis to use the M-11s and to unpack and assemble the missiles. "At least some of the M-11s that had been dispersed at military locations throughout Pakistan are now being stored at Sargodha," the intelligence report said. "But we have yet to see operational missiles on imagery. April imagery showed canisters at Sargodha similar to ones seen at the M-11 production facility in

China. But a missile-handling exercise was under way at Sargodha at that time, and the canisters were assessed to be mock-ups for use in that exercise."

Still, the State Department held back. It worried that declaring the missiles "operational" would force the administration to impose sanctions on China and Pakistan as required by anti-proliferation laws. So, to the dismay of intelligence professionals, the term "operational" was dropped in the final report.

During his Senate testimony, Oehler noted that "intelligence officials knew why the administration took the position that they did, that the imposition of Category I sanctions would have a very great impact on its relationship with China and almost any measure needed to be found to continue their negotiating flexibility, rather than automatically impose sanctions. And one of the easier outs on this is to say that the intelligence information doesn't quite meet their high standards."

Intelligence analysts throughout the government were upset by the politicization of the intelligence on M-11s. "These are people who struggle day to day to put together intelligence judgments, a collection of profiles, and everything. And they were very discouraged to see that, fairly regularly, their work was, in their view, summarily dismissed by the policy community, with a statement that 'it isn't good enough, it isn't good enough.'"

Was there any doubt that the M-11s were in Pakistan?

"There is no question in my mind whatsoever about this," Oehler said. "The evidence comes from many sources, very good sources."

Asked to explain the administration's denials about China's M-11 sale to Pakistan, Oehler said that no administration likes legislation on automatic sanctions because it limits "flexibility." Oehler continued:

> With that in mind, then they are going to try to find whatever way they can to carry out the policy that they think is best. And one of the loopholes in this is that the president must certify that this transfer has taken place. The certification has been passed down to an undersecretary of state. But then it's up to that person to decide whether the level

of evidence is sufficient to impose these—in their view—drastic or draconian sanctions.

Because of their interest in wanting to preserve their negotiating flexibility, in my view, there was going to be little likelihood that the evidence would ever be high enough to do that. Now, when you say that, you could ask, "Well, what would it take?" Obviously, if the Pakistanis were foolish enough to parade these missiles in Karachi, or to fire some of these missiles, or test them, or do something like that, then that would force their hand. But, short of that, I think that they're going to want to continue to maintain their negotiating flexibility.

Oehler echoed CIA Director John Deutch's earlier statement about the evidence obtained by intelligence agencies on the Chinese ring magnets sale. Asked if sanctions would ever be imposed for the M-11 sales, Oehler said, "It's going to be a long while."

Senate Foreign Relations Committee Chairman Jesse Helms, who presided over the hearing, recalled Clinton's comments from only two months earlier, when the president told a group visiting the White House that U.S. proliferation laws had put pressure on the government, forcing it to "fudge" in evaluating the facts. "Nowhere has this fudging of the facts been more clearly manifested than with respect to China's missile proliferation, and specifically in the instance of China's transfer to Pakistan of dozens of nuclear-capable M-11 missiles," Helms said.

The Clinton administration's policy of focusing on economic issues led to willful misconduct in America's national security affairs.

Yet, even after Oehler's startling evidence, no action was taken to force the administration to obey the law, perhaps because pro-business Republicans in Congress were reluctant to fight an administration that had adopted such a pro-business stance. In the Clinton administration, *all* national security policies were subordinated to business interests, including the intense lobbying efforts of U.S. satellite manufacturers who wanted to export their wares.

In June 1998 the White House released a series of documents to Congress on its export control policies. One of the most revealing was a December 8, 1993, memorandum produced for National Security Adviser Anthony Lake and his deputy Samuel Berger on the dispute about whether U.S. satellite exports to China should be covered by sanctions that had been imposed in August 1993. At issue were U.S. satellites worth $800 million, but which contained components that could be used for missiles. "We have consistently told the Chinese that sanctions could be waived if the Chinese would: (1) not ship any more M-11–related items to Pakistan; and (2) formally agree, in a binding international agreement, to adhere to the MTCR guidelines." But since the imposition of the sanctions, the memo noted, "Hughes Corp. and its CEO Mike Armstrong, has [*sic*] lobbied aggressively to exclude its satellites from the sanctions." To seal the matter, Armstrong added a threat. "Armstrong is now fairly directly threatening to wage a more public campaign against the administration's sanctions," the memo said. "He has secured key congressional support (e.g., Nunn, California delegation) and suggests he may prompt a congressional inquiry, write op-eds, and/or spur union opposition. He expresses a desire to work quietly with us—and has until now—but he is becoming impatient."

The connections between Loral and Hughes and the Clinton administration were highlighted in the 1998 book *Year of the Rat*, by congressional staffers Edward Timperlake and William C. Triplett II. They revealed how Loral's chairman Bernard Schwartz wrote a check to the Democratic Party for $100,000 and two months later was aboard Commerce Secretary Ron Brown's trade mission to China. Schwartz would become the largest contributor to the Clinton-Gore reelection campaign in 1996 and continued funding the president after that, giving more than $1.1 million to Democrats. In exchange, the administration gave Loral an anti-trust exemption and loosened export controls on satellites. "America's first line of defense against missile proliferation was dismantled," the authors wrote.

And while Loral was under investigation by the Justice Department for providing strategic missile technology to China, the White House issued a waiver to Loral that permitted the company to launch a satellite on a Chinese rocket.

As for former Hughes chairman C. Michael Armstrong, now chief executive officer of AT&T, Timperlake and Triplett revealed that Hughes lobbied hard to sell high-technology satellites that will be used by China's People's Liberation Army for intelligence purposes. "Armstrong persuaded the Commerce Department to allow Hughes much more free access to private discussions with Chinese rocket scientists," they said. "This is exactly what the national security apparatus didn't want to happen."

"I have no doubt," said Senator Helms at the Oehler hearing, "that concern over the impact of missile sanctions in this case has fueled the administration's efforts to contradict clear and totally unambiguous evidence that operational M-11 missiles are in fact in Pakistan."

The veil finally lifted after Pakistan detonated its first nuclear device. The Pentagon held a background briefing and disclosed not only that the M-11s were in Pakistan, but also that they could be equipped with nuclear warheads. Yet now, even the Pentagon's statement, "The fact is they do have M-11s," was later contradicted by Ken Bacon, the assistant defense secretary for public affairs. Bacon, a veteran political spinmeister, backed the State Department's dishonest position. He stated that the Pentagon did not disagree with the State Department on the issue—in other words, a final determination about the M-11s still could not be made.

WILLFUL MISCONDUCT

The Clinton administration policy of focusing almost exclusively on economic affairs (slogan: "It's the economy, stupid") led to willful misconduct in America's national security affairs. U.S. laws requiring the president to impose economic sanctions to punish nations that sell dangerous nuclear weapons and missile delivery systems were ignored with impunity. U.S. intelligence exposing the violations was perverted by dishonest policymakers who claimed the intelligence was "inconclusive." Analysts within the U.S. government who had spent careers producing honest assessments were told their conclusions were wrong. The corrosive effect was extremely demoralizing, prompting many of the CIA's best analysts to quit. And the failure of the administration to take decisive action to punish weapons proliferators was correctly interpreted in Beijing, Moscow, and elsewhere as weakness and vacillation. America's position as the sole remaining geostrategic superpower was squandered. The failure to act also emboldened proliferators and weapons developers to continue their efforts.

But in Bill Clinton's Washington, national security facts never get in the way of helping corporate friends do business.

CHAPTER EIGHT

From Russia with Technology

"One and a half years after President Yeltsin told President Clinton that ballistic missile technology transfers to Iran would stop, it still continues.... Now time is running out; the stakes are great.... Unless this problem is solved we see a potential trainwreck in our relations."

—White House National Security Adviser Samuel Berger to Russian Security Council Secretary Andrei Kokoshin during a closed-door Kremlin meeting in May 1998

*M*issile technology transfers from Russia to Iran represent one of the most egregious cases of the failed foreign policies of Bill Clinton. In the mid-1990s U.S. intelligence agencies uncovered extremely detailed information disclosing the deadly missile trade. The president at first ignored it, and then failed to take action, hoping the problem would go away. Senior Clinton aides frequently briefed Russian officials on intelligence derived from intercepts and agents, and in return Moscow's intelligence services shut down the secret channels that were providing data to U.S. spies. American diplomats talked while the Russians listened and ignored them. By 1998 Moscow had secretly boosted Iran's crash program to build missiles capable of attacking all of the Middle East and most of Central Europe with chemical, biological, and eventually nuclear weapons. Moscow denied the missile trade with Iran, then lied about it, and finally increased the trade. Clinton and his national security team, afraid to put any pressure on the Yeltsin government, adopted a blindly pro-Russian policy. Missile technology transfers to

Iran were not allowed to interfere with the president's naive arms con-
trol agenda with Russia, which seemed aimed more at limiting U.S.
power than at reducing nuclear arsenals.

By failing to promote democratic change with realistic and honest
policies toward Russia, Clinton lost the opportunity to turn a Cold War
foe into a friend. By 1999 the weak and conciliatory policy of pleading
with Russia had failed miserably. Instead of halting its arms trade,
Moscow stepped it up and began selling more weapons to America's
enemies, including nuclear technology needed by the Iranians to top
off their new long-range missiles with nuclear warheads.

The Clinton policies, such as the inaction on the Iran missile trade,
will dominate future debate on "Who lost Russia?"

When President Clinton met with Russian President Boris Yeltsin on
March 13, 1996, both leaders were up for reelection. After a few minutes
their small talk gave way to substance. Regarding Russia's elections,
Clinton said, "First of all I want to make sure that everything the United
States does will have a positive impact, and nothing should have a neg-
ative impact. The United States will work with Russia to ensure this."

Yeltsin replied that a leader of global stature like President Clinton
should "support Russia, and that means supporting Yeltsin." The two
nations' officials should think about how "to do that wisely," the
Russian said.

Clinton told him Secretary of State Warren Christopher and
Russian Foreign Minister (and former spy chief) Yevgeni Primakov
would talk about that. "The main thing is that the two sides should
not do anything that would harm the other. Things could come up
between now and elections in Russia or the United States which could
cause conflicts," Clinton said.

The president then raised one particular issue: Russia's refusal to
allow imports of American chicken because of worries the poultry
contained unacceptable amounts of bacteria. Clinton said perhaps
the commission headed by Vice President Al Gore and Russian Prime
Minister Victor Chernomyrdin could resolve such issues.

"This is a big issue, especially since about 40 percent of U.S. poultry is produced in Arkansas," Clinton said, dropping the not-so-subtle

hint that U.S. backing for the Russian president was linked to resolving the dispute, which involved his longtime political supporter Don Tyson, head of the huge Arkansas poultry producer Tyson Foods, Incorporated. "This question should be on its way to resolution, and an effort should be made to keep such things from getting out of hand," Clinton said.

"Use direct channels," Yeltsin interrupted. He then said the main thing was that U.S. inspectors had confirmed that there were violations but "now we are back in business." Within a week after the meeting in Egypt, the Gore-Chernomyrdin commission issued a statement announcing that the poultry dispute had been settled.

The 1996 encounter between the two leaders was revealed in a classified document called a "memorandum of conversation" obtained by the author. It captured the essence of the political subtlety of Bill Clinton. It also showed the lengths the president would go to satisfy crass political debts, and how cavalierly he would play politics with national security. This ploy would be seen on a different scale in the Democratic Party campaign finance scandal, when Friends of Bill Clinton transferred cash, much of it suspected of coming from the Chinese government, into campaign coffers.

> **President Clinton has gone to great lengths to satisfy crass political debts, and he has cavalierly played politics with national security.**

The private conversation between Yeltsin and Clinton also captured the essence of how the Clinton administration adopted a Yeltsin-above-all policy toward Russia. That policy, formulated and pushed by Deputy Secretary of State Strobe Talbott, Clinton's one-time college roommate, would have disastrous consequences when it came to trying to stem the flow of Russian missile technology to Iran.

THE FAILURE OF STRATEGIC COOPERATION

"Our goal, like that of many Russians, is to see Russia become a normal, modern state—democratic in its governance, abiding by its own constitution and by its own laws, market-oriented and prosperous in its economic development, at peace with itself and with the rest of the world," Strobe Talbott said in a 1997 speech at Stanford University. "There is no doubt where our own national interest lies: Quite simply, we want to see the ascendancy of Russia's reformers, those who look outward and forward rather than inward and backward for the signposts of national revival.... The essence of our policy, in short, is: give them time—give them time to consolidate the reforms that constitute the good news of the past few years; give them time to beat back the forces that have generated the bad news; give them time to work out their identity and destiny in ways that will not only best serve a modern Russia's real interests but that will also be, to the greatest extent possible, compatible with our interests as well. In other words, we need to make sure we have a policy toward Russia that contains an indispensable feature: strategic patience."

By any measure, the Talbott policy of strategic cooperation—and patience—has been a huge failure with potentially disastrous results for U.S. national security. Reformers were pushed aside by corrupt Russian officials and businessmen who plundered Western aid money to the tune of between $20 billion and $60 billion, most of which is now sitting in Swiss or French banks. The hardliner Yevgeni Primakov's rise to power in 1998 was the final blow to reform. Many of the communist or communist-style leaders of the era of Mikhail Gorbachev also came back to power. By 1999 Primakov had taken steps to place former KGB political police cronies in top positions of the government and media. He was lining up political supporters for his assumed bid for the presidency. Andrei Kokoshin, Yeltsin's key national security adviser who was sympathetic but powerless to deal with Western concerns about weapons proliferation, was ousted in 1998, as the Russian hardliners gained grounds.

Caspar Weinberger, the respected secretary of defense in the Reagan administration who can claim a large measure of credit for defeating the Soviet Union, believes the Clinton policy toward Russia in the 1990s went "extraordinarily wrong" because the president and his advisers failed to treat Russia as the defeated power it was. By coddling Moscow and Yeltsin, instead of dealing with the Russians from a position of unrivaled strength, the United States brought about the return to power of anti-Western leaders in 1998. "It seems to me," Weinberger said in a Heritage Foundation speech, "we had a very large amount to do with causing it, by our refusal to recognize Russia for what it was, a defeated former great power that needed to spend all of its time and energy on not only recovering its economic situation, but moving from tyranny of the worst kind, oppression of the worst kind, to democracy, market-oriented policies, and some basic association with the ideas of the West. And none of that was done." Western aid in the tens of billions of dollars that could have been used for industrial recovery "just disappeared entirely," he said. "And

> **The Clinton administration's Yeltsin-above-all policy toward Russia has had disastrous consequences.**

other funds went to support an extremely large program of regaining sophisticated military capabilities, what would have cost us about… $38 billion for the acquisition of such things as an underground bunker and command systems, which is basically used in a nuclear war…."

While Strobe Talbott was counseling patience with Russia, Russia was illegally doling out missile technology to the radical Muslim regime in Iran. As CIA Director George Tenet testified in February 1998, Russian assistance was a major boost to the Iranian missile program. "When I testified a year ago," Tenet told the Senate Intelligence Committee, "I said that Iran, which had received extensive missile assistance from North Korea, would probably have medium-range missiles capable of hitting Saudi Arabia and Israel in less than ten years. Since I testified, Iran's success in gaining technology and material from Russian companies, combined with recent indigenous Iranian advances, means that it could have a medium-range missile much sooner than I assessed last year." In February 1999 Tenet told the Senate that the flow of missile technology from Russia to Iran had not stopped, that it was continuing "as we speak." Tenet testified, "Especially during the last six months, expertise and material from Russia have continued to assist the Iranian missile effort in areas ranging from training to testing to components." The missile assistance, he said, "will play a crucial role in Iran's ability to develop more sophisticated and longer-range missiles."

After years of ignoring the problem, Congress finally became energized and in 1998 passed legislation requiring sanctions to be imposed on Russia for the missile trade. But President Clinton vetoed the bill in June of that year. "This bill will make it more difficult to continue our work with the Russian government in this area," Clinton said in a statement.

A month later, after months and months of denials and dissembling, the Russian government announced it had identified nine companies involved in technology export violations, and the Clinton administration finally imposed economic sanctions on the supposedly "private" Russian research institutes and companies. But the list did not include the major Russian entities involved in the missile technology transfer to Iran, including the government's state trading company, known as *Rosvooruzheniye* [pronounced "Roz-vor-oo-zhen-ye"], and the Russian Space Agency. Two other culprits that made a major contribution to Iran's missile program were also left out: The Bauman Institute and the Central Aerohydrodynamic Institute. Both were identified in classified U.S. intelligence reports as vital to Iran's program.

Besides, by the time the sanctions were imposed, it was too late. On July 22, 1998, Iran stunned the world by conducting the first test flight of a new medium-range missile called the Shahab-3. The missile is nuclear-capable and could be fitted with deadly poison gas or biological weapons. The mobile missile directly threatens American troops deployed throughout the region, including in the Persian Gulf and Turkey. "Obviously, if they were to develop an intermediate-range missile, it could change the regional stability dynamics in the Middle East," Clinton said in response. "We're very, very concerned about it, but not surprised by it," he said.

The story of Iran's Shahab missile is a tale of the development of a dangerous weapon that could have been prevented. It was a major national security failure on the part of the Clinton administration, which simply ignored the growing military danger in favor of its policy of supporting Boris Yeltsin.

RUSSIA AND IRAN

More than a year before the Iranian test, on January 29, 1997, the U.S. embassy in Moscow received a secret cable from the State Department in Washington. A delegation of Israeli military intelligence officials was in Washington and brought the alarming news that Russia was deeply involved in Iran's crash program to develop medium-range ballistic missiles based on the North Korean No Dong. The Israelis said the cooperation was "a severe threat" to Israel and the region. The cable read:

> This is shaping up as a serious problem. While we have not seen or analyzed their raw data, the Israelis seem to have established that:
>
> - The Iranians are working on two No Dong derivatives, Shahab-3 (with a 1,250 mm tube, 1,300 to 1,500 kilometer range, and 750 kilogram RV [reentry vehicle, or warhead]); and Shahab-4 (larger, more advanced guidance systems, 2,000 kilometer-range and 1,000 kilogram RV).
> - The Iranians are seeking domestic production.
> - Iranian defense industry entities have worked with the Bauman Institute in St. Petersburg, with Rosvooruzheniye, the Russian Space Agency, NPO Trud, Polyus, and other Russian firms in: Conducting wind tunnel testing of the nose cone, designing the guidance and propulsion systems and working on a solid-fuel project.
>
> The Israelis have identified [Russian Space Agency Director Yuri] Koptev and Rosvooruzheniye's aerospace director in connection with the project; they have a copy of the $7 million contract with NPO Trud (which built the Russian lunar space vehicle).

- Great Wall Industries (China) is working on telemetry infrastructure; little information.
- A prototype may be ready in two to three years.

The Israelis believe the Russians may try to justify the missiles as research devices. They have not identified a Russian-Iranian coordinating channel for missile development, nor implicated any senior figure besides Koptev, possibly suggesting a pattern of freelancing. The Israelis suspect, but have not established, that the total of relevant contracts in Russia may not exceed $20 million.

As part of their presentation, the Israelis supplied a classified report showing how Russia was helping Iran develop medium-range missiles that would enable the Iranians to strike targets as far away as Central Europe.

Details of the report were kept secret within the administration for more than seven months, until the story broke on September 10, 1997, in an article by the author, carried with a front-page banner headline in the *Washington Times*: "Russia, China aid Iran's missile program. Prototype expected within three years of weapons that could hit Central Europe."

State Department officials made light of the threat, doing no more than issuing a standard protest. "We take these reports seriously and have raised our concerns repeatedly and at the highest levels of the Russian government," spokesman Jim Foley said. "The Russian government continues to assure us that it is committed to the highest non-proliferation standards. While we appreciate such assurances, we remain disturbed by the discrepancy between these assurances and reports of Russian firms cooperating with Iran. Given the far-reaching implications of this matter, we will continue to pursue it at the highest levels." The diplomacy, of course, was a failure.

As for China, earlier statements praising China's alleged "excellent progress" in curbing weapons proliferation were left standing. Foley said that China had agreed in October 1994 to ban all exports of Missile Technology Control Regime–covered missiles and that "we have no evidence that China has conducted activities inconsistent with this commitment." So were the administration's concerns about Chinese-Iranian missile cooperation allayed? "No, I would not say that our concerns have been allayed," Foley said, but "no determination" had been made about the Beijing-Tehran missile transfers.

Were there any plans by the administration to do something other than express concern or condemn the transfers? Something substantial?

"Well, we have a concerted across-the-board effort to deny Iran not only weapons of this nature, themselves, but also the means to acquire such weapons through our economic sanctions and approach," Foley said. "So I think, in every conceivable way, we are making this one of our highest foreign policy priorities. These efforts—Iranian efforts—to acquire weapons of mass destruction and the means to deliver them indeed pose a threat to some of our closest friends and allies in the world. That's why we think everyone has a stake in addressing this issue very seriously."

While the Clinton administration was counseling patience with Russia, Russia was illegally doling out missile technology to the radical Muslim regime in Iran.

Clinton and Yeltsin twice discussed the issue of Russian involvement: first, in Helsinki, Finland, in March 1997, and again at the June 1997 economic summit in Denver. Vice President Al Gore also raised the matter during his regular secret talks with Russian Prime Minister Victor Chernomyrdin. But as the memorandum of the March 1996 conversation between Clinton and Yeltsin laid out, the two sides made sure nothing "negative" would affect relations between the two countries. The administration followed the script closely. Secretary of State Madeleine Albright "discussed" the matter with Yevgeni Primakov, the foreign minister whose contacts with Middle East dictators and terrorists went back decades.

In February 1997 Gore broached the subject of Russian firms that were supplying SS-4 ICBM technology to Iran. Despite having had the

Israeli report since January, and numerous other U.S. intelligence reports to back it up, the administration waited until the summer of 1997 before appointing Frank Wisner, a former Pentagon official and recently retired U.S. ambassador to India, as a special envoy to Russia on the matter. Wisner had a conflict of interest from the start. The company he went to work for after finishing his tenure in India had a big contract in Russia. American International Group, a major international insurance underwriter, had set up a huge private investment fund in the former Soviet Union. Wisner was appointed director and vice chairman of American International Group in September 1997— two months *after* he was appointed as a special envoy to negotiate with the Russians on ways to end the missile trade with Iran. Kenneth Timmerman, a specialist on Iran, revealed the facts in an April 1998 report in *The American Spectator*.

Whom did the Russians pick to deal with Wisner? None other than Yuri Koptev, the Russian Space Agency director and one of two Russian government officials the Israelis had identified as being directly involved in the Iranian missile trade—which White House National Security Council officials denied. During an interview, a senior non-proliferation specialist said flatly, "We don't think Koptev is involved." Did Koptev have any contacts with the Iranians? "Not related to missile transfers." Did he discuss space cooperation? "There were some contacts on space cooperation, but they were minor." Do the Iranians have a space program? "No."

But as the Israelis had predicted, the Iranian missile program was carried out undercover as a peaceful space project. The White House, apparently, was willing to go along with the ruse, solely to protect the Russians.

Aleksander Medvedchikov, a spokesman for the Russian Space Agency, said none of the agency's space experts had been to Iran and could not possibly be linked to the Iranian missile program. But, in response to the September 1997 *Washington Times* article, he told the Interfax news agency that "some three years ago" Iran had discussed "possible assistance in the construction of satellites."

Wisner led the first of several administration interagency teams to Moscow in August 1997 to discuss ways, in the State Department's words, to "work together to prevent missile technology from reaching Iran, and we expect this effort will continue."

But the day after the *Times* story broke, Russian Foreign Ministry spokesman Valeriy Nesterushkin issued the first of Moscow's categorical denials in an attempt to block American investigation. "The appropriate Russian agencies have repeatedly checked various scenarios and rumors to this effect and found no confirmation of them," Nesterushkin said. "Russia has given exhaustive explanations to its partners on several occasions" in seeking to explain its military and technical cooperation with Iran. "However, one gets the impression our explanations are not being heard."

They were being heard, just not believed by Western intelligence agencies that had developed their own information showing that the post-Soviet KGB intelligence services, the Foreign Intelligence Service, and the Federal Security Service, in charge of proliferation issues, were deeply involved in the covert missile trade with Iran. Nesterushkin asserted that Russia was faithfully following the June 1995 commitment not to violate the terms of the Missile Technology Control Regime. Prime Minister Victor Chernomyrdin went further, ridiculing reports of cooperation with Iran. "I have no intention of commenting on stupid statements," the prime minister said. Yevgeni Primakov, the former Communist Party operative who would eventually succeed Chernomyrdin, also took a hard line, but parsed his statements to leave open the possibility that the missile sales from Russia were going on behind the back of the Yeltsin government, a claim that would later be exposed as false. "Not a single such project via government channels has been undertaken by Russia with Iran," Primakov said. "No [technology] leaks of the type which could assist Iran in creating either nuclear arms or long-range missiles have taken place via non-government channels either." But, he added, Russia would not curb its sales of "peaceful" nuclear technology to Iran. "We will do this, and we will build the nuclear power station in Bushehr," he said.

"Nothing will change this stance as it has nothing to do with the existing suspicions. At the same time, it is quite important for Russia in terms of the economy."

Israel was the nation most immediately threatened by the Iranian medium-range missiles. Shortly after news of the Shahab missile cooperation was made public by the *Washington Times*, Israel announced that it would hold up its deal with Russia on the construction of a natural gas pipeline.

As for the CIA, the agency had doubted Russia's commitment to non-proliferation since at least 1994. A special analysis produced by the CIA in September of that year questioned whether Boris Yeltsin's promises for implementing non-proliferation commitments could be followed through. The analysis, labeled "TOP SECRET UMBRA NOFORN," was produced under the direction of Jack Caravelli, a veteran CIA analyst who would eventually wind up working on the White House National Security Council staff. "Despite efforts to control missile-related exports, Moscow has been unable or unwilling to prevent some Russian organizations from marketing their missile-related hardware and technologies abroad for profit, according to special intelligence," the classified intelligence report said. Special intelligence is the euphemism for information gathered by the National Security Agency's worldwide electronic eavesdroppers. "Russian missile-related enterprises have negotiated with Chinese counterparts the sale of hardware and technologies for long-range cruise missiles which are regulated under MTCR [the Missile Technology Control Regime]. Russian firms also have been involved in, or are planning cooperation with, the Brazilian MTCR Category I space launch vehicle program. Cooperation involves composite structures, guidance and control and system testing."

On the subject of Iran, the report helped explain what was to come several years later in the area of illicit missile trade. It stated that "senior Russian officials" had rejected U.S. appeals for a total arms embargo against Iran as a precondition for joining discussions on a successor to the Coordinating Committee for Multilateral Export Controls, or COCOM, which had been successful in keeping weapons technology from reaching the Soviet bloc and China during the Cold War. President Clinton had already dismantled COCOM as part of his pro-business policies. Russia's defense industrialists, legislators, and senior military officers opposed the arms embargo with Iran, but said they might agree to an embargo that permits "some or all current arms deals with Iran to be fulfilled or which does not apply to certain categories of weapons." But the Russian Duma in November 1998 passed a resolution calling for increased military cooperation with Iran, belying earlier claims by Moscow that no military cooperation existed.

The CIA report concluded that the only chance for Russia to live up to its weapons non-proliferation commitments would be if Yeltsin could resolve "ongoing rivalries among government ministries and agencies." Yeltsin could have helped the implementation by making "a stronger public show of support than he has up to now" for his government's commitments. The CIA added that Yeltsin's appointment of a new head of the Russian counterintelligence service in charge of a commission to monitor nuclear smuggling had not "invested a single official with authority to compel rival bureaucracies to cooperate and comply with Russia's many non-proliferation commitments." The Ministry of Foreign Affairs (MFA), judged by the CIA to be most sympathetic to U.S. and Western non-proliferation worries, was unable to enforce action. "The MFA has resources problems, is not fully engaged on some proliferation issues and must rely on other Russian organizations for information and expertise."

A MOUNTAIN OF EVIDENCE

In June 1997 President Clinton met with Boris Yeltsin in Denver, and at that time Yeltsin promised Clinton that Russia would halt its missile technology transfers to Iran. But the promise was hollow. Either the Russian leader could not deliver, or more than likely he chose not to.

Intelligence reports from U.S. spy agencies, primarily the eavesdropping National Security Agency, presented a picture of Russian-Iranian missile cooperation that was lucrative and dangerous.

Russian research institutes had been struggling financially since the breakup of the old Soviet Union in 1991, and for them Iran's missile program was money in the bank.

They even knew the specific amounts the Iranians were willing to spend. A CIA intelligence report labeled "Secret Specat" disclosed in March 1997 that Iranian President Ali Akbar Hashemi Rafsanjani had told senior Iranian officials he was pleased with the growing ties between Moscow and Tehran. The Iranian president "considers obtaining Russian military technology one of Iran's primary foreign policy goals." Rafsanjani further stated that "Iran had a budgetary reserve of $10 billion, much of which it is willing to dedicate towards military purchases from Russia," and directed the Iranian embassy in Moscow "to devote resources to fulfilling Iranian weapons requirements through purchases from Russia."

The discussion followed the December 1996 visit to Iran by Russian Foreign Minister Primakov, who, according to the intelligence report, "promised Rafsanjani, Foreign Minister Ali Akbar Velayati, and other high-level Iranian leaders there would be no threat to Russian-Iranian relations so long as President Boris Yeltsin and Primakov continue to direct Russian foreign relations."

Then on May 6, 1997, the director of the National Security Agency sent a cable to agency stations in Moscow and Tel Aviv, as well as to two Department of Energy nuclear weapons laboratories, the Arms Control and Disarmament Agency, the Commerce Department, and the U.S. Customs Service. The headline for the cable, which bore the mark "Secret Spoke"—a code word denoting information derived from electronic intelligence gatherers—read: "Iran-Russia/Missile Development: Iranian Missile Producer Has Contracts for Wind Tunnel and Other Projects with Russian Firms."

"Recently available information of 1996 has revealed a deeper cooperation than was previously known between Iran's Defense Industries Organization (DIO) and several Russian firms on the production of liquid-fueled ballistic missiles," the cable stated. "Contracts have been signed with one Russian firm for 'theoretical investigations,' model manufacturing and software supply, and the same firm was planning talks on the construction of probably a wind tunnel in Iran. Negotiations were taking place with a second Russian firm on a wind tunnel project, while a third Russian firm was planning to produce a number of items for DIO, including raw materials, laser-related items, large mirrors, maraging steel samples [used in missile frames] and graphite coated with tungsten."

The report identified a Russian at the Central Aerohydrodynamic Institute who contacted a "Mr. Danesh" of Iran's Shahid Hemat Industrial Group, or SHIG, in August 1996 to update him on the various contracts between the two organizations. "SHIG is responsible for development and production of liquid-fueled missiles in Iran." The contracts included three 1996 contracts for "experimental and theoretical investigation," signed on February 16; one contract for missile "model manufacturing" on April 11; and one contract for computer software on June 6. A total of five contracts were outstanding, worth a total of $135,430. The Russian institute's deputy director, V. L. Soukhanov, complained that payments had been late and that the delays had caused "considerable losses" to the institute and its subcontractors. Future contracts should be made within the two-week time frame the two sides had agreed on, he said. Soukhanov also noted that the institute was preparing for negotiations on building an "aerodynamic investigation center"—a wind tunnel for testing missile designs—in Iran, a complicated project that would cost millions of U.S. dollars.

Even more revealing was evidence in the National Security Agency report linking Russia's state trading company to the missile trade. The Russian State Corporation for Export and Import of Armament and Military Equipment, known as *Rosvooruzheniye*, "also was working with SHIG in 1996 on a 'wind tunnel' project," the report said. "Rosvooruzheniye's V. Telkov wanted SHIG's Mr. Danesh in July 1996 to provide information on the place and time of the negotiations on the project." Telkov was the state trading firm's aerospace director, who along with Yuri Koptev was one of the two Russian officials linked by the Israelis to the missile trade with Iran. The intelligence directly contradicted Russian government claims.

The intercept noted that another Russian firm, the scientific and production center known as INOR, was preparing for a number of projects with the Iranian missile program. INOR's president, identified in the National Security Agency report only as "L. Chromova," and its science director, "Y. Rodinov," had a conversation with SHIG official "Kalantarian" in March 1996 regarding the delivery of raw materials to SHIG's address in Iran. The Russian firm also planned to provide the Iranians with technology related to "laser techniques," which are part of missile testing requirements, and special mirrors. "Maraging steel" would also be provided. This ultra-high-strength steel, used in missile bodies, is durable enough to withstand the intense pressure of launch, intense cold of outer space, and intense heat associated with reentry into the earth's atmosphere. INOR specialized in producing maraging steel. The firm also planned to provide special graphite material coated with tungsten for the missile program.

Part of the deal would be concluded in September 1997 and would provide a major boost to the guidance and control program for the Iranians' Shahab missile. According to a September 1997 National Security Agency report, INOR closed the agreement to sell four special missile-related alloys to Iran. "Two months of intensive marketing efforts by a determined Russian firm appeared to have borne fruit when an Iranian inertial guidance and control organization subordinate to the Defense Industries Organization apparently agreed to purchase four alloys from the firm," the secret report stated. "The Russian firm provided the Iranian organization with a pro forma invoice for the alloys in late September 1997, which listed the prices for the alloys, as well as information about the quantity, shape and sizes for each. With an eye to establishing a long term business relationship, the Russian firm offered to give the Iranian organization a discount on the total value of the invoice."

The issue of Russian technology transfers to Iran came up during a meeting between Vice President Al Gore and Russian Prime Minister Victor Chernomyrdin in Moscow in late September 1997. After signing a number of agreements that appeared to be aimed more at bolstering the political fortunes of the two leaders than at actually producing anything of substance, Gore referred to "the possible transfer of missile technologies to Iran" as though he did not believe his own government's intelligence reports. "There is no doubt in my mind that the goals of Russia and the United States are the same," Gore insisted. "This is a partnership, and it is a productive partnership." He was also "impressed" by the Russians' efforts to "dig into" the problem. During a press conference later, Gore was asked what new information had been uncovered, and he refused to answer. "We agreed not to divulge details of the study because it involves intelligence information in both countries and for obvious reasons it cannot be made public." Then Gore said, "But perhaps Victor Stepanovich [Chernomyrdin] would want to respond to this."

"I won't tell you anything at all," Chernomyrdin barked. The prime minister, like all the Russians, was defiant. "We have discussed the questions of our relations with Iran in the military and technical field," he said. "I must tell you, as I said during our discussions, that we have our commitments and we are meeting those commitments. We are not diverging from our commitments, and even if somebody wishes to diverge from these commitments, they will not have their way. There is no question of any missile deliveries. It was not touched upon, and it is just not possible. Once again, we have obligations, and we are not dodging them."

Gore granted that Iran was making a "vigorous" effort to obtain missile components as well as the know-how to build nuclear weapons. But, he said, the United States would continue to "share information" with the Russians aimed at halting the transfer. The Wisner-Koptev investigation into the transfers "appears" to be going on in "total good faith," Gore asserted. "There is a common view by the United States and Russia about the inadvisability of ballistic missile technology or technology for weapons of mass destruction going to Iran." Yet he acknowledged, albeit indirectly, that the problem was not solved and continuing discussions were needed "for further fact finding."

Behind the scenes, however, many U.S. intelligence officials were looking at the administration's handling of the issue with dismay.

Once U.S. intelligence was shared with the Russian government, sources of information—from human agents to electronic communications links that were clandestinely monitored—would disappear. It soon became clear that the Russians were passing on information and that the targeted entities were taking steps to avoid further disclosures.

Congressman Doug Bereuter, Nebraska Republican and a member of the House Intelligence Committee, went public with his worries about the damage to U.S. intelligence as a result of the administration's cooperation with Moscow officials. "There is some evidence we did share information in the past which caused us to lose resources," Bereuter said. Bereuter went further: "In fact, there may be the intent by the Russian government to permit resources to go to the Iranian missile development program."

The congressman's remarks were based on a vast amount of extremely sensitive intelligence reporting on the Moscow-Tehran connections. The White House had ignored or dismissed the reports as inconclusive. But as the intelligence revealed, the Russian government was not a passive observer unable to stop the missile trade between "entities" supposedly acting independently of the government. It was actually deeply involved at a clandestine level.

One National Security Agency report from early February 1998, labeled "Top Secret Gamma," revealed that Russia's Foreign Intelligence Service also had a role in the Iranian missile trade. In January 1998 U.S. pressure on Russia to stop the missile technology transfers to Iran appeared to be having some effect. "The... Russians were very concerned about... illegal efforts to recruit Russian companies and experts to participate in Iran's missile program," the National Security Agency report said. "News of this concern had already been passed to Iran through various channels. The Russians pointed out that [these] actions were contrary to the spirit of cooperation that exists between Russia and Iran and could damage this cooperation in various areas. Given these concerns, the Russians stated that they believed the Iranian authorities would take the necessary actions to immediately terminate all [such] activities in Russia.... The memorandum emphasized that Russia was interested in expanding normal relations with Iran, who Moscow viewed as a neighbor and business partner.... The memorandum stated that Russia did not intend to inform anyone else of its decision...."

But according to the National Security Agency, Iran dismissed this Russian Foreign Ministry demand by noting that it had been given private assurances from the Russian Foreign Intelligence Service, known by its acronym SVR, that the missile dealings would go on: "the insistence [by the Ministry of Foreign Affairs] on the termination" of all of these activities "was contrary to SVR Head Vyacheslav Trubnikov's earlier message... that the Russians were still willing to work" with Iran's missile deployment "provided that it discontinued its current illegal practices."

Although the Russians had continually lied, the Clinton administration offered billions of dollars to get Russia to halt weapons technology proliferation.

The intelligence report confirmed that the Russians had a two-track policy toward the Iranian missile transfers. The first track involved Foreign Ministry officials asking Iran to curb all missile activities in Russia. The second track was covert, involving the head of the Russian Foreign Intelligence Service and the domestic Federal Security Service closely coordinating the activities of Iran's intelligence services in the missile trade.

Also in early February, the National Security Agency reported in a highly classified cable that Iran's intelligence chief wanted the Russian Federal Security Service to coordinate visits by Iranian missile technicians. Another report from the National Security Agency provided close-up details of Russian-Iranian cooperation in a joint "education" center. "A Russian technical university provided information to an Iranian college, affiliated with Iran's missile program, in January 1998 concerning ongoing cooperation under an established joint education center," the report said. The technical university was not simply an education institution. According to the National Security Agency, "Prior to 1990, Baltic State Technical University was known as the Military Mechanical Institute Imeni Ustinova and was a training site for both military and civilian specialists for rocket and space forces of the former Soviet Union."

RUSSIAN DEFIANCE, AMERICAN CONCESSIONS

Such detailed intelligence was not welcome news for the White House. Despite months of constant discussions that White House officials insisted were fruitful and leading to curbs on the trade, Russian arms and technology sales obviously continued.

Moreover, the White House was applauding the announcement a month earlier by Chernomyrdin that Moscow was putting new export controls in place to curb missile transfers and cooperation. A senior White House National Security Council official said the decree stated clearly that there was a government-wide ban on all missile technology exchanges. "There should not be any gray areas," this official said. In November 1997 Russia did indeed arrest and expel an Iranian "diplomat" who had been caught attempting to buy missile-related information "illegally." But U.S. intelligence officials told me that this was Russian window-dressing to please the Clinton administration.

Lurking in the background was the Missile Technology Control Regime. Russia's missile trade with Iran violated the agreement, but U.S. officials launched no protests, until Congress voted to enforce sanctions. "The Russians just don't get words," said Congressman Curt Weldon, chairman of the House National Security subcommittee on military research. "You've got to back those words with solid action; you've got to impose sanctions."

Meanwhile, Russia's Foreign Intelligence Service spokesman Yuri Kobaladze, formerly of the KGB, accused U.S. spy agencies of working against President Clinton by leaking new details of Iranian-Russian intelligence cooperation on missile transfers to the *Washington Times*. "The U.S. president, secretary of state and other influential personalities are speaking about cooperation with Russia and their satisfaction about this cooperation," Kobaladze told the Itar-Tass news agency. "Yet, some U.S. intelligence services have apparently started to work against their president and government." The CIA dismissed the comments as "nonsense."

Around the same time, Frank Wisner quit as the special envoy and was replaced by Robert Gallucci, a former State Department official and a key architect of the Agreed Framework, the administration's disastrous deal with the communist government of North Korea. By 1998 the framework had begun to unravel—fresh intelligence reports revealed that the North Koreans were secretly building nuclear weapons again.

By May 1998 it had become clear to some U.S. officials that months of begging the Russians to halt the missile trade hadn't worked. Still, National Security Adviser Samuel "Sandy" Berger went to Moscow to try again. On May 8 he met in the office of Andrei Kokoshin, the reformist deputy defense minister who was despised by most of the military and ministry hardliners.

Berger had gone to Moscow to prepare for the meeting of the G-7 economic powers in Birmingham, England, and brought with him a high-powered delegation that included Deputy Secretary of State Strobe Talbott; Leon Fuerth, Gore's national security adviser; Stephen Sestanovich, a State Department specialist on Russia; John Tefft, the charge d'affairs in Moscow; James Timbie, a senior State Department adviser on arms; and Gary Samore, the National Security Council's proliferation director. No Pentagon or CIA official was present, even though the Russian delegation included the director of Russia's domestic intelligence service and officials from Russia's Defense Ministry. It was obvious the White House did not trust the CIA or Defense Department and purposely excluded those officials from the discussions. This was an extraordinary breach of trust and demonstrated how far the administration would go to prevent any interference with its misguided Russia policies.

Berger's conversation, according to officials present, went like this: "I am here with a high-level delegation because President Clinton is concerned that the vision he and President Yeltsin had jointly developed about our relationship is in jeopardy.... I have come at a critical juncture. We encountered tough problems in the past and will do so again. Decisions will have to be made in Washington and in Moscow that will have a fundamental impact on our relationship. I personally believe that we can solve the tough issue of ballistic missile technology transfers to Iran, but only if the two presidents are involved." He added further platitudes about the United States and Russia "standing together" so that "the two presidents can plan our future agenda and launch START III negotiations."

The administration wanted Russia to ratify START II so that further arms reduction pacts could be negotiated. But the Russians were uninterested in arms reductions that bargained away the only thing separating post-Soviet Russia from being a third world nation: namely, its nuclear weapons.

"Now time is running out; the stakes are great," Berger insisted. "On the downside, unless this problem [of Russian-Iranian missile cooperation] is solved we see a potential trainwreck in our relations. On the upside, if we can solve this problem, the future holds out great cooperation in space launches and other aerospace activities. There may be $3 billion to $4 billion of economic possibilities in the aerospace field in the future."

The statement was astonishing. For many months, the Russians had lied and dissembled about the flow of missile technology. Yeltsin himself had promised President Clinton that he would halt the technology transfers. Now, Berger, the president's top national security official, was asking again for the trade to stop—and was offering billions of dollars and more as concessions. The Clinton policy was all carrots and no sticks. The threat of sanctions by Congress had only prompted the White House to go to Russia for another begging session.

Berger said Clinton was Russia's ally in attempting to waive sanctions, technically required under the Iran-Libya Sanctions Act passed in 1996. But "the issue before us is whether the administration can justify a waiver of the act," Berger said. In other words, the intelligence was too compelling to ignore, even for a White House that was working against Congress and in support of the Russian government. "We hope to treat the Europeans and Russians in the same way. There is a difference, however. None of the Europeans has helped the Iranians develop their nuclear or ballistic missile programs."

Berger added that the Clinton administration had to decide whether to implement U.S. technology transfer laws; the Senate would soon vote on a bill imposing sanctions on firms and countries selling missile technology to Iran. "The bill now has eighty-two cosponsors," Berger said. "The administration wants to beat back the bill, but needs concrete steps from Russia. We know this is difficult, but we need real progress to defend our relationship." The spectacle of a national security adviser pleading with the Russians and asking them to help him circumvent the will of Congress was almost too much for some U.S. officials and prompted disclosure of the memorandum of these talks.

Shortly after the Berger meeting in Moscow, Clinton announced he was waiving the Iran-Libya sanctions on Russia, and the Russian government announced that it had identified seven firms involved in the missile trade, and that the missile technology flow would stop. But this was far from the whole story.

During the discussion between the two delegations, Nikolay Kovalev, director of Russia's Federal Security Service, the former KGB domestic spying agency, accused the *United States* of supplying missile technology to Iran, with "provocational work" by the CIA involving Americans in Russia setting up contracts to ship equipment to Iran. "We can give you information on this," Kovalev said. Moreover, Kovalev said, Russian technical training for the Iranians would not be stopped completely. The Federal Security Service was the same spy agency that Clinton had directed the FBI to work closely with, even paying for several Russian officers to open an office in New York.

The Russians complained during the meeting about a report identifying twenty Russian firms that had been singled out by the U.S. government for sanctions. Berger denied that sanctions were going to be imposed and once again made an astonishing admission: "One of the purposes of my trip to Moscow is to prevent sanctions if we could agree what steps Russia could take to implement these export control laws."

The bottom line, Berger noted, was that "our own assessment is that assistance to Iran was still flowing."

Andrei Kokoshin requested from the American delegation—and was given—detailed information on how the United States checks on its exports, information that would obviously be useful in subverting future American monitoring of Russian trade.

In any event, the Clinton-Berger policy was a failure. Despite highly detailed intelligence pinpointing the companies, institutes, and officials involved in the missile trade, all the president did was talk. And while the talks continued, the specter of nuclear-tipped missiles capable of hitting allies in the Middle East and Europe grew alarmingly closer. By late 1998 Israeli intelligence had determined that the Iranian missile program was far advanced. A senior member of Israel's parliament, known as the Knesset, told me in August 1998, "We are in the last few months when things can be reversed." Unless Russian aid was halted, it would soon be too late to make any difference in Iran's missile program.

Asked why the United States refused to take a tough stand on Russia, the Knesset member, who asked not to be named, said he was told by Thomas Pickering, undersecretary of state for political affairs, that the United States was afraid that putting pressure on Moscow would further destabilize the country. "He made it clear that the administration was not going to sour relations with Russia. He said, 'We're not going to stretch the wire too much because if there is a greater crisis in Russia then there will be a greater danger of proliferation.'"

But what could be worse than nuclear weapons in Iran?

PART IV

Wag the Dog

CHAPTER NINE

Bombs Away

> *"The illusion of arms control is more dangerous than no arms control at all. What is being propagated by the Security Council... is such an illusion, one which in all good faith, I cannot and will not be a party to."*
>
> —UN Arms Inspector Scott Ritter, announcing his resignation from the United Nations Special Commission

After months of false starts and aborted attempts, United Nations Arms Inspector Scott Ritter had begun to succeed where other UN weapons inspectors had failed, organizing a unique intelligence operation that exposed how Iraq was blocking UN weapons inspectors from discovering illicitly stockpiled weapons of mass destruction.

Ritter, thirty-seven, a gung ho retired Marine Corps officer and Persian Gulf War veteran, began his career as an intelligence officer with the On-Site Inspection Agency, a U.S. government agency set up to monitor the 1987 Intermediate-Range Nuclear Forces Treaty between the Soviet Union and the United States. For a time he was posted to the remote Russian city of Votkinsk, where Moscow made its most modern missiles, including the world's only road-mobile operational ICBM, the SS-25. He served with distinction for the inspection agency, and his experience would serve him well after joining the newly formed United Nations Special Commission (UNSCOM) in 1991.

UNSCOM was set up after the UN Security Council, on April 3, 1991, approved Security Council Resolution 687 to end the Gulf War. It said Iraq must unconditionally accept, under international supervision, the "destruction, removal or rendering harmless" of its weapons of mass destruction and ballistic missiles with ranges of more than ninety-three miles. In June UNSCOM carried out its first inspection of an Iraqi chemical weapons site. Eventually, however, it became apparent that Saddam Hussein was keeping weapons technology in reserve for the day when he would be free to pursue nuclear, chemical, and biological military technology without UN interference. By 1994 it was impossible to ignore the suspicious regularity with which a team of UN inspectors would arrive at a suspected weapons site only to find that the Iraqis had cleaned it out.

Scott Ritter changed that when, in his words, he "took a look at the information that was recently made available to UNSCOM from Israel." Israeli military intelligence, Aman, had uncovered Iraq's "concealment mechanism"—essentially a highly efficient security task force that included Iraq's Special Security Organization, the Special Presidential Guard Units, and the Special Republican Guard, who were given the job of deceiving UN weapons inspectors. The force was run by Saddam's son Qusay. In response, Ritter set up a special UN intelligence-gathering and covert action group called the Capable Sites Concealment Investigation Teams, or CICI.

Until 1994 UNSCOM had had some success in dismantling weapons, but the international inspection teams could not verify Iraq's 1991 claim that it had destroyed all its banned weapons. Ritter recalled, "We uncovered a lot of inconsistencies in their story, and I think everybody knew there was something wrong, but we didn't have a smoking gun. So that's where we were in 1994; we could show the Iraqis were lying to us, but could not show that they still had weapons."

According to Ritter, the Iraqis were lying about all four areas of the weapons program banned by the UN: nuclear weapons, chemical weapons, biological weapons, and missiles with ranges greater than 186 miles.

By 1995 Ritter had been working with UNSCOM for four years and knew what he was doing. "I knew UNSCOM, I knew Iraq, I just knew this situation," Ritter said. He was also able to win the trust of the

Israelis, a prerequisite for winning their cooperation. In July Ritter went to work on uncovering the Iraqi method for hiding prohibited arms. His game plan consisted of a program to be carried out over six months—he needed the entire period to smoke out the Iraqis. He called the intelligence plan "Shake the Tree."

"It's basically a stimulate, collect, and assess program," Ritter said. The idea was to use UN weapons inspections by UNSCOM to trigger specific Iraqi responses. Then, using a combination of U-2 surveillance aircraft and special electronic monitoring of communications as well as new—and in many cases still secret—intelligence collection techniques, Ritter and his team could monitor how the Iraqi concealment operations responded. The plan was ambitious, but Ritter was absolutely convinced it would work. The only problem was that the support promised by the U.S. government never materialized. "They knew exactly what I was up to, they agreed to it, but they never really supported it," Ritter said. "The Israelis did their deal, and we got really good cooperation, but the Americans never followed through."

The first major inspection under "Shake the Tree" was set for November 1995. Ritter explained that the initial inspection required very specific support from the United States in the form of technical intelligence-gathering equipment, which he declined to discuss in detail since it would give away the technique to the Iraqis. Other intelligence officials described the equipment as small electronic transmitters that were used to intercept and monitor Iraqi communications among the secret services involved in the shell-game of hiding banned weapons. The devices had to be placed in proximity to Iraqi communications equipment, a very risky undertaking, and were able to pick up copious amounts of encrypted military communications that made the rounds of Iraq's security services. The transmitters automatically sent the encrypted data to U.S. spy satellites, which then transferred the intelligence to the National Security Agency. UN weapons inspectors called the devices the "black box" system, and it produced a gold mine of intelligence. Planting the devices was the job of inspectors like Ritter and others on the ground in Iraq.

The U.S. equipment was the best in the world and required unique training in its use. Ritter traveled to Washington, D.C., from New York, where UNSCOM headquarters is located, to train secretly at a safe house outside the capital city. But when the CIA officer specializing in "technical services" showed up, he had equipment different from the gear Ritter had been promised. He began explaining how to use the equipment to Ritter and another UN inspector, Nikita Smidovich of Russia, but Ritter interrupted him. "What you're offering is not acceptable," he said. "This is not what was promised." Ritter said the equipment was not advanced enough for their mission, but the CIA officer insisted that there had been a change of plans; all the U.S. government could offer was the less capable equipment. Ritter told him that, without the equipment he had asked for, the large-scale inspection could not go forward. Worse, the equipment that was offered would have compromised the inspectors, exposing them to danger from the Iraqis.

"What hurt me was that this was a huge inspection, this was the one that I had been building a case for," Ritter said. Smidovich, who was as suspicious of the Iraqis as Ritter was, asked him if they could go forward without the special equipment. Ritter said no. "This is months of planning, and we were getting ready to flush it all," he added.

Appeals to CIA Director John Deutch, who was told the operation could not go forward without the gear, were rejected. The planned inspection had to be scrapped. "It was a huge embarrassment for the United States," Ritter said. Additionally, the security of the mission had been weakened because UNSCOM had sent letters around the world notifying many UN members that the large-scale inspection was to be carried out. Providing some notice to members was standard procedure for UNSCOM, and, according to Ritter, some details of the new anti-concealment effort had leaked out. "From that point on, the relationship with the United States was a tough one," Ritter said.

UNSCOM continued to work over the next several months to obtain the right technical equipment. By February 1996, with help from countries other than the United States, UNSCOM got what it needed. In March the first "Shake the Tree" inspection began and produced good results, Ritter said. A defector provided what Ritter called "brilliant information" that helped reveal Iraq's weapons concealment program. The Iraqis had arranged the program much as terrorist organizations operate; small, ultra-secret "cells" were compartmentalized and kept secret from other organs of government to protect the security of the operations. Ritter saw his team's role "as sort of the arms control equivalent of counterterrorism."

But then another setback occurred: The target list had been leaked to Baghdad. "So when we went in in March, all the sites were 'sanitized,' and it was really frustrating," Ritter said ruefully. "Sanitized" meant the Iraqis had cleared out the facilities in advance, making it harder for the inspectors to plot the movement of contraband.

Ritter blamed the United States for compromising the specific target sites. "In UNSCOM we had five people who knew the sites," he said. "I can control those five people. But in the United States, when we coordinate with the U.S. [intelligence] community, there are several thousand people who know the site." The United States informed the Russians and the French, which according to Ritter was a bad idea.

Contrary to claims by Baghdad to have destroyed all of its missiles, Iraq had systems that could be used against U.S. forces and regional states.

The Russians were openly sympathetic to the Iraqis, as were the French. The Russians' motivation was economic. The CIA's top-secret "National Intelligence Daily" revealed that in 1997 Russia had concluded economic agreements with Iraq worth an estimated $10 billion to $12 billion. The agreements involved nine Russian oil companies, the chief of the *Rosvooruzheniye* arms exporting firm, and officials from several foreign affairs and industry ministries. The CIA report noted that the oilfield development would be used "to settle Iraq's $10 billion debt to Russia." Of course, Moscow pledged to honor the UN sanctions "but has indicated it is eager to be in a position to pursue its economic interests," the report said. "The size of these deals and the possibility other states will follow suit could generate new efforts in the UN to ease the sanctions." In early 1999 more intelligence reports indicated that Moscow was preparing to sell air defense equipment to the Iraqis—weapons that could be used to attack U.S. and British aircraft patrolling Iraqi skies. The Russians denied the reports. From the State Department came no comment; from the Pentagon came denials.

Still, Ritter was pleased that "we succeeded in doing what we wanted to do: we stimulated, and collected," valuable intelligence about Iraqi deception. UNSCOM now had firm information showing that Iraqi nuclear, chemical, and biological weapons were kept in rotated "hide sites" that moved from Baghdad to Saddam International Airport north of the city to areas near the city of Tikrit.

Ritter's team was ready for the next step, what he called the "circle of death" inspection. The objective was to cordon off Saddam International Airport, inspect several suspected arms sites simultaneously, and approach them in an aggressive manner from several different directions. "Again, it was ambitious," Ritter said. "It's not arms control like you expect.... It's a new way of doing business."

But it was not to be. After launching the encircling inspection in June 1996, the Iraqi military refused all access to the sites. Baghdad claimed the sites were off-limits because they were related to Iraq's "national security."

"They froze us out, so the inspection got stopped," Ritter said. "That was a defining moment." The earlier "Shake the Tree" inspection had met with some Iraqi resistance, but the Security Council intervened and backed up the inspectors by issuing statements condemning Iraq. Now UNSCOM had been stopped again. The Clinton administration demanded that the inspections go forward but would not act without "consensus" among other nations. "This was the beginning of the end of our policy," Ritter said.

With American resolve apparently wavering, UNSCOM Chairman Rolf Ekeus traveled to Baghdad and arranged new "modalities"—rules—for UNSCOM inspection of "sensitive" sites. The agreement was a major concession to the Iraqis, who used the new rules to continue blocking UN inspectors from entering "unsanitized" sites, going so far as to threaten inspectors with drawn guns.

Ritter spent from August 1996 through the end of the year developing a new plan to use "Shake the Tree" tactics to uncover and destroy Iraq's operational ballistic missile force.

A classified Defense Intelligence Agency report revealed that the Iraqis had kept a covert force of Scud missiles. The February 2, 1998, report, contained in the Defense Intelligence Agency's "Military Intelligence Digest," stated that Iraq was probably concealing "several dozen" Al-Hussein short-range ballistic missiles with an estimated range of 600 kilometers, or 372 miles—the same type of missile that killed twenty-eight American soldiers during the Persian Gulf War. The Iraqis also had several flatbed truck–mounted launchers and "a few" of the 900-kilometer (558-mile) range Al-Abbas missiles, both variants of the Scud missile. "Baghdad prefers to retain this force as part of long-term reconstitution, rather than use it as a short-term political or military weapon," the report said. "Saddam knows that the missile force is of limited usefulness now because launching even a single short-range ballistic missile would immediately confirm to the world that he has been evading UN restrictions for nearly seven years. However, under certain conditions, Saddam could order missiles launched against targets in Israel or Gulf Cooperation Council states."

The Iraqis, according to the Defense Intelligence Agency report, were hiding the missiles "at or near presidential or Republican Guard facilities" close to Baghdad's Abu Ghurayb area, in Tikrit, Bayji, or secure facilities in the western part of the country. "Forces associated with regime security—the Special Republican Guard and the intelligence services, in particular—are involved in Saddam's efforts to conceal Iraq's prohibited weapons-of-mass-destruction programs, including Scud missiles," the report said. They were all sites that Ritter had identified with painstaking effort through "Shake the Tree."

The Defense Intelligence Agency report concluded that the Iraqis may be concealing "missiles, launchers, propellants, and support equipment" to avoid detection by UNSCOM. "Alternatively, Saddam, in anticipation of military confrontation, could covertly deploy missiles from their concealment locations in central Iraq.... Launched from points near or in Baghdad, the missiles could strike military targets in Saudi Arabia at King Khalid Military City or Hafir al Batin, as well as all of Kuwait."

The report was alarming. It showed that contrary to claims by Baghdad to have destroyed all its missiles, Iraq had systems that could be used against U.S. forces and regional states. When President Clinton traveled to Israel shortly before launching Operation Desert Fox in mid-December 1998, the Pentagon deployed Patriot anti-missile batteries to Israel just in case the Iraqi leader decided to attack. The Pentagon would not admit publicly that the Patriots were there to deal with the Iraqi threat, but claimed they were deployed temporarily for an exercise.

THWARTING THE INSPECTIONS

Ritter continued to face Clinton administration opposition to his inspection plans in early 1997. "An inspection is a very choreographed thing," Ritter said. It requires having the right number of inspectors in the right positions and then, as the last piece, having aircraft reconnaissance. "The Americans never met the timeline with the U-2s," Ritter said. "They didn't fly the sensors we wanted them to fly, and therefore the ground and air components were never in sequence."

"In the end it was a big political black eye. We did our job," Ritter said of his inspections, "but the U.S. didn't do its job" in providing the technical support necessary to track Iraqi concealment. According to Ritter, the Clinton administration did not take a strong enough stand in backing UNSCOM in carrying out the weapons inspections. There were complaints that too much money was being spent and not enough was being uncovered, although UNSCOM's record in eliminating large portions of the Iraqi unconventional weapons program had been impressive. Large quantities of materials related to nuclear and chemical weapons were destroyed or neutralized. Missiles and biological weapons were a more difficult target for the inspectors, but

Ritter was confident that with the right backing UNSCOM could succeed in eliminating those arms as well. But the United States failed to provide the needed support.

On June 21, 1997, the UN condemned Iraq for refusing to permit weapons inspections at three sites containing weapons banned by the UN. But the resolution advised nothing, and inspectors continued to be bullied. And they watched helplessly as what appeared to the inspectors to be relevant files and documents were moved or burned as they waited to gain access to sites.

> **The Iraqis continued to bully UN weapons inspectors because they sensed weakness on the part of the United States and the United Nations.**

During September and October, UNSCOM teams were blocked from inspecting several presidential sites.

Then on October 23, 1997, a pivotal event occurred. The UN Security Council passed Resolution 1134, banning Iraqi government intelligence and security officials from traveling (and therefore disrupting inspections). The specifics of the resolution, however, were less important than the voting; though the vote was 10 to 0, Russia, China, France, Kenya, and Egypt all abstained. On November 13 Baghdad responded by ordering all American nationals on the UNSCOM inspection teams to leave Iraq within a week, claiming they were spies and saying they would not be allowed back in the country. Richard Butler, UNSCOM's new executive director, pulled out all but a handful of the forty inspectors. In Washington, Clinton appeared to stand firm. "Iraq must comply with the unanimous will of the international community and let the weapons inspectors resume their work," he said. The president pledged that "we are prepared to pursue whatever options are necessary."

Clinton's options, however, were limited by his desire for good relations with Russia. The United States had backed a deal by Yevgeni Primakov, a Russian Middle East expert and anti-Western hardliner, that regained access for the inspectors in exchange for a UN pledge to consider lifting economic sanctions against Iraq. After the Russian deal, Ritter was anxious to get going, and an inspection plan was again drawn up and approved by UNSCOM.

This time the inspection was blocked not by the Iraqis, but by the secretary of state. "Madeleine Albright stepped in and had it cancelled," Ritter said. "She didn't want to be seen as sabotaging the Primakov plan" with inspections the Iraqis would consider proactive. Moreover, while President Clinton was calling for Iraq to allow UN inspectors complete access, he was secretly sending a different message to Iraq. The duplicity was disclosed in secret intelligence collected by the National Security Agency on November 27, 1997. According to the top-secret report, a senior Russian official informed Iraq that the United States had offered not to launch air strikes if Saddam opened up restricted sites to the inspectors.

In an interview with the author, National Security Adviser Sandy Berger denied the Russians were secretly conveying a U.S. offer to the Iraqis. "That is total and complete nonsense," he asserted. But he and other White House and State Department officials would not provide any details about what the Russians were discussing with the Iraqis at the time. "We cannot account for what the Russians may have told Iraq," White House spokesman Michael McCurry told me. "We can say without equivocation that there weren't any secret deals or secret negotiations which occurred with respect to the Iraqi matter."

One administration official familiar with the intercept said the offer appeared to be a secret U.S. "carrot" for Saddam, who would regard such secret diplomacy as a concession and a sign of weakness.

A day after the Russian offer, Iraq said it would allow the UN inspectors to conduct inspections (although it would later balk). In exchange, the inspections had to be halted if nothing related to the weapons programs was uncovered after several months.

Further, the Iraqis created five categories of off-limits sites for the UN. They included presidential palaces, ministries, "sovereign sites," "sensitive sites," and private residences. In practice, this list expanded, for the Iraqis would deny access to sites on the pretext that a presidential palace was *nearby*.

In early December 1997 Ritter formulated a new inspection plan approved by UNSCOM. But shortly thereafter UNSCOM dropped some of the more controversial sites from the plan.

Ritter wanted to know why. Later, Charles Duelfer, the deputy UNSCOM chairman, revealed to Ritter that "Madeleine [Albright] pulled the plug." The reason: "She realized the Iraqis were not going to let us in, and the United States didn't want to go to war over the Christmas holidays," Ritter said.

Ritter was furious. He spent the Christmas holidays planning a new inspection, and a five-day plan was set up for early January.

On January 12, 1998, the Iraqi government announced that it was blocking Ritter's inspection team because it contained too many Americans and Britons. UNSCOM was against giving in to the demand, but Ritter agreed to it because he wanted no more delays. He wanted to call the Iraqis' bluff and "go straight for the jugular."

"We're going to go straight in and hit the presidential areas and the Special Security Organization," he said. "Then we will know if the Iraqis are serious or not about access."

But the plan hit a new glitch when the FBI accused Ritter of being an Israeli spy. The UN's most experienced and aggressive weapons inspector—the man who was close to getting at the concealed Iraqi weapons—had been sandbagged, most likely by government officials who opposed his aggressive version of arms control. The probe had been sparked after Ritter took a lie-detector test as part of an application to join the CIA. The CIA asked Ritter if he had contacts with foreign intelligence services. Considering that he was in charge of orchestrating a major international intelligence operation against Iraq with the help of Israel, he explained in detail all his exchanges with the Israelis, including allowing the Israelis to analyze classified U-2 reconnaissance photographs of Iraq. He had gone to the Israelis with the full authority of his UNSCOM superiors after the CIA refused to help him. But in the wake of the Aldrich Ames espionage case, the CIA reported the contacts to the FBI for possible espionage charges.

"I gave them many, many pages of details," Ritter explained. "And they panicked. They started asking about what I did. So I told them about 'Shake the Tree.' They never understood that this was an UNSCOM operation and not a U.S. operation. They didn't understand that I didn't have a security clearance, that everything that UNSCOM deals with, from a U.S. perspective, is unclassified. So when you start talking about areas of intelligence that are normally classified at the SCI level and cooperate with foreign governments on this, they freaked, basically." SCI stands for Sensitive Compartmented Information, and is used to protect data that are classified above the "Top Secret" level.

Ritter provided the CIA with the names of all his contacts and their phone numbers and explained that everything he had done had been approved by the U.S. government and coordinated with U.S. officials. Yet the investigators never bothered to check out the contacts. Instead, they jumped at the "inconclusive" results of Ritter's polygraph test to trigger an FBI counterintelligence investigation.

"One reason why they didn't pass me [on the lie-detector] was that they claimed I hesitated on some of my answers; I was taking a breath or shifting in my chair or I somehow gave a signal that I hesitated," Ritter said. "Well, yeah, I hesitated. I've gone around the world getting the most sensitive support made available to the Special Commission on the basis that I am *not* a U.S. government employee, and that I am an UNSCOM employee and that I won't talk about this with the United States."

Ritter had told the investigators that he would not talk about some confidential things he had learned as part of UNSCOM, but also that he would not lie about his activities and contacts. He told one CIA interviewer: "When you say, 'Can I explain,' well, the answer is, 'I don't want to explain because it's UNSCOM's business. It's not your business.'" The investigator replied, "You're an American, and now you've got to report."

Ritter believes the CIA probing had a vindictive aspect to it that may have been partly the result of his falling out with Steve Richter, the CIA's Near East operations chief. The CIA denied Richter had anything to do with the probe and insisted it reported the polygraph results to the FBI under new counterespionage rules.

Nevertheless, when UN Secretary General Kofi Anan achieved a "memorandum of understanding" with Iraq for further inspections, Scott Ritter was tapped to lead the team, over the initial objection of Secretary of State Madeleine Albright. The UN weapons inspectors, in a letter demanding that Ritter head up the team, wrote, "Only Scott Ritter has the in-depth knowledge... of the personalities and organizations that this inspection was to pursue."

So Ritter led UNSCOM 227-B in March 1998, and, in his words, "We were able to emerge from our inspection with definitive proof of how the Iraqis were hiding things," including the use of fleets of Mercedes trucks and special concealed communications equipment. Since the Iraqis were renowned for good record-keeping, the documentary proof the inspectors needed to prove Iraqi duplicity and noncompliance was close at hand.

There was only one problem: Bill Clinton. "We were going to win, except the U.S. had the big military buildup and the U.S. did some pretty silly things, like throw in demands to see sites that had no arms control value. They wanted me to provoke a war."

Since coming under political pressure in January 1998 because of revelations about President Clinton's affair with White House intern Monica Lewinsky, the administration had begun saber rattling. The threats to use military force were dubbed "Monica's War" by some cynical or disgusted military officers in the Pentagon.

By February 1998 U.S. forces were assembling for attacks on Iraq. President Clinton declared, "One way or the other, we are determined to see that [Saddam Hussein] makes good on his own promise" to destroy all weapons of mass destruction and missiles.

Based on the president's tough rhetoric, Ritter regrouped his inspection forces for a new round of aggressive inspections. "I said, 'All right, let's go, I'm ready to reconstitute my team.'" But instead of backing Ritter, the United States cut the legs out from under UNSCOM by withdrawing all technical support for the inspections, Ritter said. "The U.S. lobbied the British to withdraw their personnel support, and they put pressure on the Israelis to withdraw specific support," he said. "The people that I had on my team in Iraq were withdrawn. The British wouldn't provide them. The Americans withdrew technical support, and I was left with half a team." The White House had secretly switched policies on Iraq in early 1998, concerned that Saddam's cat-and-mouse confrontation over the inspections was damaging U.S. credibility and further weakening the already tenuous regional alliances against Iraq. The president had decided that the facade of inspections should continue but without producing big results.

The Clinton national security team had demanded and won a concession from UNSCOM that weapons inspectors could no longer act on "assessments" but had to have "hard intelligence." When Ritter claimed he had it, the Clinton administration moved the bar higher, demanding *guarantees* that an inspection would uncover banned weapons or materials.

By August, however, Ritter had developed intelligence locating about a dozen guidance and control mechanisms for Iraqi ballistic missiles of a range banned by the UN. But before Ritter could launch his inspection, he received a phone call from UN headquarters informing him that Madeleine Albright had ordered the inspection stopped. Clinton, fearing the inspection would be too confrontational, had intervened with UNSCOM Chairman Richard Butler to have it stopped. "It would have created a confrontation to force the U.S. to take action it didn't want to take," Ritter said. For Ritter, this was the end. He resigned in protest shortly thereafter.

"MONICA'S WAR"

With Ritter now permanently sidelined and under attack from the Clinton administration's well-oiled "spin machine"—Madeleine Albright, for instance, accused Ritter of having "no clue" about U.S. policy on weapons inspection—President Clinton delayed for several more months before launching a military strike. In November 1998 he even recalled U.S. bombers in flight and stopped cruise missile attacks minutes before launch, after Saddam offered another hollow promise to allow weapons inspections. When the commander in chief finally did decide to use military force, it was on December 16, a few short hours before the U.S. House of Representatives began impeachment proceedings against the president for perjury and obstruction of justice stemming from the cover-up of his sexual relations with Monica Lewinsky. In his Oval Office statement, the president emphasized that he had undertaken the action with "the unanimous recommendation of my national security team"—highlighting that President Clinton's moral authority to lead a military operation was now so weak that he had to mention that his advisers supported him.

The president notified Congress on December 18, 1998, that he had launched the military strikes "pursuant to my authority under the Constitution as commander in chief and as chief executive and to conduct U.S. foreign relations." The action, he said, was authorized by the public law enacted by President George Bush in January 1991, on the eve of Operation Desert Storm.

However, both the president and congressional Democrats, who rallied to their beleaguered president's defense by piously calling for a deferment of the impeachment vote, failed to mention that most Democratic leaders had voted *against* that resolution back in 1991. In fact, one of Clinton's most important advisers, Deputy Defense Secretary John Hamre—who had been a Senate staff member working for Sam Nunn, the Senate Armed Services Committee chairman— called the 1991 vote one of the darkest days of his life.

> **The world's sole remaining superpower was made to look foolish by Saddam Hussein, a small-time dictator who forced Clinton to back down time and again.**

Pentagon officials, disgusted by what they regarded as the blatant use of military forces for personal political gain by the president, leaked word that the attack was *not*, as the administration claimed, based on UNSCOM chief Richard Butler's report on Iraqi noncompliance, delivered to the Security Council on Tuesday, December 15, 1998. Butler's report merely provided a convenient fig leaf for the president. Rather, Clinton had notified the Joint Staff to begin updating the bombing plan for Iraq on Sunday, December 13.

The attacks drew denunciation from some Republicans. Congressman Gerald Solomon, New York Republican, said he was "outraged" that the president would use the military strikes as a political diversion from the impeachment process. Trent Lott, the Senate majority leader, also issued a statement saying that, "while I have been assured by administration officials that there is no connection with the impeachment process in the House of Representatives, I cannot support this military action in the Persian Gulf at this time."

"Operation Desert Fox" was privately ridiculed by Pentagon officials as "Operation Free Willy." Former Secretary of State Lawrence Eagleburger publicly questioned Clinton's motives: "While I approve [of] the action, I think the timing stinks, frankly." Eagleburger's remark prompted a telephone call from Albright, who insisted that the impeachment had nothing to do with the attack. For many, the whole situation seemed like something out of a movie—in this case, *Wag the Dog*, a film about an unscrupulous president and his political operatives who launch a war to cover up a tawdry sexual affair.

Ultimately, Operation Desert Fox lasted just seventy hours and ended after the House voted to approve two of the four articles of impeachment.

Clinton derided those who challenged his motives. "I don't believe any reasonably astute person in Washington would believe that Secretary Cohen and General Shelton [chairman of the Joint Chiefs of Staff] and the whole rest of the national security team would participate in such an action," he told reporters.

Cohen for his part vigorously denied any political motive, as he had been forced to do months earlier when the United States launched cruise missile strikes on terrorist targets in the Sudan and Afghanistan three days after Clinton's grand jury testimony and his televised confession that he had misled the country about his affair with Lewinsky.

Asked by the author if planning for the strike had begun before UNSCOM presented its report, Cohen would not answer directly. "Our military planning started on November 15 in terms of being prepared to carry out an operation should it become necessary," he said. Pressed to explain the timing, he said, "We have always been prepared to go during the month of December, to take action. We were not going to take any action until such time as a report was filed, we knew what was said, and the president actually called for a strike."

On Sunday, the day after strikes were halted, Madeleine Albright appeared on *Meet the Press* to defend the attacks. Albright assured the nation of the effectiveness of the strikes, saying, "The destruction was heavy and devastating." The Iraqis had announced that UNSCOM would not be allowed back into the country, to which Albright replied, "The truth is that they have not been able to do their job effectively for the last eight months."

But if UNSCOM would no longer be allowed to search for and destroy Iraq's illegal nuclear, chemical, and biological weapons, what had been gained? The only victor was Iraq. As Scott Ritter predicted in an interview with the author weeks before Clinton's air strikes, "The battle for Iraq is a battle over UNSCOM, and the Iraqis have set a wonderful trap"—a trap that was sprung by "Monica's War."

The use of military force to bolster the president's political fortune continued during the Senate impeachment trial in early 1999. As Iraq grew bolder in the wake of the ineffective air strikes of December, air defense units in both northern and southern Iraq began to systematically target and threaten the patrolling U.S. warplanes. Clinton used the Iraqi maneuvering to his political advantage by loosening the military's "rules of engagement" to permit the jets to launch more and larger attacks on Iraqi ground targets. As senators listened to the impeachment case, U.S. Air Force and Navy jets were bombing Iraq on almost a daily a basis. A coincidence? Many in the military doubted it.

In the end, the December attack had been a weak show of force that led to the complete expulsion of the weapons inspectors. Moreover, U.S. pilots continued to be at risk in the low-level conflict that followed for months after the operation. The Pentagon immediately stopped releasing video footage showing almost daily bombing raids because it would remind the American people that the United States was once again at war with Iraq.

In mishandling Saddam Hussein, President Clinton and his advisers demonstrated constant weakness and vacillating policies toward Iraq. The world's sole remaining superpower was made to look foolish by Saddam, a small-time dictator who constantly stood up to Clinton and forced him and the UN to back down time and again. And as Moscow moved closer to Baghdad, the Yeltsin-first policy again became paramount, causing Secretary of State Albright to defer to Russian leaders who were looking to recoup the billions Iraq owed them for weapons sales decades earlier. The limited air strikes that were finally launched in December 1998 showed that the president did not seriously want to defeat Saddam with force but was only trying to outsmart him—an effort that has so far failed. The handling showed a lack of leadership, an absence of the necessary determination to take forceful, effective action. Instead, the president once again wavered, further weakening respect for the United States around the world.

CHAPTER TEN
The Clinton Legacy

President Clinton's most important legacy will not be his serio-comic sex scandals, but his dead serious disarmament of the United States and his self-serving appeasement of powerful and determined foreign enemies. His flower-child "can't we all just get along" approach to global power politics has left the nation weakened and vulnerable in a dangerous and hostile world.

The president and his adversaries knowingly placed economic prosperity—and campaign contributions—above national security interests, and the damage will be felt for years to come. The administration's policies have endangered not only the United States, but the peace and security of the entire world.

A significant part of the Clinton legacy will be the dominance of "spin" over substance, a practice perfected during his tenure. No matter how disastrously a presidential decision or action turned out, White House spinmeisters managed to seduce most of the press and public into believing that the action taken was, all things considered, for the best.

One far-reaching failure was the president's policy toward Russia. Instead of supporting the elements that were working for a true democracy, the administration gave aid and comfort to a handful of corrupt ex-communists who, far from modernizing Russian socialism, turned one of the world's most resource-rich countries into a bankrupt beggar, a Mafia-dominated kleptocracy that stole upwards of $150 billion in Western aid, most of which ended up in the private bank accounts of Russian officials and organized crime figures.

In a world where nuclear weapons are proliferating and missile threats are growing, President Clinton dangerously undercut the missile defense systems needed for the nation's survival and for the protection of American troops abroad. While budget and personnel cuts made the Pentagon's primary mission—fighting wars—more and more difficult, the administration piled on more nonvital and non-military missions for which the armed forces are ill suited. Creating an entire secretariat in the Pentagon for bogus "environmental security" was a covert means to siphon defense money for nondefense programs. These kinds of activities led to sagging morale that will take years to correct.

As the military became "hollowed out" under the Clinton administration, so too did the nation's first line of defense: its unequaled electronic intelligence services. At a time when China's espionage operations against the United States were growing rapidly, the National Security Agency's research and development budget was slashed by 90 percent; the ensuing personnel reductions saw the loss of many of the most highly skilled intelligence officers. To prevent this essential world-monitoring capability from being crippled further will take five years of steady funds and focused leadership.

In the Energy Department, staffed at the highest levels largely by antinuclear activists appointed during the Clinton administration, U.S. nuclear weapons programs were severely undermined. Clinton's decision to halt underground testing threatened the viability of our strategic nuclear deterrent. Combined with the president's ideological aversion to strategic defense, this increased the danger that the United States might be attacked by miscalculation, by accident, or by a power that thinks it can get away with it, because our deterrent capability has eroded.

The president's feel-good naiveté led him to send tens of millions of dollars to Russia, ostensibly for weapons-dismantling programs. The end result, however, was quite the opposite: Moscow used American dollars as a way to pay for its strategic nuclear missile buildup. When this buildup—including new ICBMs, missile submarines, and huge underground command facilities—became known, the president and his aides brushed aside the dangers as insignificant rather than admit to their mistakes.

Perhaps the Clinton legacy of most serious concern to the American people is the nation's vulnerability to enemy missiles, thanks to the president's stubborn refusal to expedite an anti-missile defense system. For years he denied the existence of any foreign missile threat; when the threat could no longer be ignored, he switched gears and claimed that U.S. technology wasn't capable of knocking out incoming missiles with other missiles. This claim has been contradicted by numerous specialists who say the know-how could be carried out easily from either space or the ground, given the political will and leadership to do so.

Perhaps the Clinton legacy of most serious concern to the American people is the nation's vulnerability to enemy missiles.

When the growing threat of North Korean and other rogue states' missiles could no longer be dismissed, even by the White House spinners, the president in January 1999 reluctantly acknowledged the danger. It was quite an admission from the man who had repeatedly intoned, "There are no more nuclear missiles pointed at any children in the United States." In fact, Russian and Chinese missiles were and are aimed at American cities. Moreover, other states are rapidly developing their long-range missile capabilities. The president's stubborn denial of the facts succeeded in delaying the earliest possible deployment of a missile defense system by at least two years, until 2005.

This, then, is the legacy of Bill Clinton. His political heirs will have their work cut out for them.

Discouraging as this inheritance is, it can be righted by clear-sighted leaders who are not afraid to look reality in the eye and take the necessary steps. Here are some suggestions for those who are elected to deal with Bill Clinton's dismal legacy:

● *Leadership*: The United States must find and place in key positions leaders who have two fundamental characteristics: honesty and courage. The fact that no single senior U.S. official, with one possible exception (Air Force Chief of Staff Ronald Fogleman), resigned to protest the national security policies of President Clinton has revealed a crisis in leadership at all levels of government and the military. Military leaders should abandon the "business mentality" imposed on them by Clinton's corporate-government axis. Instead, leaders must be found who do and say what is right, not merely what their superiors want to hear. The military must instill in its leaders a renewed spirit of "attack and win," not the vague, flabby, corporate concepts of "dominance" and "conflict prevention" and "peacetime activities" that are common today.

- *Missile Defense*: The greatest strategic threat to the United States is not instability in southern Europe, Saddam Hussein's Iraq, or even international terrorism. It is the danger of long-range strategic missiles. Unless this most serious danger is handled, the military and civilian national security bureaucracy will have no incentive to tackle others.

- *Military Power*: For America to continue acting as a force for positive change, U.S. military capabilities—naval, airborne, spaceborne and ground-based—must be strengthened and missions refined and limited to being used when vital U.S. interests are at stake.

- *Business and Foreign Policy*: The United States has to end the Clinton administration's mercantilism by separating the too-close ties between government and the private business sector. The focus on free trade should be continued, but it cannot come before protecting U.S. national security interests.

- *China*: America must treat China as a rival for power and not as a strategic partner. Dismissing current and future threats posed by China is dangerous and could lead to devastating miscalculation and war. The 1995 threat by Communist Chinese General Xiong Guangkai to use nuclear weapons against Los Angeles if the United States came to the military defense of Taiwan should be taken as a clear warning of things to come.

- *Russia*: The United States must promote true democratic reform in Russia with economic incentives for opening up a true free-market economy. But with that carrot should be the stick of harsh sanctions for selling weapons of mass destruction to rogue states.

Defense and foreign policy are serious business. It's time America had a serious commander in chief.

APPENDIX

The Paper Trail

T he pages that follow offer a sampling of government documents that reveals how Bill Clinton and his administration have undermined America's national security. These documents, many of which are top secret, present a stark record of the Clinton administration's betrayal, and of how the world is becoming an increasingly dangerous place.

MEETING SCHEDULE

0630	AM J3 Brief	MTWTF	DDO OFC
0730	J3 Mtg	MWF	J3 Conf Rm
0800	J3 Staff Brf	MTWTF	ODCR
0815	CJCS Brf	MTWTF	ODCR
0700	J33	MTWTF	J33 CR

Top Secret
(WHEN FILLED IN)
DDO PASSDOWN LOG

TURN OVER CHECKLIST
KEYS/ INVENTORY
POLs/NMCC EQUIPMENT STATUS
VIP TOURS
OPEN TASKING
REVIEW LOG ENTRIES

DATE: 7 April 97

Time	EVENT/UPDATES
061915	**Russian Merchant Vessel Incident:** Received a report from NCC of an incident that took place on 4 Apr 97 in the Puget Sound area. At approximately 1540 EST a Russian Merchant Vessel (Kapitan Man) was transiting the inbound lane of the strait of Juan De Fuca (US Territorial Waters). This ship is known to the intel community and is suspected of having submarine detection equipment on board. At the same time, the USS Ohio (SSBN 726) was transiting the outbound lane. A Canadian unit stationed at Esquimalt, Vancouver Island, launched a CH-124A helicopter for surveillance of the merchant vessel. This is a relatively routine operation. Onboard the helicopter was a US Navy Lieutenant Intelligence Officer serving as the Foreign Liaison Officer to MARPAC HQ. The lieutenant was operating digital camera equipment for the operation. During the course of the surveillance, the helicopter crew experienced what they believed to be a laser emanation from the merchant vessel. One of the Canadian pilots and the American Lieutenant reported pain and irritation in their eyes. . The report was delayed pending medical examinations. We continued to develop as much detail as possible and began notifications with the J-3 at 2052 EDT. The entire chain of command was notified. While we were developing the details, DOS contacted us to ask what DOD intended to do about the situation. At the time, the details did not support taking action against the merchant vessel. Upon notifying the CJCS the second time, we received guidance from him to deal directly with the MARPAC HQ to develop the details. Subsequently, conversations were held with both the US Lieutenant involved in the incident and the J-3 MARPAC HQ. Additional information included - the focus of the operation was to collect pictures of the antenna array aboard the merchant vessel. A total of 30 frames were taken with frame number 16 showing definitive evidence of an emanation coming from the bridge area of the merchant vessel. Initial medical exams indicate some eye damage to both the pilot and the US Lieutenant, but none that is considered permanent. The lieutenant's injuries appear more severe than the pilot's as he was looking through a camera at the time of the incident. The J-3 also confirmed that the merchant vessel was scheduled to depart 070100 EDT and offered new information that the subject merchant vessels sister ship (Anatoliy Kolesnichenko) was currently transiting the inbound lane with an unknown destination. MARPAC HQ had this second vessel under observation earlier in the day. Subsequent actions: OT-1 transitioned during this process and managed communications and reporting that resulted in the eventual decision. **UPDATE**
070130	After discussions with Thomas Lynch, DOS Director of Russian Affairs, he stated DOS would concur with DOD if we had reason to detain the vessel. After consultation with CJCS, VCJCS, and DEPSECDEF it was determined to detain the vessel. This was based on discussion DDO had with Lt Daly, the American on the Canadian helo-there is enough evidence foul play occurred. DEPSECDEF directed us through the VCJCS to call the USCG and tell them our wishes. USCG issued the order with a legal chop to detain the vessel. ADM Spade, USCG Dist 13, called to let us know it will happen, however, the vessel isn't scheduled to depart until 0900 EDT(0600 PDT) Mon. Talked with Col John Burton, J3 legal, USCG can detain any vessel for a reasonable amount of time if we suspect foul play has been accomplished in US waters. VCJCS, J3 have been updated on everything. CJCS, SECDEF, and DEPSECDEF know everything with the exception of the 0900 EDT departure time. Issues working:

TOP SECRET
(WHEN FILLED IN)
Printed on 04/17/97 4:26 PM

1

This April 7, 1997, Pentagon report reveals that a Russian ship, the Kapitan Man, fired a laser at a Canadian helicopter, injuring the pilot and a U.S. Navy intelligence officer, Lieutenant Jack Daly. The incident was covered up by the White House and State Department, which took over the issue from the Pentagon early on in the affair. (4 pages)

MEETING SCHEDULE		
0630 AM J3 Brief	MTWTF	DDO OPC
0730 J3 Mtg	MWF	J3 Conf Rm
0800 J2 Staff Brf	MTWTF	ODCR
0815 CJCS Brf	MTWTF	ODCR
0700 J33	MTWTF	J33 CR

Top Secret
(WHEN FILLED IN)
DDO PASSDOWN LOG

TURN OVER CHECKLIST
KEYS/ INVENTORY
POIs/NMCC EQUIPMENT STATUS
VIP TOURS
OPEN TASKING
REVIEW LOG ENTRIES

-Col Mattis is aware and will work any paperwork first light Mon morning-need to update him and BG Dunn first light Mon morning
-What is reasonable amount time-ans: it depends but John Burton says maybe up to 2-3 days
-J3 called and was tasked by VCJCS-what's the way ahead after detainment?
  --the next step is finding the right people to assist the USCG Boarding party-J3 tasked me to energize the J2 community to take advantage of this opportunity to board this vessel
-Building a pkg for J3 to take to VCJCS on whole incident-told the J3 this will not be in the Exec summary or morning slides due to sensitivity of the incident-he concurred
-If we discover the equipment on board-what's the next action?
-DDI needs to energize Navy Exploitation Team, NSA, and CIA

070150 Rcvd a call from Lt Daly saying the vessel is now planning to pull out around 0700-0800 EDT-USCG will issue detainment orders to the vessel just prior to the time. Told him to make sure he has the evidence documented because his info is the basis of the detainment-no senior leaders know this info-need to tell them first light Mon. ADDO has where to contact Lt Daly and has all the times the big decisions were made-this was a fast moving train, however, when senior leadership wakes up the they are going to start what-ifs.

070315 Rcvd picture of Frame #16 of 30 which clearly shows a light coming from the bridge of the KAPITAN MAN. Building two slides with back-up data for the J3 to take to VCJCS at 0600-will have copy on DDO desk. DDI reports NSA energized on action so they will monitor, CIA notified and recommends Office of Naval Intelligence(ONI) take the lead-they have exploitation team which could take advantage of opportunity. J2 is coming in 0400 and will be briefed-J3 thinks he should have the lead on the effort to exploit the vessel.
Once everyone gets up, suspect everyone in the building we'll be coming to us for the info-ADDO has pkg on his desk with numbers(ie Lt Daly, MARPAC HQ, etc.)-we've been going through USCG Ops Center to get plugged into any body in the CG-ADM Saunders, acting asst USCG ops, issued the order to Dist 13 in Washington state. ADM Spade, Dist 13, is commander of ops in the AOR.

UPDATE: Spoke with J3. Recommended that JCS/DOD take back seat role from this point forward. This is a USCG/DOT and DOS issue. He agreed. Called NSC and relayed same. They agreed. POC is CAPT Joe Bouchard ((456-9191) – faxed info paper and USCG order to vessel. May have SVTS. Talked to J33 and told him that if SVTS, DDO can take lead JCS role. He agreed. Coordinated with DOD (Larry Prather) to ensure we agree on the way ahead – essentially that DOD takes a back seat and DOT/DOS.

POC for Ambassador Collins (U.S. Ambassador designate to Russia) is Gladys Bodula (202) 647-2160; fax (202) 647-3506. We're tied into her and will update as needed. Faxed to her the memo and the USCG notification to the ship. Told her the NSC AO is CAPT Bouchard. Then talked to LT Daly. He indicated that the U.S. agreement with Canadians is the "Canadian/U.S. Maritime Operational Plan West", signed by CINCPAC and Cdr MARPAC dtd 20 June 96 which authorizes the activities that LT Daly was engaged in. Asked him to fax us the appropriate parts of this 40+ page document. Called Ms Bodula to backbrief. DDI assures me that ONI (Office of Naval Intel) is wedded at the hip with the USCG.

TOP SECRET
(WHEN FILLED IN)

2

MEETING SCHEDULE		
0430	AM J3 Brief MTWTF	DDO OFC
0730	J3 Mtg MWF	J3 Conf Rm
0800	J3 Staff Brf MTWTF	ODCR
0815	CJCS Brf MTWTF	ODCR
0700	J33 MTWTF	J33 CR

Top Secret
(WHEN FILLED IN)
DDO PASSDOWN LOG

TURN OVER CHECKLIST
KEYS/ INVENTORY
POIs/NMCC EQUIPMENT STATUS
VIP TOURS
OPEN TASKING
REVIEW LOG ENTRIES

Then ADDO called the NDOC (Canadian version of NMCC) to update them. Also called COL John Brown (DEPSECDEF's office) to update. POC for DOD is CDR Jeff Hughes (769-9348)

Spoke with RADM Spade (USCG Cdr, 13th Dist) (206) 220-7001. He's pessimistic that we'll find anything if we're looking for a hand held laser. Concerned that the decision to augment the team in a "covert" fashion is a U.S. govt Policy decision. Told him I'd check with DOS, DOD, and NSC. Called all of the above. DOD and NSC have legal concerns and so are checking with their GC. Advised CJCS EA and J3 EA of all of the above.

1600 SVTS scheduled to guage the way ahead. Called USCGD 13 to advise of where we are. LT Teschendorf indicated that they anticipate 2 individuals arriving from Whidby Island by 1600 EST and they plan to "board" by 1800 EST. Told him that we need to defer any ONI participation in the boarding until we get the policy decision on whether or not it's OK for them to participate. SVTS will drive that so I may have decision to him before scheduled boarding time. Told him to go ahead and plan for ONI participation but not to execute until they hear from us. He said that he also had instructions to wait until USCG HQ gave them clearance as well as they are checking the legal implications. He said he'd pass all of the above to Adm Spade. I passed it all to Gladys Bodula and to DOD.

1600 SVTS participants notified: J3, J33, DDI, DOD (CDR Hughes and Mr Prather's sec'y), USCG IIQ, NSC (Bob Bell likely lead), JCS legal, CAPT McClain (J3 USCG rep), etc etc.

| 071400 | Bottom line: As of 1330 EST we're awaiting decision from NSC that there is no problem with ONI augmentation of the boarding party. Told USCGD13 that they need to delay boarding until that decision is made. Current scheduled boarding is 1800 EST anyway so we may have the decision by then. Therefore, drive on with the planning for inclusion of ONI and we'll get back to them after SVTS. |

Spoke with CAPT Bouchard (NSC) and he indicated that NSC has no problem with our augmentation of the USCG team for the purposes we described. Said this had been coordinated with DOD and USCG general counsel. Informed J3 and OSD (CDR Hughes).

SVTS would be held at 1600. Told him I'd close the loop with DOD, USCG HQ and USCGD 13 to proceed as planned. He asked that we get the distance the helo was from the vessel, number of passes, and time on station. ADDO tracking this down.

Gladys Boluda called to see if she could get a cy of our chronolog so she could update. Told her we'd do that as soon as possible.

| 071600 | SVTS time changed to 1700. Confirmed Mr. Bell will conduct at NSC. Everyone notified. |

NSC requested information on the nature of the helicopter's operations in vicinity of the merchant ship. The following details were faxed to CAPT Bouchard: Duration - 20-25 minutes; total of 5 passes, all right hand turns; Distance from vessel - 100 feet to 500 yards.

TOP SECRET
(WHEN FILLED IN)
Printed on 04/07/97 1:36 PM

3

MEETING SCHEDULE				Top Secret (WHEN FILLED IN) **DDO PASSDOWN LOG**	TURN OVER CHECKLIST
0630	AM J3 Brief	MTWTF	DDO OFC		KEYS/ INVENTORY
0730	J3 Mtg	MWF	J3 Conf Rm		POIs/NMCC EQUIPMENT STATUS
0800	J2 Staff Brf	MTWTF	ODCR		VIP TOURS
0815	CJCR Brf	MTWTF	ODCR		OPEN TASKING
0700	J33	MTWTF	J33 CR		REVIEW LOG ENTRIES

Informed by J-33 that the augmentation team would include 4 personnel (USN): O-3 intel, E-7 intel, Russian linguist, and a photomate intel specialist.

SECRET

TO: SWO - J. LeCroy

FROM: EAO - J. Kessler

Re: April 7, 1996 5:00 SVTS Conference on Russian Ship Incident

Participants From: NSC   B. Bell
                     STATE   Amb. Collins
                     OSD
                     Coast Guard
                     Naval Intelligence

Two crew members of Canadian military helicopter which flew over a Russian merchant ship, *Capt. Mann,* April 4, have eye damage. The helicopter crew reported seeing a "red light" emanating from the ship. The *Capt. Mann* is now docked at Tacoma, Washington. The ship has been held at the Port of Tacoma pending a CG/Naval Intelligence search. The search began at approximately 1815 EDT. The nine-member boarding party has instructions to search public areas of the ship for a laser. SVTS participants decided that if the crew of the vessel cooperates with the boarding party by admitting to illuminating the helicopter with a laser and shows the party the laser, the case will be handled through Naval channels, although the search party will continue to search the vessel. If the *Capt. Mann* crew is uncooperative, a second SVTS will be convened April 7 to decide on a further course of action.

cc: S/S   : JCampbell
       S/S-O: KMessner

SECRET

These 1997 internal State Department documents show that the search for a laser on the Russian ship was limited to "public" areas of the vessel, and that officials at the White House and State Department allowed the Russian ship to leave a U.S. port before medical tests on the injured military personnel could be completed. (3 pages)

From: Kessler, Jonathan
Sent: Monday, April 07, 1997 10:38 PM
To: S/S-O (Int)
Subject: RE: Boarding the Capt Mann

According to CG ops 2138 the CG/Naval Intell. team didn't board the Capt. Mann until 2030 EDT. The initial report is that the crew was helpful, but denied having a Laser on board the ship.   SVTS scheduled for 2300

From: Kessler, Jonathan
Sent: Monday, April 07, 1997 9:57 PM
To: S/S-O (Int)
Subject: Boarding the Capt Mann

From: Kessler, Jonathan
Sent: Tuesday, April 08, 1997 12:34 AM
To: S/S-O (Int); Campbell, John
Subject: RE: Boarding the Capt. Mann

The CG/Navy team aboard the Capt. Mann found no laser nor any trace of a laser. The American helo crewmember, LT. Daley, along with the Canadians left Canada at 0000 4/8 for San Antonio for further medical tests to confirm laser burns. The tests are scheduled to be completed around 1200 4/8 .

At the 4/7 2300 SVTS, the conferees could not agree on a course of action. State and the NSC opted to let the Capt. Mann leave Tacoma. DOD (except for the Coast Guard) want to detain the vessel until tests are completed on the helo crew.

NSC initiated a secure telcon at 0015 4/8 with Lodal, Steinberg, Talbot, and Collins to decide the issue.

From: Kessler, Jonathan
Sent: Monday, April 07, 1997 10:38 PM
To: S/S-O (Int)
Subject: RE: Boarding the Capt. Mann

According to CG ops 2138 the CG/Naval Intell. team didn't board the Capt. Mann until 2030 EDT. The initial report is that the crew was helpful, but denied having a Laser on board the ship. SVTS scheduled for 2300

From: Kessler, Jonathan
Sent: Monday, April 07, 1997 9:57 PM
To: S/S-O (Int)
Subject: Boarding the Capt Mann

<<File: SVTS_0407.doc>>

Intelligence Report

Office of Russian and Eurasian Analysis
Office of Weapons, Technology and Proliferation

Prospects for Unsanctioned Use of Russian Nuclear Weapons (C)

A Research Paper

This report was prepared by Jerry Sparks, Office of Russian and Eurasian Analysis, and Julie Grimes, Office of Weapons, Technology and Proliferation. The draft was reviewed by analysts in DIA and NSA, who have somewhat different views (see footnote 3). Comments and queries are welcome and may be directed to the Chief, Security Issues Division, ORE, on (703) 482-5552 or secure (93) 52625. (U)

Key findings of a 1996 CIA report show that Russian control over nuclear weapons is weak. (2 pages)

Prospects for Unsanctioned Use of
Russian Nuclear Weapons (C)

Key Findings

Information available as of 28 August 1996 was used in this report. (U)

The Russian nuclear command and control system is being subjected to stresses it was not designed to withstand as a result of wrenching social change, economic hardship, and malaise within the armed forces. Moreover, some evidence suggests that, despite their official assurances, high-level Moscow officials are concerned about the security of their nuclear inventory. Adding to our concerns are significant gaps and inconsistencies in our information about the command and control of Russian nuclear weapons:

- Some reporting indicates that echelons below the General Staff—such as SRF command posts—have the technical ability to launch without authorization by political leaders or the General Staff.

- Human sources have repeatedly warned that the controls over some tactical nuclear weapons are poor; *these appear to be the weapons most at risk.*

- There also are conflicting reports that Russian ballistic missile submarines carry valid launch codes on board for emergency use. (S NF)

We continue to assess the possibility of unauthorized launch or nuclear blackmail as low, because many of the safeguards built into the old Soviet system are still in place. A severe political crisis, however, could exacerbate existing problems in military-political relations and widen internal fissures in the armed forces, especially if control of the military—already demoralized and corrupted—were to break down. Such a crisis could raise concerns about nuclear control:

- An array of evidence indicates that political authorities could not prevent the General Staff from launching nuclear weapons on its own initiative.

- *Nuclear-armed units conceivably could become involved in conspiracies to threaten or blackmail perceived enemies or political authorities; a rogue submarine crew might have the autonomous ability to launch at least tactical nuclear weapons.* (S NF)

Handle via COMINT Channels

Reverse Blank

iii

Top Secret
ORE 96-10007CX
WTP 96-10009CX
September 1996

SECRET

Report to Congress on Detargeting (Classified Version)

(U)   At the January 1994 Moscow summit, Presidents Clinton and Yeltsin announced that they would direct the detargeting of U.S. and Russian strategic missiles, respectively, so that by May 30, 1994 none of these missiles would be targeted against any country on a day-to-day basis. The United States implemented detargeting by May 30, 1994, and the Russian government notified us that it also implemented detargeting on schedule.

(U)   This detargeting initiative was a confidence-building measure that symbolizes the improved relationship between the United States and Russia. In this regard, it is one of a series of such measures adopted in the aftermath of the Cold War, including discontinuing strategic bomber ground alert and continuous airborne command post operations, and withdrawing and eliminating certain tactical nuclear weapons.

(S)   Placing ICBMs in a non-targeted status does not remove them from combat duty and only slightly reduces their readiness. For Russian ICBMs, detargeting means that targeting and flight data have been downloaded from the missile's onboard computer and replaced with a zero or null target set. Such data, however, remains stored in the fire-control computer and can be reloaded into the missiles's onboard computer within a few minutes. The impact of detargeting on combat readiness is thus easily reversible and cannot be directly monitored by national technical means. Unless a missile is actually demated from its warheads, defueled, and removed from its launcher, the Intelligence Community is unable to monitor a change in its combat duty status.

(S)   Russian nuclear-powered ballistic missile submarines on pierside duty or on patrol in peacetime operations do have targeting data stored within the missiles. These data are stored on tapes locked in the commanding officer's safe on board the submarine. These tapes are loaded only when the submarine receives a valid shore command, which activates the fire-control computer and authorizes the ship's commanding officer to remove the tapes from his safe and initiate pre-launch preparations. The detargeting agreement thus required no change to Russian procedures and did not change Russian SLBM readiness (nor that of US SLBMs).

(U)   As political commitment, rather than a treaty obligation, there are no procedures to verify detargeting. Effective verification would not appear feasible, nor would attempts at verification make sense, given the fact that the process can be reversed within a short period of time. By the same token, however, since U.S. missile crews could quickly reconfigure equipment to prepare to launch missiles if so directed, detargeting does not in any way reduce U.S. security. The principal purpose of detargeting was to take an additional step which symbolizes the improved strategic relationship between the United States and Russia.

SECRET

This 1997 report to Congress on "detargeting" nuclear warheads reveals that the symbolic agreement reached by President Clinton and Russian leader Boris Yeltsin cannot be verified and only slightly reduces missiles' readiness to fire. (1 page)

Intelligence Report

Office of Russian and Eurasian Analysis

Rodionov's Concerns about Nuclear Command and Control (U)

Russian Defense Minister Rodionov, in disagreeing with Defense Council Secretary Baturin over the need for more defense funding, has claimed repeatedly that financial constraints are eroding the Russian nuclear command and control system. *Rodionov's statements probably reflect both frustration and genuine concern over political leaders' perceived unwillingness to address the continued degradation of the military. Raising concern about nuclear control is perhaps the hottest "button" Rodionov can push. He may hope to force the politicians either to increase resource distributions or to acknowledge responsibility for the problem and its potential consequences.* (C NF)

Rodionov--in the mold of past Soviet and Russian military leaders who have worried more about maintaining a robust launch capability than safety or an unauthorized launch--seems primarily concerned with maintaining the credibility of Russia's nuclear deterrent. Some evidence supports his concerns, such as power cutoffs to Strategic Rocket Forces' command posts, the reported obsolescence of the Cheget nuclear briefcase and Kazbek nuclear warning and retaliation system, financially-strapped command and control equipment-production facilities, and interruptions in SRF communications. In addition to system obsolescence, there is some evidence that he is worried about perceived US capabilities to interrupt a Russian launch. His expressed concern about the reliability of his own officers and other statements suggest that he also may worry about unsanctioned use of Russian nuclear weapons. (S NF)

Nonetheless, we judge that prospects for unauthorized launch of Russian nuclear weapons are very low under normal circumstances because many of the safeguards built into the Soviet system are still in place. However, if that system and its safeguards continue to degrade because of lack of funding and maintenance, our concern will increase, especially if a crisis arose that splintered the armed forces. (C NF)

ORE IR 97-40067X

TN: DO 97-02512
CL BY: 0480332
CL REASON: 1.5 (c)
DECL ON: X1
DRV FROM: Multiple Sources
Secret

This CIA report exposes how computer glitches in Russia caused nuclear missiles to "spontaneously" go on higher alert. (2 pages)

- According to a former SRF officer, command and control equipment often malfunctions and "on more than one occasion" has switched spontaneously to combat mode.[1] (S NF)

Launch Capabilities Paramount (U)

Although some of his warnings are probably overstated and their exact meaning is unclear, Rodionov, as the top official charged with maintaining the credibility of Russia's nuclear deterrent forces, probably is most worried about the ability of the command system, including its associated warning functions, to respond quickly in a crisis. Fearing system decapitation, Soviet and Russian military leaders traditionally have been more concerned with maintaining a robust launch capability over negative control (to exclude an accidental or unauthorized launch). Recent reporting indicates that Rodionov also attributes potent counter-command and control capabilities to the United States, according to a reliable source with access. (S NF)

His comments suggest that he also is worried about unauthorized nuclear use,[2] but this is probably of lesser concern. Although he thus far has not directly addressed warhead theft, other Russian military officials have, *and this probably is an additional source of anxiety.* (C NF)

Concerns About Troop Reliability (U)

Rodionov also is worried about troop morale and reliability. According to recent defense attache reporting, he personally checks, morning and evening, the status of

---

[1] *A "spontaneous" transition to combat mode would not necessarily result in an unauthorized missile launch, however. Transferring command and control equipment to combat mode is only one of several steps necessary. Also needed are unlocking codes, which, together with transfer of control equipment to combat mode, unlock the control system and enable targeting data to be passed to the missile, according to emigre reports. Without those additional data, the missile probably could not be launched and reach its target.* (S NF)

[2] See the DI Research Paper ORE 96-10007CX/ WTP 96-10009CX (Top Secret Codeword NF NC OC), September 1996, *Prospects for Unsanctioned Use of Russian Nuclear Weapons.* The DI Intelligence Memorandum OSE M 94-20095X (Secret NF NC OC), 9 December 1994, *How To Steal a Russian Nuclear Warhead: An Insider's View,* addresses the danger of nuclear theft. In addition, several ORE reports have addressed aspects of Rodionov's political problems and tenure as Defense Minister. See, for example, the DI Intelligence Report ORE IR 97-40022 (Confidential NF), 12 February 1997, *Rodionov: "Spectator" at the Destruction of the Armed Forces,* which characterizes the Defense Minister as an embittered and isolated man whose penchant for bluntness increases the odds that he will be fired or resign. The DI Intelligence Report ORE IR 97-40033 (Confidential NF), 4 March 1997, *Rodionov: Will He Survive?* concludes that he probably will not. The DI Intelligence Memorandum ORE M 97-20012 (Confidential NF), 27 March 1997, *The Two Faces of Igor' Rodionov,* addresses the inconsistency of his public statements and what they may portend about his behavior in a future crisis. (C)

4

RUSSIA: **More Strategic Underground Construction (S NF)**

According to the US defense attache and satellite imagery, work has
progressed on extending a deep subway for rapid evacuation of leaders
during wartime from Moscow; a Russian press report in 1995 described
this project. Recent satellite imagery shows construction is nearly
complete on a governmental relocation bunker outside Moscow, although
work on the bunker appeared to have stopped some time ago. Several
similar sites remain abandoned.

— Satellite imagery shows continued excavation at the deep,
   underground complex at Yamantau Mountain and new
   construction in each of its aboveground support areas.

— Work continues on a nuclear-survivable, strategic command
   post at Kos'vinskiy Mountain. (S NF)

*President Yel'tsin and Premier Chernomyrdin apparently have endorsed
such projects.* In January, authorities barring defense attaches from access
to Yamantau cited a decree Yel'tsin issued in November on maintaining
the project's security. Press reports have mentioned similar decrees.

— The federal budget for this year lists a subsidy to the closed
   city building Yamantau—*the first public reference to funding
   for the facility.*

— Chernomyrdin in 1995 sent a telegram to thank the tunneling
   company building the VIP subway and the Yamantau complex.
   (S NF)

*The underground construction appears larger than previously assessed.
Two decrees last year on an emergency planning authority under
Yel'tsin with oversight of underground facility construction suggest that
the purpose of the Moscow-area projects is to maintain continuity of
leadership during nuclear war.*

— *The command post at Kos'vinskiy appears to provide the
   Russians with a means to retaliate against a nuclear attack;
   the rationale for the Yamantau complex is unclear.* (S NF)
   -CIA, DIA, NIMA-

*This excerpt from March 1997 CIA reports on strategic underground construction shows
that Moscow continues to invest in efforts to survive nuclear war. (2 pages)*

Strategic Underground Construction Around Moscow (S NF)

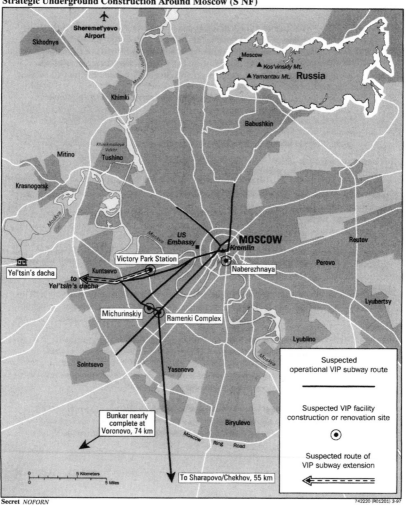

PRESIDENTIAL REVIEW THIRTY ONE

U.S. POLICY ON BALLISTIC MISSILE DEFENSES AND
THE FUTURE OF THE ABM TREATY (S NF)

Executive Summary

A. Context for Decisions

o   On September 1, 1993, the President approved the
     recommendations from the Bottom-Up Review (BUR), including
     SecDef's recommendations for a fundamental restructuring of
     ballistic missile defense (BMD) programs.

o   Specifically, the U.S. will pursue an $18 billion BMD
     program between FY95 and FY99 that will include (1) $12
     billion to provide for enhanced theater missile defense
     (TMD) capability later this decade; (2) $3 billion for
     maintaining national missile defense (NMD) as a technology
     (R&D) program; and (3) $3 billion for a modest follow-on
     technologies (FOT) and research and support (R&S) program.

o   These decisions have profound implications for U.S. policy
     in the areas addressed in this PRD:

     --   Absent the emergence of a Third World ICBM threat or a
          reversal of trends in our improving relationship with
          Russia, there will be no acquisition program for NMD
          systems. NMD will remain for the indefinite future as
          a technology program, and 10-15 years would be required
          to deploy a system were a decision taken to do so. As
          a result, for all intents and purposes NMD ABM Treaty
          amendment issues are now moot, notwithstanding the
          goals Congress articulated in the Missile Defense Act
          (MDA) as recently as one year ago.

     --   The requirement for robust TMD programs has been
          validated as a top priority of the United States; thus,
          ensuring that the ABM Treaty is updated to reflect
          changes in TMD technologies is more important than
          ever.

o   The decisions taken in this PRD also occur in the context of
     a radically transformed international political landscape.

     --   The Soviet Union has disintegrated.

     --   Russia finds many of its ABM assets on foreign soil.

     --   The Newly Independent States (NIS) are claiming co-
          equal status for the purposes of succession to the ABM
          Treaty as Ukraine and Belarus underscored at the
          recently completed five-year ABM Treaty Review
          Conference in Geneva.   -

*These excerpts from a presidential directive order a major strategic weapons review,
revealing plans for a dubious "grand bargain" with Russia to expand the 1972 Anti-Ballistic
Missile Treaty and make future treaty changes more difficult. (4 pages)*

> -- The proliferation of weapons of mass destruction (WMD) has heightened interest in early warning sharing and cooperative TMD efforts.

o Taking all of this into account, this Review recommends a comprehensive "grand bargain" for meeting U.S. national security requirements in the changed circumstances of the current international security environment and as recently validated in the BUR.

> -- In return for U.S. agreement to (1) multilateralize the ABM Treaty and (2) defer indefinitely discussion of amendments to the ABM Treaty that would allow for more robust NMD architectures beyond that currently permitted by the ABM Treaty, Russia (and other successor states intent on joining the Treaty) would agree to TMD clarifications that allow the U.S. to execute those TMD programs that the BUR has identified as essential to U.S. national security requirements.

> -- The U.S. would also be prepared to proceed with sharing of early warning data, planning for use of ATBM forces and TMD technology cooperation, recognizing that the pace of these cooperative efforts would, at least indirectly, be linked to our ability to move forward with our own TMD programs.

B. Assessment of the Threat

B.I. Threat From Russia

o The collapse of the Former Soviet Union (FSU) and the end of the Cold War has dramatically reduced the immediate potential for strategic nuclear war with Russia. Reflecting this change, U.S. strategic bombers are no longer on alert, and U.S. nuclear weapons have been withdrawn from surface ships and submarines (with the exception of SLBM warheads, which remain at sea). Also, the U.S. has canceled a number of strategic modernization programs, including rail-garrison MX and Midgetman, and has stopped production of the Advanced Cruise Missile and Trident Mark V warhead. In addition, the United States is now engaged in a broad range of strategic stability enhancement discussions with Russia, including detargeting. (S)

o Nonetheless, while the immediate potential for strategic nuclear war with Russia has dramatically reduced, Russian strategic forces (currently consisting of 10,100 weapons) remain on continuous alert and hold U.S. and NATO forces at risk. (S)

o Even without further modernization, Russia will still be able to retain a potent, but aging, strategic force through the early 2000s (between 2,600-3,500 warheads). Without further refurbishment, most of the existing strategic systems will reach the end of their service life by 2010-

3

2020; however, we expect maintaining the viability of strategic nuclear forces to remain Russia's highest military priority. (S)

o As long as Moscow maintains current security practices, the possibility of an unauthorized launch is remote. During a coup or widespread violence, there is the possibility that the Russian General Staff might misunderstand or miscalculate Western intentions and actions. Technical deficiencies and growing gaps in Russia's ballistic missile early warning and attack assessment capabilities increase the possibility of such miscalculations. (S)

B.II. Threat From China

o The Chinese intercontinental missile threat is significantly smaller than that posed by Russia, currently consisting of only seven relatively inaccurate single-warhead ICBMs. By the year 2000, Beijing probably will have some 24-28 missiles capable of reaching the CONUS, some of which may be MIRVed. China's medium and intermediate range missile force currently is composed of some 50 launchers, and is expected to double within the next 10 years. (S)

B.II. Threat From Others

o It is unlikely that any nations beyond Russia, China, and possibly Ukraine will develop ICBMs capable of striking the United States during the next 10-15 years; beyond 10-15 years, one or more nations that are hostile to the United States may be able to indigenously develop ballistic missiles that could threaten the United States. (S)

o A number of countries hostile to the United States currently possess short- and intermediate-range missile systems that are capable of threatening U.S. friends and deployed U.S. forces. Of particular concern in this regard are North Korea, Iran, Iraq, and Libya. Within the next 10-15 years, the capabilities of these countries will be increased. (S)

  -- By the turn of the century, in most cases where U.S. forces could potentially be engaged in a large-scale manner, it is likely that our adversary will potentially possess WMD in some form. Theater ballistic missiles are likely to be included in a future adversary's arsenal of weapons, especially in the Middle East and Southwest Asia, where missiles have been used in four of the last six major wars, or Northeast Asia, where North Korea deploys a number of ballistic missiles.

SECRET   4

C. **Ballistic Missile Defense Systems**

   C.I. **Assessment: Requirements and Capabilities**:

      C.1.a. **U.S. NMD**

o   Prior to completion and approval of the BUR, the Joint
      Requirements Oversight Council (JROC) adopted a requirement
      for strategic ballistic missile defense specifying an
      overall system performance high enough to ensure a threshold
      effectiveness of 100% reentry vehicle (RV) negation (with a
      probability of performance of 95%) against a 20 RV attack
      launched within 10 seconds. The objective requirement calls
      for the same effectiveness but against an attack of 200 RVs.
      In light of the BUR decision to downgrade NMD to a
      technology-only program, this JROC must be revisited. (S)

o   Should the United States decide in the future that an
      emerging Third World ICBM threat or a reversal of reform in
      Russia required elevating NMD to a systems acquisition
      program, the maximum level of defense that could be provided
      10-15 years later by a single Ballistic Missile Defense
      (BMD) site would be highly dependent on the assumed
      characteristics of the threat and the suite of sensors used
      to provide weapon targeting information. (S)

o   Using currently available or near-term technologies, a
      single site BMD architecture for the defense of the United
      States located at Grand Forks that includes 100 Ground Based
      Interceptors (GBIs) and 1 Ground Based Radar (GBR) and no
      additional sensors can protect only the central United
      States against missiles constituting a northerly threat.

      --   The cost to deploy and maintain this system for 10
           years is estimated as $15-17B in FY 88 dollars. (S)

o   Additional sensors, such as an upgraded early warning radar
      (UEWR) system, Brilliant Eyes (BE), GSTS, or additional
      (remote) GBRs, could expand coverage provided by a single
      BMD site to include the entire CONUS. Each of the
      additional sensor options could provide high levels (>90%)
      of protection against single launches from proliferant
      states. However, protection against multiple RVs from CIS
      or China would vary depending on the type of additional
      sensor system employed.

      --   The cost to deploy and maintain each of these sensors
           for 10 years is: $1B FY 88 for UEWR, $2-4B FY 88 for
           GSTS, and $5-6B FY 88 for BE for 10 years of operation.
           (S)

o   Deploying two ABM sites (each one about in the middle of
      each U.S. coast) would increase the effectiveness of
      national missile defenses.

SECRET

SECRET

SECRET

THE WHITE HOUSE
WASHINGTON

December 11, 1993

PRESIDENTIAL DECISION DIRECTIVE/NSC-17

MEMORANDUM FOR THE VICE PRESIDENT
                THE SECRETARY OF STATE
                THE SECRETARY OF THE TREASURY
                THE SECRETARY OF DEFENSE
                THE SECRETARY OF ENERGY
                DIRECTOR OF THE OFFICE OF MANAGEMENT AND BUDGET
                U.S. PERMANENT REPRESENTATIVE TO
                  THE UNITED NATIONS
                CHIEF OF STAFF TO THE PRESIDENT
                ASSISTANT TO THE PRESIDENT FOR NATIONAL
                  SECURITY AFFAIRS
                DIRECTOR OF CENTRAL INTELLIGENCE
                CHAIRMAN OF THE JOINT CHIEFS OF STAFF
                DIRECTOR OF THE ARMS CONTROL AND
                  DISARMAMENT AGENCY
                DIRECTOR OF THE OFFICE OF SCIENCE AND TECHNOLOGY
                  POLICY

SUBJECT: U.S. Policy on Ballistic Missile Defenses and the
                Future of the ABM Treaty (S)

This Presidential Decision Directive establishes and directs the
implementation of U.S. Policy on Ballistic Missile Defenses (BMD)
and the Future of the Anti-Ballistic Missile (ABM) Treaty. (S)

Background

On April 26, 1993, Presidential Review Directive (PRD)-31 tasked
a comprehensive examination of U.S. BMD policy, focusing on the
following three areas:

--   The objectives the Administration should pursue as a
      priority in BMD. (S)

--   An assessment of what, if any, changes in the ABM Treaty
      should be sought in light of these objectives and the
      modalities for achieving any changes. (S)

--   A strategy for pursuing our BMD objectives with Russia and
      with friends and allies   (S)

SECRET

SECRET

*President Clinton signed Presidential Decision Directive 17 in 1993, making it the policy of
the United States not to seek changes in the 1972 Anti-Ballistic Missile Treaty. The policy
effectively blocked the United States from building a national missile defense capable of
protecting all fifty states from long-range missile attack. (5 pages)*

SECRET   ∠   ̄ ̄ ̄ ̄ ̄ ̄

The Review was completed by the Interagency Working Group (IWG) on Arms Control and forwarded to the Deputies Committee on November 13, 1993. It was considered by the Principals Committee on November 22, 1993. (C)

U.S. BMD Objectives and Program

Consistent with the assessment of the ballistic missile threat contained in PRD-31, on August 30 1993 I approved the recommendations from the Bottom Up Review (BUR), including the Secretary of Defense's recommendations for a fundamental restructuring of BMD programs. (C)

Specifically, the U.S. will pursue a BMD program between FY95 and FY99 that will provide for:

--   . . . . theater missile defense (TMD) capability later this decade. (U)

--   Maintaining national missile defense (NMD) as a technology research and development (R&D) program. (U)

--   A modest follow-on technologies (FOT) and research and support (R&S) program. (U)

The TMD programs identified in the BUR will play a key role in minimizing two critical dangers to U.S. security: regional threats to U.S. interests and the proliferation of weapons of mass destruction (WMD). In general, our TMD forces should:

--   Provide highly effective protection against limited tactical ballistic missile attacks for forward deployed and concentrated or dispersed expeditionary elements of the armed forces of the United States and for the facilities and forces of friends and allies of the United States. (U)

--   Effectively protect allied population centers. This protection could provide the opportunity for U.S./allies to execute military options in support of national objectives with minimum interference from enemy missile forces. (U)

ABM Treaty

Consistent with U.S. BMD programmatic objectives, the following will be the policy of the United States with regard to the ABM Treaty. (S)

--   ABM Treaty interpretation The Administration has already informed the Congress that it will adhere to the traditional, or "narrow," interpretation of the ABM Treaty. (U)

--   NMD ABM Treaty issues: The United States will not seek amendments to the ABM Treaty to permit (1) expansion of the number of ABM sites and ground-based interceptors beyond

SECRET   SECRET

SECRET   3

those currently permitted (1 and 100, respectively), (2)
development, testing or deployment of space-based sensors
for direct battle management (i e., satellites capable of
substituting for ABM radars) or (3) development, testing or
deployment of space-based interceptors. The United States
will, however, reexamine these options if a decision is
taken at some future date to elevate NMD to an acquisition
and deployment program   (C)

-- Brilliant Eyes (BE) ABM Treaty issues: The objective BE
space-based sensor system is not sufficiently defined to
determine its ABM Treaty implications. If, at some future
date, the USG concludes that the ABM Treaty would prohibit
the objective BE system, the USG will determine at that time
whether to seek changes or redesign the system to make it
consistent with the USG interpretation of the ABM Treaty.
However, the United States will not negotiate at this time
ABM Treaty amendments or otherwise seek formal agreement to
the objective BE system. (C)

-- Succession: The United States will agree to negotiate a
protocol that will multilateralize the ABM Treaty, i.e., to
give each of the Bishkek signatories, as well as Georgia and
Azerbaijan, the option of becoming parties to the ABM
Treaty. (C)

-- TMD/ABM clarification: The requirement for robust TMD
programs has been validated as a top priority in our defense
planning; thus, ensuring that the ABM Treaty is updated to
reflect changes in TMD technologies is more important than
ever. (U)

The U.S. will propose to our ABM Treaty partners that for
purposes of determining treaty compliance a TMD system would
not be deemed to have been "given the capability to counter"
a strategic ballistic missile (SBM) unless it had actually
been tested against an SBM. An SBM would, in turn, be
defined as having a maximum velocity greater than 5.0
km/second. (S)

-- Linkage: The U.S. will implicitly link our positions on
succession and TMD/ABM clarification. The U.S. will not
conclude one without the other (S)

BMD Cooperation

The U.S. will be prepared to discuss (1) sharing of ballistic
missile early warning information. (2) planning for use of ATBM
forces and (3) employing technology cooperation to assist in
forging a positive security relationship between the United
States and Russia and to serve as part of a general strategy to
address the proliferation of ballistic missiles and weapons of
mass destruction. The United States will adopt a regional/
bilateral approach to BMD cooperation in each of the above three
areas. (C)

SECRET   SECRET

In general, the degree to which we are willing to share technology will depend on the country with which we propose to cooperate. In the specific case of Russia, the extent to which we would pursue missile defense technology cooperation would depend on their continued progress in political and economic reform; adherence to arms control agreements and the Missile Technology Control Regime and a willingness to enter into and abide by a bilateral agreement on cooperative activities. (C)

The United States will, however, limit these cooperative programs with Russia in two important ways.

-- First, the technology development should be generic and not involve direct cooperation in any current U.S. system development (i.e., joint space sensor technology programs should include experiments not tied to BE or other operational system development). (C)

-- Second, the United States should focus on jointly developing new technology products rather than transferring existing technology. Thus, only the carefully controlled U.S. technology necessary for specific projects would be incorporated into them. (C)

Our program with Russia will proceed on its own merits, although the pace of cooperation will be implicitly linked to our ability to move forward with our own TMD programs. That, in turn, will require a forthcoming response from Russia (and the other New Independent States that would be made Party to the ABM Treaty) on our TMD/ABM demarcation proposals (C)

Encouraging other countries to acquire Anti-Tactical Ballistic Missiles (ATBMs), and (as appro-priate) sharing U.S. technologies permitted by the MTCR, can further U S security interests in some regions of the world, reduce escalatory tendencies that unchecked offensive military capabilities can create and contribute to U.S. counter-proliferation efforts. (C)

However, potential tensions and tradeoffs exist between pursuing missile defenses and limiting or preventing proliferation. A tension between our BMD efforts and our nonproliferation goals may arise if and when we need to cooperate with a non-MTCR country in the development or sale of missile interceptors. Entering into such cooperation could easily put the U.S. in the position of engaging in behavior that we would object to -- and might have to impose sanctions on -- if it were carried out by other countries. Thus, the U.S. will strictly limit the number of non-MTCR states with which such cooperation occurs (C)

The Department of Defense and Department of State will formulate a specific proposal for (a) early-warning (b) TMD and (c) technology cooperation with Russia (and, as appropriate, other countries and/or regions) and submit it to the IWG on Arms Control no later than January 7, 1994. (C)

SECRET

SECREI

Negotiating Forum

The United States will use the Standing Consultative Commission
(SCC) as the forum for negotiating clarifications, modifications,
state succession and procedural applications of the ABM Treaty.
Meeting in the SCC will serve to reaffirm the Administration's
commitment to the ABM Treaty and will constitute a good faith
effort to cooperate with the Russians on issues over which they
have serious concerns. (C)

Higher-level political discussions should be used to reach broad
agreement on our basic implementation strategy and to set
parameters for the SCC sessions to follow. These discussions
will also be the main forum for articulating to the Russians our
revised BMD cooperation objectives, supplemented by technical
discussions in sub-level working groups. (C)

Implementation

The NSC staff will coordinate the taskings identified in this
PDD. (U)

William J Clinton

EURASIA

Russia:　　　　　　　**New Production of SA-12 SAMs for Possible Export (S NF)**

Satellite imagery suggests that a surge in production of SA-12 surface-to-air missiles is imminent; the imagery shows that last month at least 38 SA-12A canisters were moved into the production buildings at the Verkhnyaya Salda missile assembly facility, which has been almost inactive for two years.

— *Because deployment of the missiles to Russian units ended in 1992 and the forces probably do not need large numbers of new missiles, any surge in production is probably intended for export.* (S NF)

Special intelligence and clandestine sources indicate that Russia has negotiated sales with a number of countries, including China, India, the UAE, and Cyprus. There is no evidence that any contract has been signed, however.

— *The missile would provide an anti-tactical-ballistic missile capability to countries concerned about tactical ballistic missile threats.*

— *Export sales would boost SA-12 production facilities, whose domestic orders had fallen dramatically since the breakup of the USSR.* (TS U NF OC) -*CIA, NSA-*

These excerpts from two 1996 CIA reports state that Russia is increasing production of advanced air defense systems for export. Moscow used negotiations with the United States on regional missile defenses to delay and restrict U.S. missile defenses in order to enhance the marketability of Russian systems. (3 pages)

Russia: SA-12 Production Resumes
Verkhnyaya Salda, 28 May 1996 (S NF)

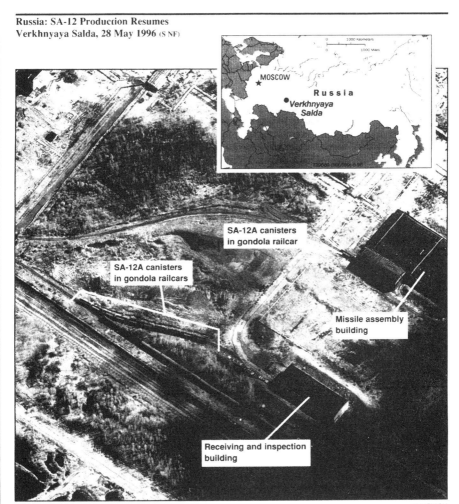

SA-12A canisters
in gondola railcar

SA-12A canisters
in gondola railcars

Missile assembly
building

Receiving and inspection
building

Secret *NOFORN*

353547PM5 5-96

Top Secret
17 June 1996

Proliferation of Advanced Air Defense Systems (U)

Special intelligence, clandestine reports, and press reports indicate Russia has recently concluded several contracts to sell modern SAM systems and their technology. Included in these sales are the first exports of the SA-15, SA-19, and SA-11 to countries other than former Warsaw Pact members.

— According to a source of the US military, a Peruvian group recently went to Russia for training on the SA-19 Tunguska gun-missile system in anticipation of receiving the system in two to three months. *The SA-19 is the first deployed system to incorporate guns and missiles on a single, self-propelled platform.*

— Satellite imagery shows that India received six SA-19 systems in February. By late March, India expected to receive another SA-19 shipment, according to special intelligence.

— Finland will soon receive Russian Buk SA-11 SAM fire units as part of an arms-for-debt-retirement arrangement worth about $210 million, according to press and US Embassy reports. Russian test range activity and press reports indicate the deal *may include a mix of SA-11 and the higher performance SA-X-17 missiles;* the latter has not yet been deployed with Russian Ground Forces. (TS U NF)

Russian press reports assert that such sales have helped the missile builders avoid collapse. *The sales also contribute to funding further air defense R&D and production.*

— The director of a radar production plant recently said that the sale of the SA-12 to the US saved the SA-12s design institute and manufacturing plants. (U) -*CIA, DIA, NSA-*

Top Secret
3 June 1996

DEPARTMENT OF DEFENSE INITIAL ASSESSMENT
OF CERTAIN DOCUMENTS CONCERNING AN INVESTIGATION BY
HUGHES SPACE AND COMMUNICATIONS COMPANY INTO THE FAILURE
OF THE LAUNCH OF THE APSTAR II ON
CHINA'S LONG MARCH 2E LAUNCH VEHICLE
December 7, 1998

(U) This is an initial assessment of information contained in certain documents provided to the Department of Defense by the Department of Commerce in July of 1998 that relate to the conduct of a failure investigation by Hughes Space and Communications Company in 1995, in connection with the failed launch of an Apstar II satellite in China. The conclusions are limited to the information that DoD derived from those documents. This initial assessment has been prepared in response to requests from Congress.

INTRODUCTION

(U) The Hughes Space and Communications Company (hereinafter referred to as "Hughes") prepared certain reports and other documents containing the findings and supporting analyses of its investigation of the January 1995 failure of the launch of a China Long March 2E (LM-2E) rocket-carrying Hughes-manufactured APSTAR II commercial communications satellite. During the course of the investigation, Hughes provided documents to, and conducted the investigation jointly with, Chinese nationals, including at least the Chinese Academy of Launch Technology (CALT), the LM-2E manufacturer, and the Chinese launch service provider, the China Great Wall Industries Corporation (CGWIC). Hereinafter, this assessment will refer to these entities collectively as the "Chinese."

(U) At various times between February and August 1995, Hughes submitted these reports and documents to the Department of Commerce for review and approval for release to China. Hughes provided copies of these documents to the Chinese. The documents indicate that some of the information contained in them was previously imparted to the Chinese in briefings and discussions prior to submission to Commerce. Commerce determined that the documents only contained information already authorized for export under the original Commerce license issued to Hughes in February 1994. Commerce did

Derived from: NAIC memo, Nov. 12, 1998
Declassify on: X1

This Pentagon report concludes that U.S. technology improved the reliability of Chinese space launchers and thus enhanced China's strategic nuclear missiles. The American company Hughes Electronics shared the technology with China during an investigation into the launch failure of a Hughes APSTAR II satellite. (4 pages)

(U) There is no indication in the Hughes/Apstar materials that the Chinese performed an independent investigation of the APSTAR II launch failure of the depth and intensity of the one conducted by and with Hughes.

(U) The conclusions outlined in the Hughes/Apstar materials provided to the Chinese (and reviewed by DoD for this assessment) were sufficiently specific to inform the Chinese of the kinds of launch vehicle design or operational changes that would make the LM-2E (and perhaps other launch vehicles as well) more reliable.

(U) Based on DoD's experience monitoring technical interchange meetings and related activities in connection with foreign launches of U.S. commercial satellites, it is reasonable to conclude that during the course of the five-month Hughes investigation there were significant interactions with the Chinese of a highly technical and specific nature that are not reflected in the Hughes/Apstar materials reviewed by DoD. It is likely that other documents exist that would shed additional light on Hughes' interactions with the Chinese. This would include information on the specific interactions at the sub-team level, and the deliberations of the Independent Team (about which DoD was only provided a one-page summary of conclusions) and the International Oversight Team (about which the documents reveal very little).

(U) Commerce has indicated it reviewed the documents supplied by Hughes in 1995 during the course of the investigation and which were provided to DoD in July 1998 for use in preparing this assessment. Commerce has stated that they determined in 1995 that the documents contained only information already authorized for export under the original Commerce license issued in February 1994.

CONCLUSIONS

(U) The provision of technical assistance in connection with the failure investigation to the Chinese by Hughes in the design, engineering, and operation of the Chinese launch vehicle and the Hughes satellite constitutes a "defense service" within the meaning of the State Department's International Traffic in Arms Regulations (ITAR) under the Arms Export Control Act (AECA). This was clearly beyond the scope of Commerce export control jurisdiction because only the Department of State is authorized to issue licenses for defense services.[3] The Commerce license issued for APSTAR II covered only the

---

[3] Section 120.9 of the International Traffic in Arms Regulations (ITAR) (22 C.F.R. Part 120.9) defines a "defense service" to include the furnishing to foreign persons of ITAR-controlled technical data or assistance (including training) in the design, development, engineering, manufacture, production, assembly, testing, repair, maintenance, modification, operation, demilitarization, destruction, processing or use of defense articles. Defense articles include a launch vehicle (ITAR Category IV) and a spacecraft, including satellites (ITAR Category XV), and specially designed or modified components, parts, attachments and associated equipment thereof. In this connection, all defense services for satellites and/or launch vehicles, including for compatibility, integration, or processing data are

10

export of the satellite and very limited technical data. There was no reasonable basis to conclude that a launch vehicle failure investigation of the scope evidenced in the documents would not be subject to State Department export control jurisdiction.

(U) The Hughes/Apstar materials reviewed by DoD reveal that the Chinese were provided with technical data and assistance from Hughes' failure investigation that enabled the Chinese launch manufacturer and launch service provider to make design and/or operational adjustments that improved launch vehicle reliability. They also reveal that the Chinese were provided practical insight into a diagnostic and failure analysis technique for identifying and isolating the cause of a launch failure.

(S/NF)

---

covered by the ITAR, even with respect to satellites subject to Commerce's license jurisdiction. (This was the case in 1994 and 1995 when Hughes sought export licenses for the Apstar II satellite launch and failure analysis, and remains true today.) Commerce's jurisdiction and licenses are limited to the APSTAR 2 satellite and technical data given to the launch provider (form, fit function, mass, electrical, mechanical, dynamic/environmental, telemetry, safety, facility, launch, access, and launch parameters) that describe the interfaces for mating and parameters for orbit (e.g. orbit, timing) of the satellite. See Note 1 to ITAR Category XV.

11

(U) The specific benefits derived from the APSTAR II launch failure investigation for Chinese missile programs did not likely alter the strategic military balance between the United States and China. However, in light of the strict standards of U.S. policy not to assist China in improving its satellite and missile-related capabilities, DoD believes that the scope and content of the launch failure investigation conducted by Hughes with the Chinese following the January 1995 APSTAR II failure raises national security concerns both with regard to violating those standards and to potentially contributing to China's missile capabilities. Therefore, the activities involved in the failure investigation warrant further inquiry to obtain a better understanding of the details of the technical assistance that Hughes provided the Chinese in order to judge the precise nature and seriousness of any impact on U.S. national security.

SECRET
24 January 1996

NOFORN

Nuclear Security and Proliferation

Control of Nuclear Weapons, Emerging Nuclear Powers, Proliferation Issues, Arms Control, Treaty Monitoring

China: Missile Technology Search

(S) Beijing may be trying to buy advanced technology associated with Moscow's SS-18/SATAN heavy ICBM. Although neither Moscow nor Kiev is likely to sell a complete SS-18 to Beijing, either might sell SS-18-related military technology or a booster for use as a space launch vehicle.

(S) East European attaches in Beijing said that when First Vice Chairman of the Central Military Commission Liu Huaqing visited Moscow in mid-December, the Chinese expressed great interest in purchasing SS-18 ICBM components. The Chinese reportedly claimed they were only interested in using SS-18 boosters for their civilian space launch programs.

UNCLASSIFIED

(C) An SS-18/SATAN in Its Launch Canister Without the Front Section. China may purchase technology related to this most lethal of Russia's ICBMs.

(S) The Ukrainian attache said the Chinese delegation approached Russian officials regarding a possible SS-18 ICBM purchase. Another East European attache, however, said Kiev was discussing an SS-18 deal with China.

Comment

(S) Ukrainian President Kuchma signed a space technology cooperation agreement with Beijing during his December visit to China. This arrangement reportedly creates a standing Sino-Ukrainian coordinating committee, but the two sides have not publicized specifics of this accord. Kuchma is a former director of the Yuzhnoye SS-18 production facility in Ukraine.

Military Intelligence Digest

SECRET

This 1996 Pentagon intelligence report reveals Chinese government efforts to buy SS-18 nuclear missile technology from Russia and Ukraine. (2 pages)

(S) Beijing has tested a series of Long March space launch vehicle (SLV) boosters and has invested heavily in its latest heavy-lift Long March 3B and 3C programs and the Long March 4-B booster. China's interest in using SS-18 boosters in its civilian space program seems odd because SS-18 engine characteristics may be incompatible with many sensitive satellite payloads. Beijing could be planning to develop a manned space vehicle under its new 5-year plan; Chinese interest in the Russian missile's engines may be linked to such a program.

(S) Even though Beijing claims it is pursuing SS-18 technology for its SLV program, any Chinese interest in the SATAN missile has military implications. Its inquiries are taking place as China is updating its strategic missile forces. Beijing is working on an improved version of the CSS-4 ICBM and seems to be planning to incorporate MIRV technology into its missile force.

(S) China's interest in Russian SS-18 military technology probably is linked to Beijing's strategic force modernization, particularly the areas of missile guidance, accuracy, rocket engines, and warhead improvements. Incorporating SS-18-related military guidance or warhead technologies into China's Strategic Missile Forces would greatly improve Beijing's ability to threaten targets in the United States.

"...SS-18-related military guidance or warhead technologies...would greatly improve Beijing's ability to threaten targets in the United States."

(S) Beijing already has a strong military technology-sharing arrangement with Moscow. Much of the missile and other arms-related technology flows from Russia to China outside official channels. Chinese scientists and institutes have approached Russian institutes directly for technology — including that related to ballistic missile guidance and control — that is unavailable through official channels. Many of these scientists have been recruited by the government to support its military upgrading plans. Russia has made no discernible effort to curtail these exchanges.

(S) Arms agreements permit other countries to use former ICBMs as SLV boosters as long as the nation of origin maintains control of all launch procedures. Considering the current scope of Russian arms and technology sales to China, however, Moscow may sell SS-18-associated military technology to Beijing.

(S) Neither Moscow nor Kiev is likely to sell a complete SS-18 ICBM to Beijing because neither would see such a sale as being in its national interest. Russia or Ukraine may be willing to transfer some sensitive military technologies associated with the SS-18 to support combined SLV and military projects with the Chinese. Many of these technologies could enable China to improve the reliability and accuracy of its strategic nuclear forces.

— Mr T. Woodrow and Mr M. Gorman, NMIPC, STU III (202) 231-4197,
DISTS 981-1873; MID 023-4A

* * *.* SECRET * * * *

NAIC–1442–0629–97 (10 December 1996)

 **Table of Contents** ➡ **Next Section** ❎ **Feedback**

Summary

(U) China has designed an upper rocket stage called the "Smart Dispenser" (SD) for a new space launch vehicle, derived from the CZ–2C, for the purpose of accurate and simultaneous deployment in orbit of two US–made Iridium mobile–telecommunications satellites. China currently has contracts for six such launches plus options for five more. A demonstration launch is currently planned for early 1997.

(U) The technology built into the SD stage has many potential uses beyond the Iridium mission. The SD stage will contain its own solid– and liquid–propulsion systems, avionics (including a guidance system), and telemetry systems which will provide the Chinese with new on–orbit maneuvering capabilities not previously available with past Chinese space launch vehicles.

(S) An initial NAIC study determined that a minimally–modified SD stage could be used on a ballistic missile as a multiple–reentry vehicle post–boost vehicle (PBV) but it would have poor capability in terms of its crossrange and downrange footprint. However, the stage could be developed into a credible PBV with a few relatively minor changes. Thus, the SD stage can be considered a "technology bridge" to a viable PBV. The same could be said for an orbital rendezvous platform for future manned missions or a co–orbital anti–satellite payload.

(C) The new space launch vehicle that will use the SD stage for launching Iridium satellites is currently called the CZ–2C/SD. Although all current Chinese launch vehicles use related technologies and sub–systems, the Iridium CZ–2C/SD launch vehicle is effectively a new launch vehicle, significantly modified from the original CZ–2C. Major differences include upgraded first and second–stage engines, a stretched second stage, an additional third stage (the SD stage), modified equipment bay, and a new fairing. The same designator was possibly kept in order for China to claim the reliability statistics of the CZ–2C.

❎ **Table of Contents** ➡ **Next Section** ❎ **Feedback**

* * * * SECRET * * * *

These excerpts from a 1996 Air Force National Air Intelligence Center report show how a Chinese commercial satellite launcher, built under contract with America's own Motorola, can be converted into a launcher for multiple nuclear warheads. (2 pages)

(S) An assessment was done on the SD stage to determine its viability for use as low performance post–boost vehicle (PBV) on the Mod CSS–4 ICBM. This effort was to assess the PBV performance of the SD stage with a minimum number of modifications. There is no data, whatsoever, that the Chinese have embarked on the development of a PBV based on the SD stage. This is simply an initial determination of feasibility. To date, the Chinese have expressed an interest in developing a multiple reentry vehicle capability that a PBV would provide, however, no known testing of such a system has occurred.

(S) The overall conclusion of this initial feasibility study shows that a minimally modified SD stage could be used to deploy multiple reentry vehicles (RVs). However, when compared to U.S. or Russian PBVs, it would be one of the least capable in terms of its crossrange and downrange footprint. However, with a few relatively minor changes beyond the ones mentioned below, the SD could easily become a credible PBV. Thus, it is concluded that the SD stage can be considered a "technology bridge" to a viable PBV.

(S) The following assumptions were made to constrain the SD–stage modifications. First, only the minimum number of changes would be allowed to the stage to get the job done. The system would not be needed for range extension since the missiles which would most likely use this system, the Mod CSS–4 and the DF–41, would have sufficient range already. The system would deploy three 470–kg Dong Feng 31 (DF–31) RVs. The system would not contain penetration aids (penaids). In addition, all 12 pitch/yaw thrusters would be used for axial thrust. Furthermore, it was assumed that these 70 N thrusters could withstand the full 128 second continuous burn. Additionally, the modified SD stage would have 20 degree/second rotation and turn rate. Lastly, the payload shroud would have a mass of about 200 kg and would be jettisoned early during second stage burn.

(S) Three modifications were identified, two significant and one minor. First, the 163–kg solid propellant kick stage was removed because of the no–range–extension assumption. Secondly, the six pitch and six yaw thrusters were rotated through 180 degrees to turn the PBV into a tractor system, minimizing the amount of fuel required for the deployment maneuvers. Lastly, the 15–kg thermal control system was removed. The masses of the conceptual PBV are shown in Table 3.

Table 3.
Modified SD PBV Mass Breakout (U)

Parameter	Value
Structure (Incl 3 RV ejectors)	260 kg
Guidance System	90 kg
Telemetry & Tracking System	40 kg
Attitude Control System (ACS, total)	80 kg
ACS (Dry)	28 kg
ACS Total Loaded Propellant	52 kg
Other	60 kg
Total	530 kg

SECRET

(S) A deployment scenario similar to that of the SS–19 Mod 3 PBV was used as it is relatively simple and effective. The RVs are evenly spaced on the PBV deck and mounted a triangular pattern. After booster burn–out, the PBV would rotate to the first null–range axis (NRA) or 180 degrees if a range extension is required. After rotation, the PBV would begin thrusting up the NRA. After a brief settling period, the first RV is deployed. The PBV would then continue to fly along the NRA (away from the just–separated RV) for three seconds. Next, the PBV would rotate and fly to the next

SECRET

NAIC-1030-098B-96
November 1996

Foreign Missile Update

(U) The purpose of this newsletter is to provide a timely update of the activities and developments of foreign countries in the area of ballistic missiles. Included is a list of current published products. Future issues of this newsletter will be published at least two times per year. If you have any questions on a technical highlight or are interested in any of the documents listed, please contact NAIC/TAB; commercial & Stu III (513) 257-2640, DSN & Stu III 787-2640.

Chinese ICBM Capability Steadily Increasing (S)

The DF-31 ICBM will give China a major strike capability that will be difficult to counterattack at any stage of its operation. It will be a significant threat not only to US forces deployed in the Pacific theater, but to portions of the continental United States and to many of our allies (S)

(S) After many delays, Beijing is proceeding with late-stage development of its DF-31 ICBM (Figure 1). This newest generation Chinese ballistic missile will narrow the gap between current Chinese, US, and Russian ballistic missile designs. The DF-31's mobility and defense-penetration ability will allow it to threaten parts of the continental United States and many US allies, as well as US forces in the Pacific theater.

(S) A probable payload test associated with the DF-31 has been postponed; possibly cancelled. By mid-October, the booster for this test had been removed from Pad D at Wuzhai. Simultaneously, two cold-launched ejection tests of DF-31 mass simulators, one of very high fidelity, were conducted. An integrated missile flight-test is likely within the next six months.

(S) The DF-31 development program is highly ambitious. Beijing's desire for a mobile 8000-km range ballistic missile (See Figures 2 and 3) incorporating many new or advanced technologies is presenting Chinese designers with substantial challenges. The DF-31 quite likely incorporates design aspects similar to those of current-generation Russian missiles. These could include upgraded mobility for the transporter-erector-launcher; advanced materials for the booster and payload; use of penetration aids such as decoys or chaff; and an improved solid propellant.

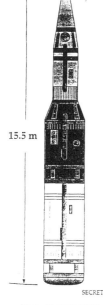

15.5 m

SECRET

Fig. 1 (S) DF-31 ICBM

Fig. 2 (S) Range of the DF-31 ICBM

1

SECRET

This November 1996 Air Force National Air Intelligence Center report exposes the threat posed by China's new mobile DF-31 intercontinental ballistic missile. (2 pages)

SECRET

NAIC-1030-098B-96
November 1996

(S) Since the 1991 Gulf War, China probably has reemphasized accuracy and defense penetration as primary goals for its developmental ballistic missiles. The Chinese gave evidence of this intent by testing two probable endoatmospheric reentry decoys on each of their two most recent ballistic missile R&D flight tests: a CSS-5 Mod 2 on 10 November 1995 and a CSS-5 Mod 1 on 10 January 1996. The de-

coys are designed to survive harsh atmospheric reentry conditions, and to simulate characteristics of the actual RV. The DF-31 ICBM is likely to use similar decoys and other types of penetration aids.

(S) The DF-31 ICBM will give China a major strike capability that will be difficult to counterattack at any stage of its operation, from pre-flight mobile operations through the terminal flight phase. After

the Chinese start to deploy DF-31s, about the turn of the century, Beijing probably will begin to decommission its operational force of CSS-3's. China will then be on its way to a ballistic missile force based around road-mobile systems. Road-mobility will greatly improve Chinese nuclear ballistic missile survivability and will complicate the task of defeating the Chinese threat.

Fig. 3 (S) Probable Launch Crew Training and TEL Checkout at Kangzhuang

2

SECRET

SECRET

R 070810Z AUG 98
FM AMEMBASSY SEOUL
TO SECSTATE WASHDC 2727
INFO AMEMBASSY BEIJING
AMEBASSY TOKYO
AMEBASSY MOSCOW
AMCONSUL SENYANG
AMCONSUL HONG KONG
AMEBASSY LONDON
AMEBASSY PARIS
AMEBASSY BONN
AIT TAIPEI 5359
SECDEF WASHDC//ISA//
CJCS WASHDC
USCINCPAC HONOLULU HI//FPA//
COMUSKOREA SEOUL KOR//J5//
USCINCUNC SEOUL KOR//UNCMAC/SA//

SECRET
EXDIS
SPECAT
E.O. 12958:DECL: (AFTER KOREAN REUNIFICATION)
TAGS: PGOV, PINS, PREL, ECON, KN

SUBJECT: THROUGH A GLASS DARKLY: REFLECTIONS ON NORTH KOREA

REF: SEOUL 3724
CLASSIFIED BY AMBASSADOR BOSWORTH. REASONS: 1.5 (B), (D)

INTRODUCTION AND SUMMARY

1.(C) THIS IS AN END-OF-TOUR ESSAY BY POL/EXT CHIEF LARRY ROBINSON, WHO HAS BEEN THE EMBASSY'S NORTH KOREAN WATCHER FOR THE PAST THREE YEARS. IT IS IN SOME SENSE A COMPANION PIECE TO REFTEL, WHICH ANALYZED PRESIDENT KIM DAE-JUNG'S "SUNSHINE POLICY TOWARD NORTH KOREA AND WHY THE NORTH WAS LIKELY TO VIEW IT AS MORE OF A THREAT THAN AN OPPORTU-NITY.

2. (S) THIS ESSAY FOCUSES ON NORTH KOREA'S INTERNAL SITUATION AND ITS RELATIONSHIP WITH THE U.S. IT CONCLUDES THAT:

— KIM JONG-IL IS A WEAK LEADER WHOSE SAVING GRACE IS HIS AWARENESS OF HIS OWN INADEQUACIES. HE KNOWS WHAT IS WRONG IN THE DPRK, BUT LACKS THE VISION, THE STRENGTH OF CHARACTER, AND THE LEGITIMACY TO CHANGE POLICY. ACCORDINGLY, HE APPEARS ALSO TO LACK THE ABILITY TO THINK SYS-TEMATICALLY, TREATING EACH OF THE ISSUES THAT COMES ACROSS HIS DESK IN ISOLATION. AT 56, HE CANNOT REALISTICALLY BE EXPECTED TO CHANGE PERSON-ALITY.

— OF KIM JONG-IL'S THREE MAIN POWER BASES — THE KOREAN WORKERS PARTY

These text excerpts from a 1998 cable from the U.S. embassy in South Korea reveal a looming crisis: North Korea is gradually disintegrating as a nation, and the Clinton administration's attempts at diplomacy have failed to adequately prepare the U.S. for the growing threat of North Korean collapse. (10 pages)

(KWP) APPARATUS, THE SOCIALIST YOUTH LEAGUE AND THE KOREAN PEOPLE'S ARMY (KPA) — ONLY LATTER IS FUNCTIONING NORMALLY. HIS CONTROL OVER THE KPA LOOKS SOLID, BUT THIS MAY BE DECEPTIVE; KIM HIMSELF DOES NOT APPEAR TO BELIEVE HE HAS A FIRM GRIP ON MILITARY LOYALTY.

— THE REST OF THE DPRK GOVERNMENT HAS LARGELY CEASED TO FUNCTION. THERE IS NO EVIDENCE THAT ANY OF THE MAJOR ORGANS OF STATE POWER HAS MET SINCE 1994. MINISTRIES GO THROUGH THE MOTIONS WITH NO CENTRAL COORDINATION . THE KWP HAS BEEN REDUCED TO THE ROLE OF CHEERLEADER AND HAGIOGRAPHER. A TOTALITARIAN SYSTEM CANNOT FUNCTION WITHOUT A PLAN, AND NORTH KOREA HAS NEITHER A PLAN NOR EVEN A BUDGET. A BYZAN-TINE FORM OF BUREAUCRATIC POLITICS IS PLAYED, THOUGH NOT ALONG THE SIM-PLE MFA VS KPA SPLIT THAT DPRK DIPLOMATS CLAIM.

— WITH NO SYSTEMATIC ALLOCATION OF RESOURCES, THE DPRK'S FORMAL ECON-OMY IS EFFECTIVELY DEFUNCT. PER CAPITA GNP MAY BE AS LOW AS THE $239 THAT PYONGYANG REPORTED TO THE UN LAST YEAR. FOOD SHORTAGES ARE JUST THE MOST VISIBLE SYMPTOM OF THIS UNPRECEDENTED COLLAPSE. IN ORDER TO ENABLE PEOPLE TO SURVIVE, NORTH KOREAN AUTHORITIES HAVE GRUDGINGLY ALLOWED THE EMERGENCE OF AN INFORMAL ECONOMY BASED LARGELY ON COR-RUPTION. THE UNTRAMMELED WORKINGS OF THIS PROTO-CAPITALIST ECONOMY HAVE HAD A DEVASTATING IMPACT ON SOCIAL ORDER AND STABILITY AND MAY HAVE REINFORCED NORTH KOREANS' AVERSION TO GENUINE MARKET REFORMS.

— NORTH KOREAN ELITES HAVE TO COPE WITH AN EXTRAORDINARY DEGREE OF COGNITIVE DISSONANCE: ALL THE INFORMATION THAT REACHES THEM ABOUT THE STATE OF THEIR COUNTRY AND THE REST OF THE WORLD IS IN FUNDAMENTAL CONFLICT WITH WHAT THEY ARE REQUIRED TO BELIEVE. AN APPARENTLY LARGE AND GROWING NUMBER OF THEM HAVE LOST THEIR FAITH IN THE OFFICIAL IDE-OLOGY. SOME ARE BEGINNING TO RISK DISCUSSING THE COUNTRY'S PROBLEMS WITH RELATIVES AND CLOSE FRIENDS. WITH THE SECURITY SERVICES INCREAS-INGLY SUSCEPTIBLE TO CORRUPTION, THESE DISCUSSIONS ARE LIKELY TO SPREAD AND INCREASE POLITICAL VOLATILITY.

— DESPITE ITS AVOWED POLICY OF "JUCHE," OR SELF-RELIANCE, NORTH KOREA HAS ALWAYS DEPENDED ON THE KINDNESS OF STRANGERS. KIM IL-SUNG WAS A MASTER AT MANIPULATING COLD WAR AND SINO-SOVIET TENSIONS TO KEEP THE SUBSIDIES-FLOWING. KIM JONG-IL HAS LOST THE LEVERAGE TO DO THIS, AS THE VIEWS OF ALL THE MAJOR OUTSIDE POWERS HAVE CONVERGED. BUT INSTEAD OF TAKING THE ADVICE THAT ALL THESE OUTSIDERS PRESS UPON HIM, KIM IS STILL LOOKING FOR A NEW, UNDEMANDING PATRON. AT HIS FATHER'S DIRECTION, HE HAS TRIED TO CAST THE U.S. IN THIS ROLE. THE UN AND THE SOUTH KOREAN CHAEBOL MAY BE THE NEXT TARGETS.

— PREDICTING THE TIMING AND NATURE OF A DPRK POLITICAL COLLAPSE IS IMPOSSIBLE. GENUINE REFORM IS CONCEIVABLE, IF UNLIKELY, AS IS AN EXTENDED PERIOD OF MUDDLING THROUGH, AND A DECISION TO GO TO WAR CANNOT BE RULED OUT. OF THE NUMEROUS OTHER SCENARIOS, MOST INVOLVE SOME KIND OF COUP AT SOME STAGE. WE DO NOT WANT THAT OUTCOME, AND SHOULD SEEK TO AVERT IT; BUT ASSUMING THAT OUR POLICIES WILL PREVENT IT IS A DANGEROUS TRAP.

— THERE IS NO "MAGIC BULLET" THAT WILL BRING ABOUT A MAJOR BREAK-THROUGH IN U.S.-DPRK RELATIONS. NEW INITIATIVES ARE LIKELY TO CONFUSE DPRK LEADERS AND ENCOURAGE THEM TO HOLD OUT FOR MORE. THE OFFERS WE HAVE ON THE TABLE ARE GOOD ONES. IF THE DPRK MAKES A FUNDAMENTAL DECISION TO COOPERATE, THE CURRENT OFFERS WILL BE MORE THAN ADEQUATE TO TRANSFORM THE RELATIONSHIP; ABSENT SUCH A DECISION, NOTHING IS GOING TO WORK. WE SHOULD BE FIRM, PATIENT AND PREDICTABLE IN PURSUING OUR CURRENT INITIATIVES; AND WE SHOULD DO A BETTER JOB OF FOLLOWING THROUGH ON OUR COMMITMENTS. AT THE SAME TIME, HOWEVER, WE NEED TO SUPPLEMENT PURSUIT OF OUR POSITIVE GOALS WITH PREPARATIONS FOR COLLAPSE—JUST AS OUR MILITARY PREPARATIONS FOR WAR SUPPLEMENT DETERRENCE.

END INTRODUCTION AND SUMMARY

THE INADEQUATE LEADER

3. (S) KIM JONG-IL REMAINS ONE OF THE MOST ENIGMATIC OF NATIONAL LEADERS. LIKE THE WIZARD OF OZ, HE HIDES BEHIND A SCREEN AND ISSUES PRONOUNCEMENTS THROUGH A MEGAPHONE. ENOUGH ANECDOTAL INFORMATION HAS SEEPED OUT OF NORTH KOREA THROUGH DEFECTORS AND VISITORS, HOWEVER, THAT WE CAN PIECE TOGETHER A REASONABLY COHERENT PICTURE OF THE MAN. WE KNOW, FOR INSTANCE, THAT HE HAS BEEN LIVING A LIE THROUGH MOST OF HIS LIFETIME: HIS "BIRTHPLACE" ON MT PAEKTU HAS BEEN RELOCATED AND REBUILT TO GIVE IT GREATER SYMBOLIC WEIGHT. BUT THE OLD GUARD AND MANY OF KIM'S INNER CIRCLE KNOW THAT HE WAS REALLY BORN IN KHABAROVSK, WHERE HIS FATHER WAS BUSY LIBERATING KOREA FROM JAPANESE RULE AS A MAJOR IN THE RED ARMY. WE KNOW THAT KIM JONG-IL HAD AN UNHAPPY CHILDHOOD, LOSING HIS ADORED MOTHER, AND YOUNGER BROTHER AS A BOY AND HATING HIS STEPMOTHER. HIS CAMPAIGN IN LATER 1997 TO DEIFY HIS MOTHER, AND HIS PERSISTENT EFFORTS TO MARGINALIZE HIS STEPMOTHER AND SIBLINGS, INDICATE THAT THIS ENMITY PERSISTS. HIS SISTER, KIM KYUNG-HEE, HAS PROBABLY BEEN HIS CLOSEST CONFIDANTE, THOUGH A REPORT IN FEBRUARY CLAIMED EVEN SHE HAD BEEN PURGED.

4. (C) IT IS ALSO REASONABLE TO ASSUME THAT KIM JONG-IL IDOLIZED HIS FATHER, WHO ENJOYED THE GENUINE ADULATION OF VIRTUALLY ALL NORTH KOREANS (AND THE GRUDGING ADMIRATION OF MANY IN THE SOUTH). IT DOES NOT APPEAR THAT THIS RESPECT WAS RECIPROCATED: THERE ARE NUMEROUS STORIES OF PUT-DOWNS BY FATHER TO SON, INCLUDING KIM JONG-IL'S OWN CURIOUS ADMISSION IN HIS SPEECH AT KIM IL-SUNG UNIVERSITY IN DECEMBER 1996 THAT HIS FATHER ALWAYS TOLD HIM TO LEAVE ECONOMIC DECISION-MAKING TO OTHERS. AND ACCORDING TO THE FORMER PLAYMATE OF KIM JONG-IL'S OLDEST SON, WHO LIVED IN HIS HOUSE FOR SEVERAL YEARS, KIM IL-SUNG NEVER ONCE CAME TO VISIT.

5. (S) KIM IL-SUNG WAS EVERYTHING HIS SON WAS NOT — PHYSICALLY IMPOSING, AN ELOQUENT PUBLIC SPEAKER, A CHARISMATIC LEADER, A COMMANDER WHO LED FROM THE FRONT WITH GENUINE (IF EXAGGERATED) MILITARY CREDENTIALS. KIM JONG-IL, BY CONTRAST, IS SO UNPREPOSSESSING THAT RUSSIAN AND CHINESE DIPLOMATS TELL US THEIR LEADERS HAVE MET HIM FREQUENTLY IN COMPANY WITH HIS FATHER, BUT NONE CAN REMEMBER HAVING DONE SO. WHILE SEVERAL PEOPLE WHO HAVE MET THE YOUNGER KIM IN PRIVATE DESCRIBE HIM AS AN

INTELLIGENCE AND ARTICULATE INTERLOCUTOR, THE FACT THAT HE HAS NEVER ATTEMPTED MORE THAN ONE SENTENCE IN A PUBLIC VENUE LENDS CREDENCE TO THE PERSISTENT RUMORS THAT HE STUTTERS UNDER PRESSURE. HE IS CLEARLY A VERY SHY PERSON, SKIPPING MOST PUBLIC CEREMONIES (EVEN FOR HIS OWN BIRTHDAY) AND SOCIALIZING ONLY WITH A TINY COHORT OF FRIENDS. HIS SON'S PLAYMATE SAID HE ALMOST INVARIABLY TOOK BOTH LUNCH AND SUPPER AT HOME, AND HER BROTHER SAID KIM WORKED ALMOST EXCLUSIVELY AT NIGHT, WITH SHIFTS OF TYPISTS TO TRANSCRIBE AND DISTRIBUTE HIS ORDERS.

6. (S) ACCORDING TO HWANG JANG-YOP, KIM IL-SUNG AND KIM JONG-IL WERE ACUTELY AWARE OF THE LATTER'S LIMITATIONS, AND SPENT TWO DECADES CON-STRUCTING A GOVERNMENTAL STRUCTURE THAT HE — AND ONLY HE — COULD CONTROL. KIM JONG-IL RULES MOSTLY BY TELEPHONE AND FAX, SELDOM SEEING EVEN SENIOR PARTY OFFICIALS. HIS PUBLIC APPEARANCES ARE CAREFULLY SCRIPTED SET-PIECES, MORE LIKE THOSE OF THE BRITISH ROYAL FAMILY THAN HIS FATHER'S "ON THE SPOT GUIDANCE."

7. (C) DESPITE HIS SECLUSION, KIM JONG-IL APPEARS TO HAVE A REASONABLY GOOD GRASP OF NORTH KOREA'S PROBLEMS, AS EVIDENCED BY HIS DECEMBER 1996 SPEECH. HE REPORTEDLY DISTRUSTS OFFICIAL REPORTS (WITH GOOD REA-SON), AND MAINTAINS SEPARATE INFORMAL CHANNELS THROUGH CLOSE AIDES. NUMEROUS REPORTS INDICATE HE ALSO FOLLOWS WORLD EVENTS AVIDLY THROUGH TRANSLATED TRANSCRIPTS OF INTERNATIONAL BROADCASTS AND PRINT MEDIA. IN CONVERSATIONS WITH KIDNAPPED SOUTH KOREAN FILM DIREC-TOR SIN SANG-OK IN THE MID-1980'S, KIM ACKNOWLEDGED THAT THE LACK OF MATERIAL INCENTIVES UNDER SOCIALISM GUARANTEED POOR ECONOMIC AND CULTURAL PERFORMANCE, AND NORTH KOREA COULD SUCCEED ONLY BY OPEN-ING UP TO THE OUTSIDE WORLD.

8. (C) BUT WHILE KIM'S ANALYSIS CAN BE PERCEPTIVE, HE SELDOM FOLLOWS HIS OWN LOGIC IN PRESCRIBING SOLUTIONS. IN HIS CONVERSATIONS WITH SIN, HE PROPOSED REINVIGORATING DPRK FILM-MAKING NOT BY INTRODUCING MATER-IAL INCENTIVES, BUT BY KIDNAPPING MORE SOUTH KOREAN ARTISTS. THE PRE-SCRIPTIVE PART OF HIS DECEMBER 1996 SPEECH FOLLOWED THE SAME PATTERN: INTENSIFICATION OF THE POLICIES THAT HAD ALREADY FAILED. WHETHER THIS DISCONNECT FLOWS FROM A LACK OF IMAGINATION, WEAKNESS OF CHARACTER, A PERCEPTION THAT HIS LEGITIMACY IS TOO WEAK TO CHALLENGE HIS FATHER'S LEGACY, OR SOME COMBINATION OF THESE REMAINS AN OPEN QUESTION.

9. (S) ONE OF THE MOST STRIKING INSIGHTS PROVIDED BY HWANG JANG-YOP — AND CONFIRMED BY OTHER SOURCES — IS THAT KIM JONG-IL HANDLES EACH OF THE MYRIAD ISSUES FOR DECISION THAT CROSS HIS DESK IN ISOLATION, WITH LIT-TLE OR NO THOUGHT TO THEIR IMPACT ON EACH OTHER. TOLD OF A PARTICULAR PROBLEM IN ONE FACTORY OR CITY, HE ISSUES INSTRUCTIONS TO GIVE TOP PRIOR-ITY TO SOLVING IT — THEN PROCEEDS TO GIVE TOP PRIORITY TO OTHER PROB-LEMS THAT DEMAND THE SAME RESOURCES. THIS IS REFLECTED IN OFFICIAL POLICY STATEMENTS OVER THE PAST FOUR YEARS THAT GIVE TOP PRIORITY TO OTHER PROBLEMS THAT DEMAND THE SAME RESOURCES. THIS IS REFLECTED IN OFFICIAL POLICY STATEMENTS OVER THE PAST FOUR YEARS THAT GIVE TOP PRI-ORITY TO AGRICULTURE, LIGHT INDUSTRY AND EXPORTS, BUT CONTINUE TO GIVE THE SAME TOP PRIORITY TO MINERAL EXTRACTION AND HEAVY INDUSTRY. THE

RESULT IS A CHAOTIC SITUATION IN WHICH PRIORITIES ARE CONSTANTLY SHIFT-
ING AND NO PROBLEM RECEIVES SUSTAINED ATTENTION.

10. (C) SIMILARLY, KIM APPEARS TO PRACTICE TO A DEBILITATING DEGREE THE
CLASSIC POLITICIAN'S PRACTICE OF TELLING EACH AUDIENCE WHAT IT WANTS TO
HEAR. WE HAVE HEARD SEVERAL SECOND-HAND ACCOUNTS OF HIS ASSURANCES
TO REFORM-MINDED INTELLECTUALS THAT HE PLANS TO CONDUCT CHINESE-
STYLE REFORM AND OPENING AS SOON AS THE TIME IS RIGHT. YET EVERY MAJOR
OFFICIAL POLICY STATEMENT SINCE HIS FATHER'S DEATH ECHOES HIS PLEDGE
AFTER THE FUNERAL: "DON'T EXPECT ANY CHANGES FROM ME." THIS MAY HELP
EXPLAIN TWO COINCIDENCES THAT DESTROYED REFORM INITIATIVES: THE 1996
SUBMARINE INCURSION JUST AS THE RAJIN-SONBONG INVESTMENT FORUM
CLOSED, AND THE 1998 INCURSIONS IMMEDIATELY AFTER HYUNDAI CHAIRMAN
CHUNG JU-YONG'S VISIT.

11. (S) EVEN IF THIS PSYCHOLOGICAL PROFILE OF KIM IS ACCURATE, THERE
REMAINS THE QUESTION OF WHETHER HE CAN CHANGE AS HE MATURES IN OFFICE
AND CONSOLIDATES HIS POWER. THERE IS SOME EVIDENCE OF SUCH CHANGE.
SOME REPORTING INDICATES HE HAS CUT BACK ON HIS PREVIOUSLY HEAVY
DRINKING SINCE HIS FATHER'S DEATH, AND THAT HE PARTICIPATES LESS IN WILD
PARTIES. MORE IMPORTANTLY, HIS PREVIOUS REPUTATION FOR IMPETUOUSNESS
HAS BEEN BELIED BY THE CAUTIOUS, RISK-AVERSE APPROACH HE HAS TAKEN TO
MAJOR DECISIONS SINCE HIS FATHER'S DEATH. BEYOND THIS, HOWEVER, IT IS
UNREALISTIC TO EXPECT FUNDAMENTAL PERSONALITY SHIFTS FROM A 56-YEAR-
OLD MAN WHO HAS BEEN RUNNING HIS COUNTRY ON A DAY-TO-DAY BASIS FOR
TWO DECADES.

SHAKY POWER BASES

...

14. (C) KIM'S RELATIONSHIP WITH THE REVOLUTIONARY OLD GUARD OF HIS
FATHER'S GENERATION APPEAR TO BE SOMEWHAT UNEASY, GIVEN THE EXTENSIVE
PURGES HE AND HIS FATHER CONDUCTED OF ALL THOSE WHO OPPOSED HIS
DYNASTIC SUCCESSION. HE HAS STRESSED THE NEED TO RESPECT ELDERS, BUT IN
PRACTICE HE APPEARS TO BYPASS THEM ALMOST ENTIRELY , WORKING INSTEAD
THROUGH THE SECRETARIAT AND LOWER RANKING OFFICIALS MORE NEARLY HIS
OWN AGE.

15 (C) THAT LEAVES THE KOREAN PEOPLE'S ARMY, THE MOST POWERFUL, MOST
FAVORED AND PROBABLY MOST EFFECTIVE ORGAN OF STATE POWER. KIM BECAME
SUPREME COMMANDER OF THE KPA AND CHAIRMAN OF THE NATIONAL DEFENSE
COMMISSION IN THE EARLY 1990'S, AND HAS BEEN ACTING CHAIRMAN OF THE
KWP MILITARY AFFAIRS COMMITTEE SINCE HIS FATHER'S DEATH. SINCE, 1994 HE
HAS RULES PRIMARILY THROUGH THE MILITARY, USING IT INCREASINGLY TO MAN-
AGE OR SUPERVISE NORMALLY CIVILIAN FUNCTIONS SUCH AS INFRASTRUCTURE
DEVELOPMENT AND AGRICULTURE. MOST OF HIS PERSONAL APPEARANCES HAVE
BEEN AT MILITARY INSTALLATIONS, EVEN AFTER HIS ACCESSION TO GENERAL SEC-
RETARY OF THE KWP IN OCTOBER 1997. DPRK USES THE TITLE OF "RESPECTED AND
BELOVED GENERAL" FOR KIM ALMOST AS OFTEN AS THE MORE EXALTED "GREAT

LEADER," AND IN RECENT YEARS HAS INTRODUCED A NEW FORMULATION EQUAT-
ING THE ARMY WITH THE PEOPLE, THE STATE AND THE PARTY. SEVERAL SOUTH
KOREAN ANALYSTS HAVE ASSESSED THAT HE WAS CONVERTING THE DPRK INTO A
MILITARY DICTATORSHIP.

16. (S) THE KPA WOULD THUS APPEAR TO BE THE MAIN BULWARK OF KIM JONG-IL'S
RULE. HWANG HAS CONFIRMED THIS, CLAIMING THAT THE ARMY FOLLOWS HIS
ORDERS BLINDLY AND WITHOUT QUESTION, AND EVEN SOME KPA DEFECTORS
INSIST THAT KIM IS A BRILLIANT MILITARY COMMANDER. BUT THESE APPEAR-
ANCES MAY BE DECEPTIVE. THERE IS EXTENSIVE EVIDENCE OF A MAJOR COUP
ATTEMPT BY ELEMENTS OF THE VI CORPS IN 1995, WHICH APPEARS TO HAVE BEEN
CRUSHED ONLY WITH SOME DIFFICULTY. THERE HAVE BEEN RUMORS OF OTHER
LESS SERIOUS MILITARY UPRISINGS AND ASSASSINATION ATTEMPT. AND WHILE
THE KPA HAS FIRST CALL ON ALL THE NATION'S RESOURCES, IT TOO HAS SUF-
FERED FROM THE FOOD SHORTAGES AND ECONOMIC COLLAPSE. RECENT DEFEC-
TORS CONSISTENTLY ASSERT THAT MILITARY DISCIPLINE HAS ERODED, AND THAT
GANGS OF SOLDIERS ROUTINELY PREY ON CIVILIANS.

17. (C) MORE SPECULATIVELY, ONE HAS TO WONDER ABOUT THE REACTION OF ANY
MILITARY ESTABLISHMENT TO A SUPREME COMMANDER WHO (UNLIKE MOST OF
THE MALE POPULATION) NEVER SPENT A DAY IN UNIFORM UNTIL HIS APPOINT-
MENT AS MARSHAL, WHO HAS A SPECTACULAR LACK OF MILITARY BEARING, WHO
HAS NEVER OBSERVED A MILITARY EXERCISE, AND WHO DEVOTES MOST OF HIS
TIME WITH THEM TO WATCHING SONG AND DANCE PERFORMANCES. TO THE
EXTENT THAT THERE ARE GENUINELY PROFESSIONAL SOLDIERS IN THE UPPER
REACHES OF THE KPA (AS OPPOSED TO PARTY HACKS IN UNIFORM), THEY MUST BE
CONCERNED ABOUT HIS LACK OF EXPERIENCE AND QUESTIONABLE JUDGEMENT.
MOST TELLINGLY, KIM HIMSELF DOES NOT ACT IN THE WAY ONE WOULD EXPECT
OF A CONFIDENT COMMANDER. THE FACTS THAT HE HAS PROMOTED 922 OFFICERS
TO MAJOR GENERAL OR ABOVE SINCE 1992 (A PERIOD DURING WHICH SENIOR
LEVEL PROMOTIONS IN THE CIVILIAN BUREAUCRACY HAVE BEEN ESSENTIALLY
FROZEN), AND THAT HE HAS LAVISHED CARS AND OTHER EXPENSIVE PRESENTS ON
FIELD COMMANDERS, MAY INDICATE MERELY HIS FASCINATION WITH THINGS MIL-
ITARY, BUT THEY CAN ALSO BE INTERPRETED AS AN ATTEMPT TO BUY OFF AN
ESTABLISHMENT WHOSE LOYALTY IS VITAL TO REGIME SURVIVAL, BUT OF WHICH
HE IS NOT CONFIDENT.

AD HOC GOVERNANCE

18. (C) APART FROM THE KPA IT IS DIFFICULT TO FIND MUCH EVIDENCE THAT THE
DPRK GOVERNMENT IS FUNCTIONING....

21 (C) THE MOST STRIKING FEATURE OF NORTH KOREA'S GOVERNANCE IS THAT IT
IS A PLANNED ECONOMY WITHOUT A PLAN. IN THIS, IT IS UNIQUE IN THE HISTORY
OF LENINIST STATES (WITH THE POSSIBLE EXCEPTION OF CHINA DURING THE CUL-
TURAL REVOLUTION). ...

24. (C) WITH NO PLAN OR BUDGET, AND WITH PRIORITIES CONSTANTLY SHIFTING
AT THE WHIM OF KIM JONG-IL, NORTH KOREA'S OFFICIAL CIVILIAN ECONOMY HAS
EFFECTIVELY GROUND TO A HALT....

26 (C) INTERNATIONAL ATTENTION TO THE DPRK ECONOMY HAS FOCUSED MAINLY
ON ITS FOOD SHORTAGES. WHILE MOST CURRENT ANECDOTAL REPORTING INDI-
CATES A SOMEWHAT BETTER SITUATION THIS SUMMER THAN IN THE PREVIOUS
TWO YEARS, THERE IS NO QUESTION THAT THE SHORTAGE REMAINS SEVERE, AND
THE CUMULATIVE IMPACT OVER THE PAST SEVERAL YEARS MAY ULTIMATELY
PROVE TO BE ONE OF THE MOST LETHAL FAMINES OF THE CENTURY. NO GOOD
STATISTICAL EVIDENCE IS AVAILABLE (THE NORTH KOREANS LIE EGREGIOUSLY IN
SEVERAL DIRECTIONS AT THE SAME TIME), BUT SEVERAL INDEPENDENT SOURCES
— HWANG JANG-YOP, ANOTHER DEFECTOR FROM THE DPRK'S MISSION TO THE
FAO, A SURVEY OF REFUGEES IN CHINA BY THE KOREAN BUDDHIST SHARING
MOVEMENT, AND MOST RECENTLY A CHINESE ANALYSIS OF VOTER ROLLS FOR THE
UPCOMING SPA ELECTIONS — ALL INDICATE A TOTAL PREMATURE MORTALITY
COUNT SINCE 1995 IN THE 2-3 MILLION RANGE, SOME 10-15 PERCENT OF THE POPU-
LATION. THAT WOULD BE TWICE AS BAD, ON A PERCENTAGE BASIS AS THE HOR-
RENDOUS CHINESE FAMINE OF 1959-62.

30. (C) … WHILE THERE IS LITTLE MONEY IN THE ECONOMY, THERE APPEARS TO
HAVE BEEN MASSIVE TRANSFER OF WEALTH, ALONG THREE DIFFERENT DIMEN-
SIONS. MONEY AND GOODS HAVE FLOWED FROM PREVIOUSLY FAVORED INDUS-
TRIAL WORKERS TO THE PEASANTS, AS TOWNSPEOPLE SELL OR BARTER
WHATEVER THEY HAVE TO GET FOOD. WEALTH HAS FLOWED FROM NORTH KOREA
INTO CHINA, AGAIN IN EXCHANGE FOR FOOD, AND THE MOST RUTHLESS AND COR-
RUPT TRADERS AND OFFICIALS MILK THE REST OF THE POPULATION, PRODUCING
GREATER DISPARITIES IN LIVING STANDARDS THAN THE DPRK HAS EVEN SEEN.
DEFECTOR REPORTS INDICATE THAT THESE FLOWS ARE BITTERLY RESENTED BY
THE LOSERS, ACCELERATING THE BREAKDOWN OF SOCIAL ORDER AND RESPECT
FOR AUTHORITY. IN ADDITION TO THE OBVIOUS PROBLEMS THIS POSES FOR
REGIME STABILITY, THERE IS ALSO A RISK THAT NORTH KOREANS WILL EQUATE
MARKETIZATION WITH MISERY, BUTTRESSING IDEOLOGICAL RESISTANCE TO GEN-
UINE REFORMS….

COGNITIVE DISSONANCE

33. (S) THERE IS A GROWING BODY OF REPORTING THAT INDICATES PEOPLE IN
NORTH KOREA ARE LOSING FAITH IN KIM JONG-IL AND MUCH OF THE BELIEF
STRUCTURE OF WHICH HE IS THE LINCHPIN. MOST OF THESE ACCOUNTS COME
FROM DEFECTORS, AND HENCE HAVE TO BE DISCOUNTED SOMEWHAT. BUT THE
INCREASING FLOW OF DEFECTORS ITSELF (AND FROM INCREASINGLY ELITE BACK-
GROUNDS) INDICATES THAT THE PROCESS IS UNDERWAY. RECENT DEFECTORS
TALK OF WIDESPREAD MUTTERING THAT KIM JONG-IL'S REIGN HAS BEEN A DISAS-
TER, THAT KWP CADRES ARE UNIVERSALLY CORRUPT, AND THAT EVEN A LOSING
WAR WOULD BE PREFERABLE TO THE CURRENT SITUATION. EVEN HWANG JANG-
YOP, WHO DISMISSES MOST NORTH KOREANS AS MINDLESS SLAVES, CLAIMS
THERE ARE SIGNIFICANT ELEMENTS WHO WANT REVOLUTIONARY CHANGE. EVI-
DENCE FROM WITHIN NORTH KOREA IS UNDERSTANDABLY SCANTY, BUT IT DOES
EXIST. IN ONE CASE A SENIOR AGRICULTURAL OFFICIAL TOLD AN AMERICAN VISI-
TOR THAT ALL GOVERNMENT AGRICULTURAL STATISTICS WERE LIES. ANOTHER
OFFICIAL ACKNOWLEDGED THAT THE OFFICIAL PROPAGANDA WAS NONSENSE,
BUT MAINTAINED IT WAS NECESSARY TO KEEP THE MASSES QUIET.

35. (S) IT IS IMPOSSIBLE TO ASCERTAIN AT THIS POINT HOW FAR THE LOSS OF FAITH HAS SPREAD OR THE EXTENT TO WHICH PEOPLE ARE BEGINNING TO RISK SHARING THEIR DOUBTS WITH OTHERS. UNTIL RECENTLY, THIS WOULD HAVE BEEN INCONCEIVABLE, GIVEN NORTH KOREA'S HUGE AND OVERLAPPING SECURITY APPARATUS. BUT WE KNOW THAT SOME DISCUSSIONS ARE TAKING PLACE — HWANG WAS PART OF ONE CONSPIRACY, OTHER DEFECTORS HAVE MENTIONED CONVERSATIONS WITH RELATIVES AND FRIENDS. THERE IS GROWING EVIDENCE OF THE SUSCEPTIBILITY OF POLICE AND STATE SECURITY OFFICIALS TO CORRUPTION. AT SOME POINT IF CHINA'S EXAMPLE IS A GUIDE, IT WILL BE POSSIBLE TO BRIBE OR OTHERWISE PERSUADE THEM TO LOOK THE OTHER WAY. WHEN THAT HAPPENS, THE LOSS OF FAITH IS LIKELY TO SPREAD VERY RAPIDLY. THE DPRK HAS A HIGHLY DEVELOPED, RIGID AND COMPREHENSIVE IDEOLOGY, AND A BELIEF STRUCTURE OF THAT SORT MIGHT TEND TO SHATTER RATHER THAN EVOLVE. WHAT, IF ANYTHING, THE DISAFFECTED ELITES WILL DO ABOUT THEIR LOSS OF FAITH IS HARD TO SAY, BUT IT WILL CERTAINLY CONTRIBUTE GREATLY TO POLITICAL VOLATILITY.

LOOKING FOR MR. GOODBAR

...

37. (C) AT SOME POINT IN THE EARLY 1990'S, KIM IL-SUNG APPARENTLY CONCLUDED THAT HIS FORMER FRIENDS WERE NO LONGER WILLING OR ABLE TO HELP, AND HE BEGAN CASTING ABOUT FOR A NEW PATRON. THIS DECISION PROBABLY EXPLAINS MUCH OF THE FLURRY OF DPRK DIPLOMATIC OUTREACH IN THE FIRST HALF OF THE DECADE, INCLUDING THE NORTH-SOUTH BASIC AGREEMENT, NORMALIZATION TALKS WITH JAPAN AND THE DIALOGUE WITH THE U.S. THAT PRODUCED THE AGREED FRAMEWORK. AT THE TIME OF KIM IL-SUNG'S DEATH, ALL THREE INITIATIVES LOOKED LIKELY TO PROVIDE LARGE-SCALE BENEFITS. KIM JONG-IL HAS BEEN FAR LESS ADEPT AT MANIPULATING EXTERNAL POWERS. LIKE HIS FATHER, HE TRIED TO USE BOTH CARROTS AND STICKS, BUT THEY HAVE TENDED TO CANCEL OUT RATHER THAN REINFORCE EACH OTHER. HE HAS ALSO BEEN STYMIED BY THE GROWING CONVERGENCE OF VIEWS ABOUT THE KOREAN PENINSULA BY ALL THE MAJOR POWERS., FROM CHINA, RUSSIA, SOUTH KOREA, THE U.S., JAPAN, AND THE EU, HE NOW GETS ESSENTIALLY THE SAME MESSAGE — WE'LL PROVIDE MODEST HUMANITARIAN AIDE, AND ARE WILLING TO GIVE MUCH MORE, BUT ONLY IF YOU REFORM.

PROSPECTS

40. (S) PREDICTING REGIME COLLAPSE IN NORTH KOREA HAS PROVEN AN EMBARRASSMENT TO A VARIETY OF OFFICIALS AND ACADEMICS FROM THE ROK, THE U.S. AND ELSEWHERE. FORMER ROK PRESIDENT KIM YOUNG-SAM EXPECTED THE COLLAPSE DURING HIS ADMINISTRATION AND ACCORDING TO SOME REPORTS, LAUNCHED COVERT ACTIONS TO FACILITATE IT. FORMER USFK CINC GENERAL LUCK TOLD CONGRESS TWO YEARS AGO THAT A COLLAPSE WAS LIKELY WITHIN A YEAR OR TWO. MANY OTHER SUCH PREDICTIONS HAVE BEEN SIMILARLY REFUTED BY EVENTS. THERE ARE SIMPLY TOO MANY UNKNOWN VARIABLES — THE RESILIENCE OF THE NORTH KOREAN PEOPLE, THE COERCIVE POWER OF THE REGIME, THE LEVEL OF OUTSIDE AID — TO MAKE FORECASTS OF NORTH KOREA'S FUTURE ANYTHING BUT A GAME FOR FOOLS. IT IS STILL CONCEIVABLE (THOUGH HIGHLY UNLIKELY) THAT KIM WILL LEAD THE DPRK TOWARD GENUINE REFORM

AND OPENNESS, AND SUCCEED AS CHINA AND VIETNAM HAVE DONE. WITH LESS FAR-REACHING REFORMS, THE DPRK COULD PROBABLY MUDDLE THROUGH FOR A CONSIDERABLE NUMBER OF YEARS, AND IT IS DANGEROUS TO RULE OUT THE POSSIBILITY OF A QUIXOTIC INVASION OF THE SOUTH, SHOULD KIM CONCLUDE THAT THE ODDS AGAINST MILITARY SUCCESS ARE NO LONGER THAN THOSE FOR OTHER ALTERNATIVES.

41. (S) WHILE ALL THESE ARE POSSIBILITIES, AND THERE IS NO SINGLE OUTCOME THAT APPROACHES A 50-50 PROBABILITY, THE LARGEST SINGLE SET OF FORESEEABLE SCENARIOS INVOLVE SOME FORM OF INTERNAL SYSTEM TRANSFORMATION THROUGH A COMBINATION OF COLLAPSE AND REVOLUTION. THERE IS A WIDE RANGE OF PATHS THIS PROCESS COULD TAKE, INCLUDING ANARCHY, FACTIONAL CONFLICT AND REGIONAL WARLORDISM. ALL OF THESE SCENARIOS, HOWEVER INVOLVE A CHANGE OF TOP LEADERSHIP AT SOME POINT. IF KIM JONG-IL FAILS TO LEAD NORTH KOREA IN A NEW DIRECTION, IT IS NEARLY INEVITABLE THAT HE WILL BE REPLACED BY SOMEONE WHO WILL. GIVEN THE FACT THAT HIS LEGITIMACY AS LEADER IS SO CLOSELY TIED UP WITH KIM IL-SUNG'S LEGACY, IT IS HIGHLY UNLIKELY THAT ANY OTHER MEMBER OF THE KIM CLAN CAN TAKE OVER; NONE OF THEM HAS ANY MORE PERFORMANCE LEGITIMACY THAN HE, AND NONE WAS KIM IL-SUNG'S CHOICE. THE ORIENTATION OF A SUCCESSOR REGIME CANNOT BE PREDICTED, BUT IT WOULD QUITE LIKELY HAVE TO INCLUDE A LARGE MILITARY COMPONENT.

42. (S) A NORTH KOREAN COLLAPSE INTO REVOLUTION WOULD BE A HUMANITARIAN DISASTER AT BEST, A GRAVE SECURITY THREAT TO THE REGION AT WORST. THERE IS NOT QUESTION THAT IT SHOULD RANK VERY LOW IN EVERY OTHER GOVERNMENT'S HIERARCHY OF PREFERRED OUTCOMES, AND THAT ALL OF US SHOULD DEVOTE OUR EFFORTS TO AVERT IT, AS THE KIM DAE-JUNG GOVERNMENT HAS PLEDGED TO DO. BUT IT IS A DANGEROUS TRAP FOR ANY OF US TO ASSUME THAT COLLAPSE WILL NOT HAPPEN BECAUSE NO ONE WANTS IT TO. AS LONG AS NO OUTSIDE POWER IS PREPARED TO TAKE ON THE RESPONSIBILITIES OF PROPPING UP THE KIM REGIME REGARDLESS OF ITS ACTIONS, COLLAPSE WILL REMAIN A DEFINITE POSSIBILITY AT SOME POINT IN THE INDEFINITE FUTURE.

U.S. RESPONSE

43. (S) IF THE EXPERIENCE OF OUTSIDE POWERS IN DEALING WITH NORTH KOREA HAS TAUGHT US ANYTHING, IT IS THAT THERE IS NO "MAGIC BULLET" THAT WILL TRANSFORM OUR RELATIONSHIP WITH THE DPRK INTO A GENUINELY COOPERATIVE ONE. IT IS IN THE NATURE OF AMERICAN POLITICAL PSYCHOLOGY TO SEEK SUCH A BREAKTHROUGH, BUT NOTHING WE KNOW ABOUT THE DPRK OFFERS ANY REASON FOR OPTIMISM THAT WE CAN ACHIEVE ONE. A MAJOR STUDY BY THE COUNCIL ON FOREIGN RELATIONS RECENTLY PROPOSED A GREATLY EXPANDED "PACKAGE DEAL" THAT WOULD TRADE COMPREHENSIVE SANCTIONS EASING AND LARGE-SCALE AID FOR DRAMATIC DPRK STEPS TO STOP THREATENING ITS NEIGHBORS. ONE OF THE STUDY'S AUTHORS TOLD US THE CFR GROUP TOOK THE AGREED FRAMEWORK'S NEGOTIATIONS AS A MODEL, AND PARTICULARLY FORMER PRESIDENT CARTER'S DRAMATIC VISIT TO PYONGYANG WHERE THE ELEMENTS OF THE DEAL WERE AGREED. BUT THIS COMPARISON IS FALLACIOUS. IT IGNORES THE FACT THAT WE ARE NOW DEALING WITH A MUCH WEAKER DPRK LEADER, AND THAT THE AGREED FRAMEWORK ALREADY STRETCHED THE LIMITS OF WHAT IS

POLITICALLY DOABLE IN THE U.S. ROK AND JAPAN. IT ALSO IGNORES THE FACT THAT NOTHING IN THE KIM-CARTER AGREEMENT WAS NEW — ALL OF THE ELEMENTS HAD BEEN UNDER NEGOTIATION FOR A YEAR, AND THE ONE CENTRAL ELEMENT (THE LIGHT WATER REACTOR) WAS A DPRK PROPOSAL. THERE IS NO REASON TO BELIEVE THAT A FULLY-FLEDGED INITIATIVE PROPOSED BY THE USG WOULD MEET WITH ANYTHING BUT PROFOUND SUSPICION, PARTICULARLY IF IT REQUIRED PYONGYANG TO GIVE UP THE ONLY THING THAT MAKES IT OF INTEREST TO THE REST OF THE WORLD — ITS ABILITY TO CAUSE TROUBLE.

44. (S) WHILE NORTH KOREA IS CLEARLY IN DIRE STRAITS, ITS LEADERS DO NOT AT THIS POINT APPEAR DESPERATE ENOUGH TO ACCEPT THE RISKS TO REGIME STABILITY THAT WOULD BE INHERENT IN A DECISION TO MOVE TO A FUNDAMENTALLY COOPERATIVE RELATIONSHIP WITH THE U.S. OR ROK. IF THEY MAKE THAT DECISION, WE ALREADY HAVE AMPLE MECHANISMS IN PLACE TO MOVE FORWARD ON ALL FRONTS AT WHATEVER SPEED THE DPRK CAN ACCOMMODATE. UNTIL AND UNLESS THAT DECISION IS MADE, NO INITIATIVE ON OUR PART IS GOING TO PRODUCE SATISFACTORY RESULTS.

45. (C) RECOGNIZING THE RISK-AVERSE NATURE OF THE DPRK'S CURRENT LEADERSHIP, WE SHOULD STRIVE TO BE AS PREDICTABLE AS POSSIBLE. FIRMNESS AND PATIENCE IN PURSUING REASONABLE DEMANDS FOR RECIPROCITY ARE MORE LIKELY THAN ANY OTHER APPROACH TO CONVINCE KIM JONG-IL THAT HE CANNOT HOPE TO REPLICATE HIS FATHER'S ONE-SIDED PATRONAGE DEALS. SIMILARLY, THE BEST WAY TO BUILD TRUST WITH THE DPRK IS TO DO A BETTER JOB OF FULFILLING OUR OWN OBLIGATIONS UNDER THE AGREED FRAMEWORK. FAR-REACHING NEW INITIATIVES AT THIS POINT WOULD ONLY CONFUSE THE DPRK, AND WOULD PROBABLY ENCOURAGE IT TO REMAIN INTRANSIGENT IN THE EXPECTATION THAT WE WILL EVENTUALLY PROPOSE SOMETHING TO ITS LIKING.

46. (S) OUR CURRENT STRATEGY OF ACTIVE AND POSITIVE ENGAGEMENT WITH THE DPRK, WITH THE GOAL OF MAXIMIZING THE PROSPECTS FOR DPRK REFORM, OPENING AND RECONCILIATION WITH THE ROK, IS UNDOUBTEDLY THE BEST APPROACH. IF IT SUCCEEDS, WE WILL ACHIEVE THE BEST OF ALL POSSIBLE OUTCOMES FOR EVERY CONCERNED GOVERNMENT. AS AND WE SAID OF KIM DAE-JUNG'S "SUNSHINE POLICY," EVEN IF IT DOES NOT SUCCEED IN THOSE TERMS, THE ANCILLARY EFFECTS OF EXPANDED CONTACTS WITH NORTH KOREANS WILL FOSTER DEMANDS FOR AND ACCEPTANCE OF THE KIND OF CHANGES WE SEEK.

47. (S) BUT A POSITIVE ENGAGEMENT STRATEGY ALONE IS INCOMPLETE. OUR MILITARY POLICY TOWARD NORTH KOREA RELIES ON BOTH A POSITIVE GOAL OF DETERRENCE AND A CONTINGENCY PREPAREDNESS TO WAGE WAR; WITHOUT THE LATTER, THE FORMER CANNOT BE EFFECTIVE. IN THE SAME WAY, WE NEED TO BE PREPARED TO COPE WITH OUTCOMES OTHER THAN THE ONE WE WANT. THERE ARE SOME INDICATIONS THAT THE KIM DAE-JUNG ADMINISTRATION'S EXPECTATION THAT THE DPRK WILL NOT COLLAPSE SOON HAS LED TO A LOSS OF MOMENTUM IN PLANNING TO DEAL WITH TERMINAL INSTABILITY. WE SHOULD NOT MAKE THE SAME MISTAKE, AND INDEED SHOULD ENCOURAGE THE ROKG TO CONTINUE QUIET BUT INTENSIVE COLLAPSE PLANNING EVEN AS WE WORK TOGETHER TO AVERT THAT OUTCOME.

BOSWORTH

SECRET

TOP SECRET CODEWORD/EXDIS

DPRK: All the Fine, Young Cannibals (SS)

Incidents of cannibalism have begun to punctuate reporting on North Korea's deepening food shortage. Reported occurrences so far have been limited to the far northeast, a remote and chronic food-deficit region. (SS)

The North's internal security apparatus has provided details of three cases—one of which prompted Kim Jong Il personally to demand that those responsible be severely punished, according to special intelligence. Lurid rumors are causing paranoia and apprehension among the populace. Kim Jong Il reportedly has ordered the party's central inspection committee to investigate the scope of the problem, thus elevating it to a national-level concern. (SS)

Senior South Korean officials are aware of the cannibalism—the ROK Defense Security command collected the information—and the reports are too sensational not to leak. When they do, President Kim Young Sam, who has adopted a hard-line stance and played down the seriousness of the North's food shortage, could have a political problem. Public opposition to more food aid has already begun to soften; this story could accelerate the trend, raising serious questions about Kim's judgement and—more important for Koreans—his morality. (SS)

(SECRET SPOKE)

TOP SECRET CODEWORD/EXDIS   February 29, 1996

The text of this 1996 U.S. intelligence report discloses that North Korea's widespread famine has led to cannibalism in parts of the country, revealing the troubled state of the nation. (1 page)

TOP SECRET UMBRA NOFORN ORCON GAMMA

Central Intelligence Agency

Washington, D.C. 20505

14 September 1996

MEMORANDUM

SUBJECT: China and Pakistan Discuss US Demarche on Nuclear Assistance

1. Chinese officials—probably from the China Nuclear Energy Industry Corporation (CNEIC)—recently met with Ghulam Kibria, Pakistan's nuclear and missile procurement officer in Beijing, to discuss the 30 August US demarche on China's sale of diagnostic equipment and a furnace to unsafeguarded nuclear facilities in Pakistan, according to an intercepted message. Kibria said Chinese personnel were already in Pakistan to install the equipment, which an intercept in August indicated was to be delivered on 2 September.

— A Chinese nuclear official informally told our Embassy on Wednesday that the equipment was sent late last year or early this year, but he claimed not to know the final end user at the Pakistani Atomic Energy Commission.

— The Pakistanis' expectation of the 2 September delivery, however, indicates either that the Chinese shipment scheduled in January did not occur or that it may have been only a partial shipment. (TS U NF OC G)

2. In the aftermath of CNEIC's ring magnet sale to Pakistan and China's 11 May commitment not to provide assistance to unsafeguarded nuclear facilities, senior-level government approval probably was needed for this most recent assistance. The Chinese told Kibria they needed end user certificates for the sale and all future dual-use shipments and other equipment for Pakistan's unsafeguarded facilities and vowed to discuss the certificates only with "a third party"—apparently the US—probably to demonstrate that Beijing is complying with its May commitment. (TS U NF OC G)

3. The PAEC's chairman told Kibria any decision to share documents with others would require the approval of Pakistan's President or Prime Minister. Kibria suggested possible language for the false end user certificates to make it appear that one item—possibly the diagnostic equipment—was intended for the safeguarded Chasma nuclear power plant, which Chinese firms are building.

— The intercept indicates Kibria also suggested to the Chinese that all remaining contracts, apparently for unsafeguarded facilities, be canceled and new ones drawn up naming unobjectionable end users.

— Kibria claimed the Chinese reacted positively to the idea, but added this kind of agreement is "dangerous." Such a subterfuge probably would require the approval of senior Chinese Government leaders. (TS U NF OC G)

This memorandum was prepared by Ken Sichel and Ray Bogusz of the Office of Weapons Technology and Proliferation with a contribution from Ted Clark from the Office of East Asian Analysis. The author can be reached on 70481 secure.

TOP SECRET UMBRA NOFORN ORCON GAMMA

This September 1996 CIA memorandum reveals that China secretly continued to sell nuclear weapons–related equipment to Pakistan after promising the United States it would halt such transfers. (2 pages)

US Intelligence Collection Jeopardized

4. The Chinese reportedly told Kibria the "secret"—apparently the latest sale—had leaked in Pakistan. In response, Islamabad ordered Kibria to stop using telephones and faxes and to confine future messages to the diplomatic pouch.

— If implemented, the order will severely limit our ability to monitor Chinese-Pakistani nuclear and, to a lesser extent, ballistic missile cooperation.

— It also could slow down Pakistani procurement. (TS U NF OC G)

Pakistan: M-11 Update

Pakistan has ordered a further payment to China on the 1988 M-11 deal, and Chinese engineers plan soon to provide further M-11 training to the Pakistani army. Though we continue to receive reports that M-11s are in Pakistan, the army has made no plans for field deployment and is just beginning to formulate an operational doctrine for the system.

Pakistan on August 22 made arrangements to pay China Precision Machinery Import/Export Corporation $15 million on the 1988 contract for M-11 missiles, launchers, and support equipment, according to special intelligence. We have no indication of upcoming shipments or other events that would explain the timing of this payment. The last known payment on this contract—$83 million—was in late 1992 for unspecified "goods" shipped at that time; subsequent reporting has provided strong evidence that missiles were part of the cargo.

A Chinese team is expected to arrive at Pakistan's Sargodha missile facility in September to provide training on the M-11, probably on the handling of spare parts, according to special intelligence and a clandestine source. This team probably is separate from one that reportedly will arrive later this year—once the Sargodha facility is complete—to unpack and assemble M-11s. This latter team's arrival has been repeatedly delayed by the Pakistanis, ostensibly because of the need to complete construction at Sargodha, but almost certainly also because of the greater likelihood of US detection of the missiles once assembled.

At least some of the M-11s that had been dispersed at military locations throughout Pakistan are now being stored at Sargodha, according to a clandestine source. But we have yet to see operational missiles on imagery. April imagery showed canisters at Sargodha similar to ones seen at the M-11 production facility in China. But a missile-handling exercise was under way at Sargodha at that time, and the canisters were assessed to be mock-ups for use in that exercise.
(TOP SECRET UMBRA/NOFORN/NOCONTRACT/ORCON/EXDIS)

The text of this 1994 U.S. intelligence report shows that China secretly sold M-11 missiles to Pakistan. (1 page)

CONFIDENTIAL   CUNCLASSIFIED   9635

NATIONAL SECURITY COUNCIL
WASHINGTON DC 20506

December 8, 1993

INFORMATION

MEMORANDUM FOR ANTHONY LAKE
ROBERT E. RUBIN
SAMUEL BERGER

FROM: ROBERT D. KYLE
ELISA D. HARRIS

SUBJECT: M-11 Missile Sanctions

Declassified/Released on 7-14-98
under provisions of E.O. 12958
by L. Salvetti, National Security Council

The Administration will need to make a decision in the very near
future whether to prevent the transfer of two satellites related
to the M-11 missile sanctions against China. This memorandum
provides background on the subject and presents the issues for
decision.

Background

As you know, the Administration imposed sanctions against China
in August in response to a growing body of evidence that China
had transferred M-11-related equipment to Pakistan, a step that
violates U.S. missile sanctions law. However, because the U.S.
did not have precise knowledge of what items were shipped, the
U.S. imposed "Category II" sanctions, which are less onerous than
those under "Category I" and are to be used when controlled
missile components have been transferred.

The Category II sanctions prohibit the export, for two years, of
items on the Missile Technology Control Regime (MTCR) list.
Satellites themselves are not on the MTCR list, but many
satellites contain MTCR components. The sanctions potentially
could have covered as many as seven satellites, totalling $800
million. We have consistently told the Chinese that the
sanctions could be waived if the Chinese would: (1) not ship any
more M-11-related items to Pakistan; and (2) formally agree, in a
binding international agreement, to adhere to the MTCR
guidelines.

Subsequently, State and Commerce expressed conflicting views on
which satellites were covered by the sanctions, based on their
different interpretations of what constitutes an MTCR-controlled
item (which is therefore subject to the sanctions). Satellites
are referred to State or Commerce, depending on the
sophistication of the satellite or its technology. For
satellites under its jurisdiction, State applies a "see-through"
rule, which holds that the satellite transfer should be
prohibited if the satellite itself contains an MTCR component

CONFIDENTIAL
Declassify on: OADR CONUNCLASSIFIED   A 001626

*This December 1993 internal White House memorandum warns that C. Michael Armstrong,
chairman of the U.S. satellite manufacturer Hughes, had threatened to go public in opposing
administration missile sanctions on China. (4 pages)*

even though the satellite itself is not an MTCR item. On this basis, all seven satellites would be denied. Commerce applies an "end product" test, and would deny no satellites, as satellites themselves are not MTCR items.

Prior to the APEC summit, the President authorized Commerce to license the two satellites under its jurisdiction, totalling $205 million. This approach made sense; if Commerce had adopted State's "see-through" rule, it would have affected Commerce's other export licensing functions, forcing it to require licenses for a broad range of less sophisticated products (e.g., aircraft, medical equipment).

In Seattle, Secretary Christopher informed the Chinese that the sale of even these two satellites was contingent on some sign of movement by the Chinese on the proliferation front (e.g., China agrees to enter formal discussions on the M-11 issue). The Chinese were not forthcoming, so we have not yet decided to transfer the two Commerce satellites.

Since the sanctions announcement, Hughes Corporation, and its CEO Mike Armstrong, has lobbied aggressively to exclude its satellites from the sanctions. The sanctions cover two of Hughes satellites, totalling $220 million. None currently are within Commerce's jurisdiction, so they would not be freed by the President's decision to license two satellites.

Armstrong is now fairly directly threatening to wage a more public campaign against the Administration's sanctions. He has secured key Congressional support (e.g., Nunn, California delegation) and suggests he may prompt a Congressional inquiry, write op-eds, and/or spur union opposition. He expresses a desire to work quietly with us -- and has until now -- but he is becoming impatient.

One final point is important: fewer than seven satellites are actually at stake here, as the attached chart shows. The first two satellites listed are under Commerce's jurisdiction and therefore would be authorized, at the latest, when the Chinese show movement.

The next two satellites might be able to wait out the sanctions because the launch date for these satellites is not until 1996. They could afford to wait to secure their licenses until after August 1995, then ship. Therefore, these two satellites may feel no real bite.

The next satellite already has the necessary licenses. It would need additional licenses if MTCR replacement parts were required, but is fully authorized otherwise. We are told that the chances of replacement parts being required is low.

The last two satellites, the Hughes products, are under State and have the least likelihood of being authorized (perhaps explaining why Hughes is so active). However, Hughes apparently is attempting to convert at least one of these satellites (Apstar 2)

to put it under Commerce's jurisdiction, and has already
submitted a license application to Commerce. Therefore, even
this satellite may avoid the sanctions. Hughes could do the same
conversion on the second satellite, but no Commerce license has
been applied for yet.

To summarize:

> Two satellites: Commerce rules apply.
> Two satellites: Launch in 1996/Able to wait?
> One satellite: Already has licenses/New parts required?
> Hughes satellites: Sanctions bite/Commerce convertible?

If the first two satellites are approved, only the Hughes
satellites probably would feel the bite of the sanctions. If the
approval of the first two satellites means all Commerce-
controlled satellites should be approved, would Hughes benefit
from subsequent conversion of its satellites to being Commerce-
controlled? If so, the sanctions would have very little, if any,
bite.

Issues/Options

The immediate question is whether we should prevent the sale of
the two satellites under Commerce's jurisdiction. Quite apart
from the MTCR sanctions, the export of any satellite to China
requires a "Tiananmen Square" Presidential waiver. One satellite
has already received this waiver. Once Commerce is formally told
the M-11 sanctions do not apply - or it becomes public - Commerce
will be under pressure to issue the license. It may also lack
legal authority not to issue. However, to stop the transfer, the
President would need to revoke the waiver. The second satellite
has not yet received the Tiananmen Square waiver; the President
has complete discretion.

There are essentially three options:

Option 1 - Authorize Transfer of Two Satellites: This approach
would be responsive to U.S. commercial interests, allowing $205
million worth of sales to proceed. It would undercut our M-11
strategy in that China has not met the conditions we imposed for
the transfer of even the two satellites. This decision might
inflame Hughes even more since their satellites were not freed.
On the other hand, if the decision means all Commerce-controlled
satellites are freed, Hughes' might benefit if it is successful
in downgrading its satellites to being Commerce-controlled. (To
the same extent, it undercuts the strength of the sanctions, of
course.)

Option 2 - Authorize One Satellite: We could permit transfer of
the one satellite ($55 million) that has already received the
Tiananmen Square waiver. (The waiver was granted before the M-11
sanctions were imposed.) But the President would not waive the
Tiananmen Square sanctions on the second Commerce satellite ($150
million). Justifying the second waiver would be difficult, given
the small progress we have made with the Chinese.

CONFIDENTIAL   UNCLASSIFIED

Option 3 – Do Not Authorize the Two Satellites: This option
continues the toughest approach toward China. We would continue
to insist on some movement prior to licensing the two satellites,
but none would be freed in the meantime. It does the least for
U.S. commercial interests, denying millions of dollars of sales
that might otherwise occur. It does nothing for Hughes – risking
more public opposition by them – and undercuts their efforts to
free their satellites through conversion.

Other options do not seem attractive. Allowing all transfers
immediately would undercut our M-11 strategy. Legally, it would
also require the President to issue a national security interest
waiver, which would be difficult to defend, given our M-11
policy.

Concurrence by: Alan Kreczko

ATTACHMENT
TAB I   Chart

Subsidiary of GM Hughes Electronics

C. MICHAEL ARMSTRONG Chairman and Chief Executive Officer

29 October 1993

The President
The White House
Washington, D. C.   20500

Dear Mr. President:

You asked me to support your economic package. I did.

You asked me to work hard to improve the California economic environment through legislative change. I did.

You asked me to support your changes to export policy and controls. I did.

You asked me to support NAFTA more strongly in California. I am.

I am respectfully requesting your involvement to resolve the China sanctions at the upcoming Seattle APEC meeting November 18-20. PRC State Councilor Song has told me they are "positive to do this". It's a tragic situation that potentially thousands of California people could lose their jobs, hundreds of millions of dollars of American business lost and a potential strategic alliance forced on our competitors in order to send a foreign policy message.

The economic consequences are already beginning to turn into reality. We have recently learned that the Chinese government is now in the process of sourcing two Hughes satellites to the Germans (DASA) that are worth $80-100M and hundreds of California jobs. In addition, we are spending $250,000 a day on another satellite that could be canceled. Due to the circumstances, this will be public and political shortly.

Thank you for your consideration.

Sincerely yours,

C. Michael Armstrong

cc: R. Brown
        W. Brown
        D. Feinstein
        A. Gore
        J. Harman
        P. Wilson

Corporate Offices
P.O. Box 80028, Los Angeles, CA 90080-0028
7200 Hughes Terrace, Los Angeles, CA 90045-0066
(310) 568-6117

These 1993 letters from Hughes chairman C. Michael Armstrong to the White House reveal that he had discussions with Chinese officials about ending U.S. missile sanctions. (2 pages)

Subsidiary of GM Hughes Electronics

C. MICHAEL ARMSTRONG Chairman and Chief Executive Officer

16 November 1993

The Honorable Samuel Berger
 Deputy Assistant to the President
 for National Security Affairs
 Washington, D.C. 20501
 Fax: 202/456-2883

Mr. Leon Fuerth
 Assistant to the Vice President
 for National Security Affairs
 Washington, D.C. 20501
 Fax: 202/395-6042

        Subject: Visit 11/16/93 at Hughes with PRC Vice Premier
                   Qian Qichen

This will confirm my conversation Tuesday AM 11/16/93 with PRC Vice Premier Qian
Qichen.

I briefly described that in meetings with the Chinese and the USG over the past several
months, it was obvious that both sides were in agreement i.e., (1) the Chinese are
committed not to proliferate missile technology (2) and with the Chinese commitment,
the USG is prepared to drop sanctions. The problem is who/when takes the first step.

I related the recent press reports that the U.S. was considering initiating a waiver, if
serious negotiations could take place. Vice Premier Qian then asked "should we
consider these press reports as representative of Washington position". I replied yes,
the press reports are valid.

Corporate Offices.
7200 Hughes Terrace, Los Angeles, CA 90045
P.O. Box 80028, Los Angeles, CA 90080-0028
(310) 568-6117

CONFIDENTIAL

IMMEDIATE
O 220127Z MAR 96
FM SECSTATE WASHDC
TO   AMEMBASSY MOSCOW IMMEDIATE 0000

ZYUW RUEHCAA8403 0820137

C O N F I D E N T I A L STATE 058403

EYES ONLY FOR AMBASSADORS PICKERING AND COLLINS

E.O. 12958: DECL: 03/15/08
TAGS: PREL, RU
SUBJECT: (C) CLINTON-YELTSIN MEMCON 3/13/96

1. CONFIDENTIAL CLASSIFIED BY: JOHN HERBSTR ACTING,
S/NIS, DEPARTMENT OF STATE REASON: 1.5 (B) AND (D)

TO::T OF MEMCON FROM CLINTON-YELTSIN 3/13/96 MEETING
FOLLOWS FOR YOUR INFORMATION

BEGIN TEXT

MEMORANDUM OF CONVERSATION

SUBJECT: MEETING WITH PRESIDENT BORIS YELTSIN OF
           RUSSIA (C)

PARTICIPANTS: UNITED STATES:
           THE PRESIDENT
           SECRETARY CHRISTOPHER, SECRETARY OF STATE
           JOHN DEUTCH, DIRECTOR OF CENTRAL
           INTELLIGENCE
           ANTHONY LAKE, ASSISTANT TO THE PRESIDENT

           FOR NATIONAL SECURITY AFFAIRS
           RADM JOHN LEUCKE, DIRECTOR, STRATEGIC
           PLANS AND POLICY, USCENTCOM
           H. ALLEN HOLMES, ASSISTANT SECRETARY FOR
           SPECIAL OPERATIONS AND LOW INTENSITY
           CONFLICT, DEPARTMENT OF DEFENSE
           ANDREW SENS, EXECUTIVE SECRETARY,
           NATIONAL SECURITY COUNCIL
           DIMITRI ZARECHNAK (INTERPRETER)

           RUSSIA:
           PRESIDENT YELTSIN
           FOREIGN MINISTER PRIMAKOV
           SECURITY ADVISOR RURIKOV
           MICHAIL BARSUKOV, DIRECTOR, FEDERAL
           SECURITY SERVICE

JOINT STAFF Y1   2
ACTION   (U)
INFO   CMAS(1) SHAPE LNO(1)
       +NATS PENTAGON WASHINGTON DC
       -CDR 4TH PSYOP GP//AOCP-POG-SB//

SECDEF V2   14
ACTION   (U)
INFO   CHAIRS(1) SECDEF-C(1) OASD:C3I-ADN(1)
       .ATSD:PA-SARAH(1) DIR:FAE-EPF(1) OASD:C3I-C2(1)
       USDP:DASDEUR(1) USDP:OSAA(1) USDP:SR(1)
       USDP:PK/PE(1) USDP:FSUNA(1) USDP:NAC(1) USDP:CTR(1)
       USDP:RUE(1)
       +USDP:OTSA

DIA V3   0
ACTION   (U/B)
INFO   +USCINCTRANS INTEL CEN SCOTT AFB IL//J2-J//
       +SAFE

CINC/SVC CHF V5   1
ACTION   (U)
INFO   CSAMS(1)
       +CCSA WASHINGTON DC
       +CSAF WASHINGTON DC
       +ETC ...

VCN=96082/C1879   TCR=96082/C152Z   T4D=96082/C154Z   CCSN=MAK590
                                                    PAGE 1 OF 2
                                                    220127Z MAR 96

S. BEREZHKOV (INTERPRETER)

PRESIDENT YELTSIN WAS IN A GOOD MOOD AND LOOKED WELL (HE
SAID AT THE END THAT HE HAD LOST 12 KILOGRAMS). HE
CONGRATULATED THE PRESIDENT ABOUT HAVING RESOLVED
EVERYTHING OVERNIGHT AND HAVING ALREADY DRAFTED THE
CONFERENCE COMMUNIQUE. (C)

THE PRESIDENT GAVE YELTSIN A COPY AND APOLOGIZED THAT IT
WAS ONLY IN ENGLISH. (C)

FOREIGN MINISTER PRIMAKOV SAID THAT HE COULD READ IT,
AND YELTSIN JOKED THAT SINCE PRIMAKOV KNEW ENGLISH,
SECRETARY CHRISTOPHER SHOULD NOW LEARN RUSSIAN. THE
RUSSIANS WOULD BE GLAD TO PROVIDE THE SECRETARY WITH A
YOUNG ATTRACTIVE INSTRUCTRESS WHO WOULD WORK WITH THE
SECRETARY NIGHT AND DAY. (C)

THE PRESIDENT JOKED THAT THIS WOULD CHANGE THE
SECRETARY'S IMAGE IN THE UNITED STATES. (C)

THE PRESIDENT ASKED YELTSIN HOW HIS ELECTION CAMPAIGN
WAS GOING. (C)

YELTSIN REPLIED THAT BILL CLINTON'S CAMPAIGN WAS GOING
WELL, AND HE WOULD BE ELECTED IF THE ELECTION TOOK PLACE
NOW (C)

THE PRESIDENT AGREED, BUT NOTED THAT THERE WERE STILL
EIGHT MONTHS TO GO. (C)

FOREIGN MINISTER PRIMAKOV, HAVING LOOKED AT THE
COMMUNIQUE, INDICATED THAT IT WAS A GOOD ONE. (C)

THE PRESIDENT THANKED YELTSIN FOR COMING TO THE SUMMIT
THIS WOULD BOOST THE PEACE PROCESS AND HELP PERES AND
ARAFAT CONFIDENCE IN ISRAEL HAD PLUMMETED AFTER THE
BOMBINGS, AND THIS WOULD HELP TO IMPROVE THE SITUATION
(C)

YELTSIN AGREED HE SAID HE HAD NO RESERVATIONS ABOUT
COMING, ESPECIALLY SINCE RUSSIA WAS A COSPONSOR OF THE
PEACE PROCESS HE THEN SAID THAT HE WANTED TO REPLY TO
THE PRESIDENT'S QUESTION ABOUT THE ELECTION CAMPAIGN IN
RUSSIA. (C)

YELTSIN'S PEOPLE HAVE BEGUN TO GET GEARED UP STAFF,
COMMITTEES, PERSONNEL HAD BEEN PUT TOGETHER THROUGHOUT
RUSSIA -- DOWN TO THE VILLAGES THE OFFICIAL
REGISTRATION OF CANDIDATES WOULD TAKE PLACE APRIL 5. A
CANDIDATE NEEDED ONE MILLION SIGNATURES TO BE ON THE
BALLOT. HE, YELTSIN, HAD OVER 6 MILLION AND YELTSIN'S
TAX DECLARATION, SUBMITTED TO THE CENTRAL ELECTION
COMMITTEE, DID NOT CONTAIN ANYTHING TO RAISE QUESTIONS,
JUST AS PRESIDENT CLINTON'S DID NOT. (C)

THE PRESIDENT OBSERVED THAT WORKING FOR THE GOVERNMENT
DOES NOT GIVE ONE A BIG SALARY (C)

YELTSIN CONTINUED THAT HE WOULD GIVE A SPEECH OUTLINING
HIS PLATFORM TO ABOUT 5,000 SUPPORTERS AND THEN GET DOWN
TO THE NUTS AND BOLTS OF THE CAMPAIGN ON APRIL 6.
FORTY-NINE CANDIDATES HAD DECLARED, BUT YELTSIN DID NOT
THINK THAT MORE THAN 5 OR 6 OF THEM WOULD BE ABLE TO GET
THE NECESSARY NUMBER OF SIGNATURES. THE AIM OF YELTSIN
AND HIS SUPPORTERS WOULD BE TO CONVINCE THE CANDIDATES
ONE-BY-ONE TO WITHDRAW FROM THE RACE AND TO THROW THEIR
SUPPORT BEHIND YELTSIN. THE ONE CANDIDATE WHO WOULD NOT
AGREE TO DO THIS WAS ZYUGANOV. HE IS A DIE-HARD
COMMUNIST, AND YELTSIN WOULD NEED TO DO BATTLE WITH
HIM. GORBACHEV WAS NOT A SERIOUS CANDIDATE -- HE HAD
AWOKEN ONE MORNING AND DECIDED TO RUN AND WOULD WAKE UP
ANOTHER MORNING AND DECIDE TO WITHDRAW HIS CANDIDACY.
THIS WOULD BE BETTER FOR HIM BECAUSE HE NOW HAD SOME
STANDING, AND IF HE PARTICIPATED IN THE ELECTIONS, HE
WOULD LOSE ANY REPUTATION HE HAD LEFT. (C)

CONFIDENTIAL

This official "memorandum of conversation" of a 1996 meeting between President Bill Clinton and Russian President Boris Yeltsin shows that Clinton promised to adopt pro-Russia policies to help Yeltsin's reelection bid in exchange for Moscow's agreeing to end a Russian ban on U.S. chicken imports—revealing how cavalierly Clinton would play politics with national security. (2 pages)

CONFIDENTIAL

YELTSIN CONTINUED THAT HE WOULD NEED TO TRAVEL INTENSELY THROUGHOUT RUSSIA FOR TWO MONTHS TO TALK TO THOUSANDS OF PEOPLE, TO GET HIS MESSAGE TO EVERY APARTMENT, HOUSE AND PERSON. (C)

YELTSIN'S PROGRAM WOULD ONLY BE AIMED AT INCREASING DEMOCRACY AND DEEPENING REFORMS. HE WOULD NOT DEVIATE FROM THAT PATH. TO IMPROVE HIS RATINGS, HIS PEOPLE HAVE CREATED THEIR OWN POLLING ORGANIZATION, TO OFFSET THE COMMUNIST POLLING ORGANIZATIONS, WHICH FABRICATE THINGS THAT DON'T EXIST. (C)

YELTSIN CONTINUED THAT AS RECENTLY AS A MONTH AGO, HE STILL HAD DOUBTS ABOUT RUNNING, BUT AFTER HE SAW THE COMMUNIST PLATFORM, HE DECIDED TO RUN. THE COMMUNISTS WOULD DESTROY REFORM, DO AWAY WITH PRIVATIZATION, NATIONALIZE PRODUCTION, CONFISCATE LAND AND HOMES. THEY WOULD EVEN EXECUTE PEOPLE. THIS WAS IN THEIR BLOOD. IT WOULD BE A DISASTER FOR RUSSIA AND MANY OTHER COUNTRIES. SO YELTSIN AGREED TO RUN AND NOW FELT BETTER AND MORE OPTIMISTIC ABOUT THE SITUATION HE HAD TRAVELED THROUGH RUSSIA AND HAL) FELT THE PUBLIC'S SUPPORT. BUT HE ADMITTED THAT HE SHOULD NOT BE OVER CONFIDENT (C)

THE PRESIDENT INDICATED THAT THERE WAS NOT MUCH TIME, PUT HE WANTED TO SAY A FEW THINGS ABOUT THE? ELECTIONS. FIRST OF ALL, HE WANTED TO MAKE SURE THAT EVERYTHING THE UNITED STATES DID WOULD HAVE A POSITIVE IMPACT, AND NOTHING SHOULD HAVE A NEGATIVE IMPACT. HE WAS ENCOURAGED THAT THE SECRETARY OF STATE WAS HEADING TO MOSCOW TO MEET WITH MINISTER PRIMAKOV, AND HE WANTED THE APRIL SUMMIT TO BE A POSITIVE EVENT. THE UNITED STATES WOULD WORK WITH RUSSIA TO ENSURE THIS, SO THAT IT WOULD REINFORCE EVERYTHING THAT YELTSIN HAD DONE IN THIS REGARD (C)

YELTSIN NOTED THAT PREPARATIONS FOR THE MULTILATERAL SUMMIT IN MOSCOW ON APRIL 20 WOULD OCCUPY HIM FULLY ON APRIL 19, BUT AFTER THE SUMMIT ON APRIL 20, HE WOULD BE HAPPY TO MEET FOR THREE TO FOUR HOURS WITH PRESIDENT CLINTON TO DISCUSS BILATERAL ISSUES. HE ADDED THAT A LEADER OF INTERNATIONAL STATURE SUCH AS PRESIDENT CLINTON SHOULD SUPPORT RUSSIA AND THAT MEANT SUPPORTING YELTSIN. THOUGHT SHOULD BE GIVEN TO HOW TO DO THAT WISELY. (C)

TUE PRESIDENT REPLIED THAT SECRETARY CHRISTOPHER AND MINISTER PRIMAKOV WOULD TALK ABOUT THAT. THE MAIN THING IS THAT THE TWO SIDES NOT DO ANYTHING THAT WOULD HARM THE OTHER. THINGS COULD COME UP BETWEEN NOW AND THE ELECTIONS IN RUSSIA OR THE UNITED STATES, WHICH COULD CAUSE CONFLICTS. PERHAPS THE GORE-CHERNOMYRDIN PROCESS COULD BE RELIED ON MORE TO RESOLVE THESE ISSUES, SUCH AS

THE POULTRY ISSUE WHICH RECENTLY AROSE. THIS IS A BIG ISSUE, ESPECIALLY SINCE ABOUT 40 PERCENT OF U.S POULTRY IS PRODUCED IN ARKANSAS. ON THE OTHER HAND OF COURSE, RUSSIA HAD LEGITIMATE ISSUES ABOUT INSPECTIONS OF U.S. PRODUCE, BUT THIS QUESTION SHOULD BE ON ITS WAY TO RESOLUTION, AND AN EFFORT SHOULD BE MADE TO KEEP SUCH THINGS FROM GETTING OUT OF HAND. (C)

YELTSIN INTERJECTED "USE DIRECT CHANNELSR " THEN WENT ON TO NOTE THAT THE MAIN THING WAS THAT THE U.S. INSPECTORS CONFIRMED THAT THERE HAD BEEN VIOLATTIONSR AND NOW WE WERE BACK IN BUSINESS. BUT LET THE GORE-CHERNOMYRDIN CONTACTS CONTINUE ON THIS. (C)

THE PRESIDENT CONCLUDED THAT HE WAS LOOKING FORWARD TO TODAY'S MEETINGS AND THE ONES IN APRIL. (C)

END OF CONVERSATION
TALBOTT ST

MCN=96082/01873   TOR=96082/01517   TAD=96082/0154Z   CDSN=MAK590

CONFIDENTIAL

AT THE REQUEST OF THE NATIONAL SECURITY AGENCY, THE PUBLISHER HAS WITHDRAWN AN INTERCEPTED COMMUNICATION THAT WAS TO HAVE APPEARED ON THIS PAGE.

These National Security Agency reports reveal that Russia was secretly selling missile technology to Iran. (6 pages)

AT THE REQUEST OF THE NATIONAL SECURITY AGENCY, THE PUBLISHER HAS WITHDRAWN AN INTERCEPTED COMMUNICATION THAT WAS TO HAVE APPEARED ON THIS PAGE.

AT THE REQUEST OF THE NATIONAL SECURITY AGENCY, THE PUBLISHER HAS WITHDRAWN AN INTERCEPTED COMMUNICATION THAT WAS TO HAVE APPEARED ON THIS PAGE.

AT THE REQUEST OF THE NATIONAL SECURITY AGENCY,
THE PUBLISHER HAS WITHDRAWN AN INTERCEPTED COM-
MUNICATION THAT WAS TO HAVE APPEARED ON THIS
PAGE.

AT THE REQUEST OF THE NATIONAL SECURITY AGENCY, THE PUBLISHER HAS WITHDRAWN AN INTERCEPTED COMMUNICATION THAT WAS TO HAVE APPEARED ON THIS PAGE.

AT THE REQUEST OF THE NATIONAL SECURITY AGENCY, THE PUBLISHER HAS WITHDRAWN AN INTERCEPTED COMMUNICATION THAT WAS TO HAVE APPEARED ON THIS PAGE.

EURASIA

Russia: **Economic Agreements To Be Signed With Iraq (TS U NF)**

A Russian delegation headed by Energy and Fuels Minister Rodionov left yesterday for Baghdad with $10-12 billion in economic agreements to be signed. The delegation includes the directors of at least nine oil companies, the chief of the Rosvooruzheniye arms exporting firm, and officials from the Foreign Economic Relations, Foreign Affairs, and Industrial Ministries, according to special intelligence.

> — *The large number of oil industry executives reflects the focus the Russians have given to oil projects.* (TS U NF)

Russian officials have said publicly the pacts to be signed involve Russian development of the West Kurna and North Rumayla oilfields, two of the Middle East's largest, as well as expansion of the Haditha-Rumaila oil pipeline and Nasiriyah-Baghdad gas pipeline, all Soviet-era projects interrupted by the Gulf war.

> — According to press reports, production from the fields will be used to settle Iraq's $10 billion debt to Russia. (C NF)

Moscow has pledged to honor UN sanctions but has indicated it is eager to be in position to pursue its economic interests. Iraqi Deputy Prime Minister Aziz recently assured Russian officials when he was in Moscow that Iraqi officials would give priority to Russians in the execution of strategic projects.

> — *The size of these deals and the possibility other states will follow suit could generate new efforts in the UN to ease the sanctions.* (C NF) -CIA, DIA, NSA-

9

This excerpt from a 1997 CIA "National Intelligence Daily" report shows that Russia arranged $10 billion to $12 billion in economic deals with Iraq. (1 page)

Regional Issues

Military Assessments, Foreign/Defense Policy, Defense Economics/ Infrastructure

Iraq: Saddam's Ballistic Missile Options

(S) The Iraqis may be concealing several dozen 600-km-range Al-Hussein SRBMs and several mobile launchers, as well as a few 900-km-range Al-Abbas SRBMs. Both SRBMs are variants of the SCUD missile. Baghdad prefers to retain this force as part of long-term reconstitution rather than use it as a short-term political or military weapon. Saddam knows that the missile force is of limited usefulness now because launching even a single SRBM would immediately confirm to the world that he has been evading UN restrictions for nearly 7 years. However, under certain conditions, Saddam could order missiles launched against targets in Israel or Gulf Cooperation Council states.

CONFIDENTIAL

(S) Two extended-range SCUD SRBMs are ready for launch from domestically produced Al-Nida mobile erector-launchers, probably in late 1990. The marks where the propellant tank extensions were welded are clearly visible.

(S) Iraq is believed to be hiding the SCUD-variant SRBMs at or near Presidential or Republican Guard facilities, most likely near Baghdad (such as the Abu Ghurayb area), Tikrit, Bayji, or secure facilities in the western part of the country. Forces associated with regime security — the Special Republican Guard and the intelligence services, in particular — are involved in Saddam's efforts to conceal Iraq's prohibited weapons-of-mass-destruction programs, including SCUD missiles.

(S) Besides hiding missiles at Presidential and Republican Guard facilities, the Iraqis may be concealing missiles, launchers, propellants, and support equipment near southern or western launch areas. Hiding them there may be an attempt to avoid detection by United Nations Special Commission (UNSCOM) personnel and to reduce response time if a launch becomes necessary. Alternatively, Saddam, in anticipation of military confrontation, could covertly deploy missiles from their concealment locations in central Iraq to sites near these launch positions. If SRBMs were used in this manner, they probably would display no improvement in accuracy over that achieved in 1991 because the Iraqis have been unable to test improvements to these SRBMs since 1990.

(S) Al-Hussein launch areas would be the same as those used during the 1991 Gulf War. Launched from points near or in Baghdad, the missiles could strike military targets in Saudi Arabia at King Khalid Military City and Hafr al Batin, as well as all of Kuwait.

This 1998 Pentagon intelligence report exposes Iraq's hidden arsenal of Scud missiles. (1 page)

ACKNOWLEDGMENTS

Many people helped me with this book. They include numerous officials inside the U.S. government, including the intelligence community, the armed services, and the policy-making community. Most of them provided help at some risk and cannot be named for fear of political retribution, or because they simply wished to remain anonymous. To them I offer many thanks.

I would like to thank the *Washington Times* for its assistance, in both time and resources, especially the *Times*'s founders, Reverend and Mrs. Sun Myung Moon, who created a great newspaper, and my editors, Wesley Pruden, Bill Giles, Francis B. Coombs, Jr., and Ken Hanner, who offered their support.

I also want to thank the Social Philosophy and Policy Center at Bowling Green State University and its executive director, Fred D. Miller, Jr., for their support. And I am indebted to the Hoover Institution on War, Revolution, and Peace at Stanford University, especially Hoover fellows Thomas H. Henriksen and Arnold Beichman, for the help and support they provided. Others who contributed valuable inspiration, advice, help, and support include: Dan Fefferman, Robert Morton, David Braaten, Don Lambro, Rowan Scarborough, and Steve Gertz. Finally, I am grateful to Regnery Executive Editor Harry Crocker for his help.

INDEX